Learning
SUPERCHARGED

Digital Age Strategies and Insights from the Edtech Frontier

Lynne Schrum
with Sandi Sumerfield

International Society for Technology in Education
PORTLAND, OREGON • ARLINGTON, VIRGINIA

Learning Supercharged
Digital Age Strategies and Insights from the Edtech Frontier
Lynne Schrum with Sandi Sumerfield

Director of Books and Journals: **Colin Murcray**
Acquisitions Editor: *Valerie Witte*
Editor: **Emily Reed**
Copy Editor: **Barbara Hewick**
Proofreader: **Corinne Gould**
Indexer: **Wendy Allex**
Book Design and Production: **Kim McGovern**
Cover Design: **Edwin Ouellette**

Library of Congress Cataloging-in-Publication Data
Names: Schrum, Lynne, author. | Sumerfield, Sandi, author.
Title: Learning supercharged : digital age strategies and insights from the edtech
    frontier / Lynne Schrum with Sandi Sumerfield.
Description: Portland : International Society for Technology in Education, [2018]|
    Includes bibliographical references and index.
Identifiers: LCCN 2018016639 (print) | LCCN 2018026335 (ebook) | ISBN
    9781564846778 (mobi) | ISBN 9781564846785 (epub) | ISBN 9781564846792
    (pdf) | ISBN 9781564846860 (pbk.)
Subjects: LCSH: Educational technology.
Classification: LCC LB1028.3 (ebook) | LCC LB1028.3 .S374 2018 (print) | DDC
    371.33—dc23
LC record available at https://lccn.loc.gov/2018016639

First Edition
ISBN: 978-1-56484-686-0
Ebook version available.

Printed in the United States of America.

ISTE® is a registered trademark of the International Society for Technology in Education.

About ISTE

The International Society for Technology in Education (ISTE) is the premier nonprofit organization serving educators and education leaders committed to empowering connected learners in a connected world. ISTE serves more than 100,000 education stakeholders throughout the world.

ISTE's innovative offerings include the ISTE Conference & Expo, one of the biggest, most comprehensive ed tech events in the world—as well as the widely adopted ISTE Standards for learning, teaching and leading in the digital age and a robust suite of professional learning resources, including webinars, online courses, consulting services for schools and districts, books, and peer-reviewed journals and publications. Visit iste.org to learn more.

Join our community of passionate educators

ISTE members get free year-round professional development opportunities and discounts on ISTE resources and conference registration. Membership also connects you to a network of educators who can instantly help with advice and best practices.

Join or renew your ISTE membership today! Visit iste.org/membership or call 800.336.5191.

Also by Lynne Schrum

Levin, B. B., & Schrum, L. (2017). *Every Teacher a Leader: Developing the Needed Dispositions, Knowledge, and Skills for Teacher Leadership.* Thousand Oaks, CA: Corwin Press.

Schrum, L., & Levin, B. (2015). *Leading a 21st century school: Harnessing technology for engagement and achievement* (2nd ed). Thousand Oaks, CA: Corwin Press.

Solomon, G., & Schrum, L. (2014). *Web 2.0 How-to for Educators, Second Edition.* Portland, OR: ISTE.

To see all books available from ISTE, visit iste.org/books.

About the Authors

Lynne Schrum, Ph.D., is a professor in the Abraham S. Fischler College of Education at Nova Southeastern University in Broward County, Florida. Previously, she served as dean of the College of Education and Human Services at West Virginia University. Her research and teaching focus on appropriate uses of information technology, preparing school leaders and teachers for the digital age, and effective and successful online teaching and learning. She has written and edited 16 books and numerous articles, and she's a past editor of the *Journal of Research on Technology in Education* (JRTE) (2002–2012; 2016–2018). Schrum is also a past president of the International Society for Technology in Education (ISTE).

Sandi Sumerfield, Ed.D., has been a classroom teacher, literacy coach, administrator, adjunct faculty, and education consultant. Her research and teaching focus on visual literacy skills to empower students as writers and thinkers. She's passionate about supporting educators in creating a classroom community that embraces social justice and develops a culturally responsive pedagogy that lifts student voice through writing.

Acknowledgements

We would like to thank the wonderful educators around the globe who gave of their time and expertise willingly; their professionalism and dedication to their learners make us proud to call ourselves educators. We also thank our ISTE supporters who helped improve this book in many ways, and our editors (Valerie Witte and Emily Reed) who provided guidance and inspiration.

Dedications

Lynne:

As always, I dedicate my efforts to the wonderful family members who support me: my two amazing daughters, Marcy and Kelly, and my two unbelievably awesome granddaughters, Cassandra and Josephine.

Sandi:

For Ed, who dreams big, believes sincerely, inspires passionately, thinks deeply, and loves unconditionally; you are my rock, my friend, and my love.

Contents

Contents

CHAPTER 4

Digital Citizenship

CHAPTER 5

Pedagogical Changes: Project-Based Learning and Personalized Learning

CHAPTER 6

CHAPTER 7

CHAPTER 8

Contents

Foreword

Educational technology is complex and nuanced. Schools will often focus heavily on devices and networking, without clearly looking at the pedagogic impacts of technology in the classrooms. Others insufficiently plan their school infrastructure which limits student learning potential. In the most effective schools, teachers and leaders think of educational technology as an interconnected and supportive system of tools, teachers, and learning.

Imagine educational technology, whether in a school or a classroom or in a single lesson, as a three-layered pyramid with each level reliant on the one below.

At the base of the pyramid, we have "Access." Access to devices, infrastructure, and learning resources that are the foundation of educational technology's impact in a school. Each student, teacher, and leader must have sufficient and reliable access to tools and information for technology to enhance learning. Without sufficient access, a school inhibits educational technology's full potential to enhance teaching and learning. And that is just what educational technology offers; potential, not promise. Putting computing tools in teachers' hands or providing reliable connections to the Internet can have great effects on teaching and learning, but those effects are not guaranteed. Often, schools that end their planning and support at the access level experience detrimental impacts on teaching and learning that can take years from which to recover.

The middle level of the pyramid, "Teaching," both mitigates these risks and helps us draw upon the learning potential of technology. The most effective schools use their access to technology as a foundation for developing dynamic and constructive teaching. They understand that focusing on teachers and their craft is at the core of student learning with technology. They see quality teaching with digital resources as enhancing curriculum, pedagogy, and the instructional role of teachers with an eye towards both personalized consumptive learning and knowledge construction.

This leads to the top level of the pyramid, "Learning." Learning with educational technology provides students the knowledge, skills, and competencies they need to be effective and empowered beyond school. Effective schools use the teaching at the middle level of the pyramid that draws upon the access at the foundation to achieve specific learning goals for students. With clarity of outcomes, students at these schools can realize the potential impact of educational technology on learning and enjoy the promise of our contemporary connected world.

In essence, a strong educational technology program starts broad with the "what" of access then builds on that for the "how" of teaching and ends with the "why" of learning.

In this book, Dr. Schrum and Dr. Sumerfield take the reader through the heart of what is most important in educational technology today by focusing on the junction of "Teaching" and "Learning" in our educational technology pyramid. They discuss teaching strategy that draws upon powerful tools to engage in personalized and dynamic learning experiences. They focus on the teacher as a sage of learning, rather than owners of content, utilizing digital resources and modern teaching strategies to maximize the value of technology in the classroom. They show us what teaching and learning, both academically and non-academically, can look like when passion, knowledge, and cooperation are blended with educational technology.

—*Matt Harris*

Matt Harris, Ed.D. is an international educational consult specializing in Educational Technology. Living in Asia, he works with schools, companies, and Ministries of Education around the world to maximize the use of technology for school operations and academics. Dr. Harris also leads the Blueprint for Technology in Education project.

Introduction

The goal of all educational enterprise is to increase student achievement, but always within the context of preparing citizens for the world; both goals must remain at the top of all educators' priority lists. This is a crucial goal for everyone involved in education—teachers, students, parents and families, support staff, and leaders. This book is intended to create a dialogue surrounding the newer technology implementations, as seen through the lens of, and balanced within, the important forces and wicked problems that face our educational system. The 2017 Horizon Report raises awareness of several important lessons: "Fluency in the digital realm is more than just understanding how to use technology" and "Advancing progressive learning approaches requires cultural transformation" (Freeman, Adams Becker, Cummins, Davis, & Hall Giesinger, 2017, p. 4). Many of the examples discussed in this book are focused on improving instruction and engaging learners, while others are focused on addressing the complex challenges that schools face. This book offers educators some important tools for teaching and learning that digital age students and teachers are already familiar with, but that are just gaining a foothold in schools today. The book is about teaching and learning tools, strategies, and ideas that will engage your students, help them acquire and practice the digital age skills and content standards they need, and involve them in their learning all at the same time.

As the name implies, it is also about digital strategies. These are not the technologies themselves, but instead represent the manner in which software or devices are used, "in both formal and informal learning; what makes them interesting is that they transcend conventional ideas to create something that feels new, meaningful, and 21st century" (Freeman, et al., 2017, p. 38). This book looks deeply at the ways these tools can be used to affect and even transform today's educational environments.

Who Should Read This Book?

The main audience for this book is anyone in a position of educational leadership, or who has some responsibility or ability to implement new ways of conceptualizing education now. This includes educators at every stage of their professional life, central office administrators, technology directors, as well as building-level leaders, including principals, technology coordinators, and teacher leaders, who strive to be 21st century leaders in their schools (Levin & Schrum, 2017). This book can be used for professional enhancement for educators at all levels, ongoing professional development of practitioners and leaders in an academy class, as a book club selection for a professional learning community, as a textbook in a preservice teacher preparation, graduate-level leadership program, or as part of any school's professional library. This book can be used to find answers to the many who-what-when-where-why questions about using new tools that a digital age school leader will need in order to lead successfully. Educators will use this book to guide them in becoming instructional leaders by developing capacity at the school or district level, and for building new skills to be successful in using technology effectively.

What Is the Rationale Behind this Book?

Three significant and intertwined themes provided the impetus for writing this book. First, the educational community is under increased pressure, perhaps as never before experienced, from students, parents, teachers, employers, and the larger community to solve problems of equity and access, and to accomplish this with multiple challenges. Funding remains a significant barrier to strong and reliable internet access (Consortium for School Networking, 2017), as only 31% of school districts surveyed said they have "sufficient internet bandwidth for today and the coming 18 months" (Consortium for School Networking, 2014, p. 12). And yet, according to the 2017 Horizon Report, "The widespread use of technology does not translate into equal learner achievement" (Freeman et al., 2017, p. 4). We also know that as many as seven out of ten teachers assign work that requires access to digital resources (Aspen Institute, 2016, cited in Center for Digital Education, 2017), yet large numbers of students have no access at home or outside of school.

Second, we now live in a world of globalization and increasingly rapid technological change. Although this has certainly been true previously, it has taken a large leap forward given the ways in which we can interact, share resources, and communicate with others. Schools must enable and require that our students develop all digital age skills, such as computational thinking, critical thinking and problem-solving, communication and collaboration, and creativity and innovation, in order to be well prepared to live and work in the digital age. To accomplish this, we must move to a student-centered educational system. However, many colleges of education programs do not prepare educators to promote digital age skills for harnessing digital technology in their classes and schools. Furthermore, we are facing a severe teacher shortage in many areas of the U.S. and around the world. Most teachers being hired today grew up with digital devices, and they expect to have access to and be able to use technology tools they need to help them teach their digital age students, although many may not have been prepared to teach effectively with the technology.

Third, there are forces at work that strive to assist educational professionals in their efforts and these are worth considering when designing or redesigning an educational system that, after all, is part of a larger community. We see the blending of formal, nonformal, and informal institutions that want to work with us to accomplish shared goals. These include libraries, museums, for-profit and not-for-profit organizations, home schooling, and online learning schools; each has its own perspective, and it is time for the educational system to lead in these areas. If we do not, we may find ourselves obsolete. Therefore, this book is designed to assist educators to acknowledge, understand, and work collaboratively to ensure the best education in the world for each and every learner.

How Is This Book Organized?

Chapters 1, 2, and 3 bring to light some of the technological innovations that are driving conversation, research, and instruction. Chapter 1 investigates the STEM, STEAM, coding, and robotics efforts currently taking place. It presents many examples of how these subjects are woven into a wide variety of curriculum areas and also offers ideas for getting started.

Chapter 2 presents the makerspaces and the maker movement, and offers insights into the purpose and goals of this movement, as well as steps that can be taken to offer this opportunity to many learners, even without designating new buildings or even a separate room. The creative examples demonstrate innovative ways to problem-solve and involve learners in this movement.

Chapter 3 looks at the idea of gamification, digital game-based learning, and the use of gaming strategies in multiple areas. The reality is that our world has become gamified—how many stars can you earn on your loyalty card if you race to buy certain products in a timely fashion? Thus, it is not surprising to find that educational institutions are following suit.

Chapter 4 brings together and presents information on digital citizenship efforts around the globe; after all, if we are digital citizens, then we recognize the importance of addressing how students stay safe, protect their privacy and that of others, avoid bullying, and guard the devices that play a preeminent role in their lives. Organizations and schools are working to promote these ideals, and this chapter offers a wide variety of examples.

Chapter 5 looks deeply at the pedagogical efforts toward project-based learning (PBL) and how it can enhance and influence learning, especially with digital resources and devices. Because personalized learning (PL) is a parallel pedagogy and strategy, often employed within project-based learning or as a stand-alone goal for each, we have placed them both in this chapter.

Chapter 6 presents information about the ongoing challenges of the digital divide and the efforts to solve the concerns of digital access and equity; this topic represents a significant area of concentration and has not disappeared, as some have suggested it has or soon will. Having a web-enabled device is certainly a start, but if a family does not have access to the internet at home, transportation to take advantage of programs in their city, or equal access to experts and digital resources, they are still at a disadvantage; multiple organizations and schools have continued to address these issues.

Chapter 7 is organized around the nonformal and informal institutions and opportunities, including after-school clubs that schools provide; these currently offer resources, programs, classes, and virtual field trips that can be connected to the educational goals and curriculum in the classroom. Learning about how these programs are supported and operate will be useful to assist educators in taking advantage of them; collaborating with them will prove to be even more beneficial to all.

Chapter 8 brings together the lessons learned through interviews, observations, investigations, and organization of the materials in the previous seven chapters. Through identification of themes, this chapter offers ways that educators may personalize their plans. They are encouraged to take good ideas, reframe them in light of their own culture and circumstances, and then begin to implement them.

What Special Features Are in This Book?

Throughout this book, we bring to light what educators want to know about current efforts in many states and several countries regarding redesigning learning to be successful in its goal of preparing our students for their futures, whatever that may be. One feature of each chapter is a list titled "In This Chapter" that provides an advanced organizer of the chapter. Next, the chapter reviews briefly what is known about the background and scholarship on the topic. The heart of each chapter is the lessons and reflections (called *Spotlights*) from teachers, principals, superintendents, and other thought leaders who have started a program, revised a curriculum, followed an idea to fruition, or encountered success. We use these stories to exemplify how your colleagues are already addressing the foci of this book. We realize that each of you reading this book will find nuggets of information that will resonate with your circumstances and you may perhaps want to reach out to the educators; when possible, we have provided Twitter handles to help you connect. We also know that your context may require modifications or adaptations, but we have great confidence in the creativity of our readers!

The ISTE Standards for students and educators included at the end of each chapter provide the foundation to guide your practice and frame your work with students. The standards represent a lens through which to consider the implementation of any one project, a class project-based experience, a schoolwide initiative, or even a district plan. They provide an excellent framework that guides discussion and planning for educators, but also with learners and the larger educational community. Using the standards—along with the topic-specific information, activities, and resources provided in each chapter—will strengthen the experiences and outcomes for both the learners and the educators.

We also suggest discussion questions for a PLN, a graduate course, or simply to provoke thought and action. Finally, each chapter has a list of resources; we include and identify those that are free and differentiate those available for a fee or to purchase. At the end of the book we include a list of references, to assist you in using the book as a springboard to further reading.

It is important to recognize that any book can only present a snapshot of some of the amazing things going on in the educational environment at this moment in time; the decision of which stories to tell or schools to celebrate was extremely difficult. Each person reading this book will likely know of a teacher, a school leader, or a district doing amazing things for learners. We hope you will take the time to recognize them for their work, and we wish we could have included each and every one of them in this book. They absolutely deserve our recognition and congratulations.

CHAPTER 1

Stem Initiatives, Robotics, and Coding

The role of the teacher is to create the conditions for invention rather than provide ready-made knowledge.

—Seymour Papert

If you haven't failed yet, you haven't tried anything yet.

—Reshma Saujani, CEO, Girls Who Code

In This Chapter:

- What is the STEM movement about?

- What is the purpose and pedagogical drive to include coding and robotics in schools?

- How are schools implementing STEM, coding, and robotics?

- How can you get started including STEM, robotics, and coding in your classroom or school?

What Is the STEM Initiative?

STEM—typically Science, Technology, Engineering, and Mathematics—has become a guiding star for education. STEM is a curriculum based on the idea of educating students in these four specific disciplines using an interdisciplinary, hands-on approach that relates to real-world applications. An integrated STEM approach is designed to bring students into the world of authentic contexts, to investigate realistic problems that have no simple answers, using active learning and teaching approaches. Moreover, this model of STEM education is designed to develop learners' conceptual knowledge of the interrelated nature of science and mathematics, as they develop their understanding of engineering and technology (Hernandez et al., 2014).

For many reasons, this integrative approach is an area of great interest and importance to business and industry, as well as to the education profession and families. Tracing back to the Sputnik era, when suddenly the Soviet Union beat the U.S. into space, science content became more urgent in educational efforts. Then in the early 2000s, reports raised the alarm regarding schools and their efforts to engage students in the four areas of STEM. In *Rising Above the Gathering Storm* (National Academies of Science, Engineering and Medicine, 2005), the authors stated that U.S. student proficiency in STEM was trailing behind other countries. They projected that, if we were to succeed as a global leader, our future workforce would need to be better prepared in STEM disciplines. Subsequently, teaching about STEM became an imperative; in 2015, the White House launched the Educate to Innovate partnership aimed at strengthening STEM education and diversifying the STEM talent pool (The White House, 2015).

From 2014 to 2024, the number of STEM jobs will grow 17%, as compared to 12% for non-STEM jobs (Change the Equation, 2015). Yet, in a study by Google and Gallup (2016), only 18% of school administrators in grades 1–6 reported computer science as a top priority in their schools. Further, "Even fewer have access to computer science (CS) courses that teach coding: just 40 percent of K–12 principals in a 2016 Google/Gallup survey said their school offers CS courses with computer programming/coding. Exposure to coding at the elementary level is even rarer" (McKibben, 2017, p. 2). Overall, only 24% of K–12 principals and 29% of superintendents identified it as a top priority. Their top reasons for not implementing it in their schools included a lack of funds for a new teacher, lack of availability of computer science teachers, and an undeniable focus on the subjects that are typically tested.

Yet, there are more than 500,000 open computing jobs in the U.S.; nine out of ten parents want their children to learn coding and computer science (Code.org, 2018).

However, those schools and educational facilities (e.g., libraries, museums) that have decided to devote resources and dedicate space to STEM curriculum and labs tend to go about them in a positive manner. One researcher found,

> Recent construction models reflect the eagerness to develop STEM/STEAM programs, with an increase in makerspaces, special labs and experiment-friendly classrooms. And more schools are creating areas where students can gather and collaborate as project-based learning continues to spread. Specially designed nooks and study spots are proving popular with learners. (Bendici, 2017, p. 32)

While STEM has become the buzzword, the teaching of STEM content has recently taken a focus on coding and robotics.

Many organizations are fostering robotics competitions, and these have been studied for educational outcomes. For example, in studying the outcomes from the Robofest robotics competition, researchers said,

> The characteristics of robotics-based pedagogy provide at least the following five key advantages over traditional pedagogy in teaching the theory and practice of STEM: (1) integration of STEM topics in a multidisciplinary fashion, 2) efficient transformation of abstract concepts into concrete learning modules for students, (3) combination of STEM theory with its practice, (4) hands-on learning that is active and engaging, and (5) a highly enjoyable and motivating learning environment. (Chung, Cartwright, & Cole, 2014, p. 24)

The goal of this competition is to be open to everyone, so the entry price is $50 per team. The rules are relatively simple: Robofest students are required to program an onboard computer to physically control the robot to achieve its missions without human assistance—absolutely no joysticks or remote controls are allowed.

Dr. Pavlo "Pasha" Antonenko developed a collaborative project to infuse focused STEM learning experiences into classrooms based on the practice of integrative science and STEM activities. Titled iDigFossils, this project is funded through an ITEST grant from the National Science Foundation. He describes this project as very rewarding and says,

I collaborate with paleontologists, geologists, computer scientists, and, of course, teachers, to design curriculum and apps that engage students in the 3-D scanning and printing practices of real-life paleontologists. Paleontology is a truly integrative science—it studies biodiversity and evolution in deep time using mathematical models, and a bunch of cool technologies such as 3-D scanners. The fossils that our participants scan are added to a virtual collection accessible to anyone at myfossil.org. The 3-D printed fossils are used by schools in a wide variety of classes. (Antonenko, 2017, personal communication)

Coding and Robotics

Coding is considered an essential element of computer science, STEM, and the overarching goal of creativity. According to Fluck et al. (2016),

Coding is about thinking. Putting a process into a particular code (writing a program for a computer) requires precision. This is analogous to the precision required in literacy skills of writing, but while people can understand intent or infer spelling, computers are far more literal. Therefore a child skilled at coding, may by transference, be more precise in their thought and have greater capacity to communicate. The beneficence is immediate and personal to the learner. (p. 42)

According to Campbell (2016), "Coding involves learning basic logic (Boolean logic, conditionals), which has applications in other aspects of life" (p. 334). In addition,

The recent introduction of computer science (CS) education into schools in many countries has led to a surge in interest in programming tools and approaches which make CS concepts and tasks engaging, motivating and accessible to all. There is renewed interest in supporting learning through physical computing, which has been shown to be motivational whilst offering opportunities for collaboration and creativity. (Sentance, Waite, Hodges, MacLeod, & Yeomans, 2017, p. 531)

Costa (2017) notes that robotics instruction moves from traditional teacher-driven instruction to hands-on learning in which collaborative teams of students use STEM knowledge to solve real-world problems. In the latest revision of the Elementary and

Secondary Education Act (called the Every Student Succeeds Act) passed in December 2015, CS is named an essential part of "well-rounded education subjects." During the last decade, robotics has attracted the high interest of teachers and researchers as a valuable tool to develop cognitive and social skills for students from "pre-school to high school and to support learning in science, mathematics, technology, informatics and other school subjects or interdisciplinary learning activities" (Alimisis, 2013, p. 63).

> The role of Educational Robotics should be seen as a tool to foster essential life skills (cognitive and personal development, team working) through which people can develop their potential to use their imagination, to express themselves and make original and valued choices in their lives. Robotics benefits are relevant for all children; the target groups in robotics projects and courses should include the whole class and not only the talented in science and technology children. (Alimisis, 2013, p. 69)

Based deeply on the ideas of Papert (1980, 1987), robotics and coding provide hands-on and creative opportunities for learners to invent, solve problems, and create. "Pioneering efforts in school classes during the last decade have shown that children are enthusiastically involved in robotics projects achieving learning goals and/or developing new skills" (Alimisis, 2013, p. 64). Studies in the field (e.g., Benitti, 2012; Eguchi, 2010) have begun to report the ways in which robotics potentially affect different subject areas including physics, mathematics, and others. More interestingly, the research suggests that learners also gain skills in research, social skills, creative thinking, and communication/team collaboration. Evidence of this is clear. Nugent, Barker, Grandgenett, and Adamchuk (2010) researched the impact of robotics and geospatial technology intervention with 288 students aged 11–12; those who attended a 40-hour intervention increased their knowledge of science, technology, engineering, and mathematic concepts. In another study, 12 elementary school teachers taught science for one year according to traditional curriculum and the following year they incorporated LEGO design challenges. Results showed that the learning of science content was greater for students who were taught the program using robotics (Wendell & Rogers, 2013). Bers, Flannery, Kazakoff, and Sullivan (2014) have suggested that when children of elementary age learn about computer science their experiences benefit not only their academic and technical learning but also their social and emotional development. Thus, it has become clear once again that computer science and coding are extremely important for multiple reasons.

Where Are the Examples?

Many organizations and schools are taking up the challenge and embedding coding and robotics into their programs. Code.org is a nonprofit dedicated to expanding access to computer science and increasing participation by women and underrepresented minorities: "Our vision is that every student in every school should have the opportunity to learn computer science, just like biology, chemistry or algebra" (code.org, 2018). Code.org organizes the annual Hour of Code (hourofcode.com) campaign, which has engaged 10% of all students in the world, and provides the leading curriculum for K–12 computer science in the largest school districts in the U.S.

Schools are growing their programs, and several are discussed below. MC2 STEM is a school that is part of the Cleveland Metropolitan School District, one of the most economically challenged school districts in the country, where the average high school graduation rate was just 60% in 2011. The school was created through a public-private partnership among several organizations, with the intention of providing about 400 students, all of whom are eligible for free or reduced-price meals, with an integrated curriculum that is informed by real-world experiences. Students attend their classes at campuses embedded in business and school sites around the city: the Great Lakes Science Center, General Electric (GE) Lighting's Nela Park campus, Cleveland State University, and various college campuses.

The McLean School outside Washington, DC is proud of its robotics curriculum, which provides "21st century skills of technology, teamwork and creativity" to the K–12 population (mcleanschool.org/page/academics/robotics). It offers students the opportunity to use LEGO WeDo, LEGO Mindstorms EV3 robots, and free-form robotics as they progress through the grades, and also provides them with the opportunity to participate in national competitions.

South Fayette School District in Pennsylvania approached inclusion of STEM, coding, and robotics in a unique manner, by restructuring the curriculum in a purposeful manner; the district began with a focus on computational thinking and held a series of discussions that involved everyone in the system. The district has been recognized for the dramatic changes to the entire system, but, as explained below, this transformation did not happen overnight.

SPOTLIGHT 1.1

Computational Thinking and Transformation

South Fayette School District (@InnovationSFSD)

Billie P. Rondinelli, Superintendent, and Aileen Owens, Director of Technology
and Innovation, South Fayette School District, South Fayette, Pennsylvania

In our school system, we began by identifying computational thinking as the
new literacy and then embedded this process into STEAM learning (science,
technology, engineering, and math, plus the arts). We started by defining what
this might include and identified three aspects. The first aspect is the problem-
solving process used in computer science, which is the ability to think logically,
algorithmically, abstractly, and recursively. The second aspect addresses essential
skills, such as habits of mind and the characteristics of intelligent and successful
problem-solvers, which also encompass complexity, persistence, and toler-
ance for ambiguity. This aspect also covers human-centered design thinking
strategies and visible thinking routines. We developed these concepts from the
works of Art Costa and Bena Kallick (habitsofmindinstitute.org), the LUMA
Institute (luma-institute.com) and Project Zero (pz.harvard.edu/projects/visible-
thinking) at Harvard University. The final aspect of our model covers career
vision, which is an awareness of career contexts in which the problem-solving
processes, dispositions, and attitudes apply. This helps students understand and
envision how those careers reflect their learning.

Remaking education may seem like a monumental task, but we have learned that
systemic and fundamental change can happen incrementally and be transformative without being drastic. Over the last eight years, we have systematically
incorporated engineering and design problem-solving, or computational
thinking, into the district's K–12 curriculum while developing a STEAM studio
model for innovation.

Together, with the support of our board of directors and community, we have
transformed traditional education by embedding computational thinking
into the existing curriculum for students in all grade levels. Local foundations
assisted us in addressing equity through outreach to schools in southwestern
Pennsylvania. This began as a grassroots effort but has spread to encompass the
entire community.

Beginning in August 2017, we added Python programming to the grade 8 curriculum through a mandatory rotation. In February 2017, we began to offer the curriculum in an eight-week after-school incubator project. An incubator is a place to safely test new ideas in a controlled setting for the purpose of creating a scalable, sustainable solution. Current eighth grade students are participating in the incubator, led by graduate students from Carnegie Mellon University and a software developer from Google Pittsburgh.

Our high school student Python programming team will act as mentors to the new class. A computer science consultant will observe each session and, based on observations of students and input from student mentors, she will make adjustments to the course and build appropriate assessments before implementation in the fall. The teacher assigned to teach the course joined the incubator to learn with the students, then attended a summer Python course at Carnegie Mellon University to gain additional expertise.

We did not build this model alone. We relied heavily on local and national experts. We sought the advice of professors and researchers from Carnegie Mellon University, the Learning Research Development Center at University of Pittsburgh, the MIT Media Lab, the MIT App Inventor Team, the Create Lab at Indiana University, and others. We received support and guidance from the Grable Foundation, Digital Promise: League of Innovative Schools, Allegheny Intermediate Unit 3, the Arts Education Collaborative, nonprofit organizations, and local businesses. Partnerships, our school board, and community support have been essential elements to our success.

After a few years of this iterative process of embedding computational thinking into teaching and learning, we created a system that has become the mechanism for delivering and sustaining innovation. Over a three-year period, the district hired STEAM teachers and facilitators for our elementary, intermediate, and middle school buildings and changed existing positions and schedules to support STEAM learning and computational thinking. Positions such as a STEAM literacy teacher and technology education teachers have been reimagined and work in tandem with STEAM teachers to support innovation. In the high school, two teachers co-taught our newly designed Innovation Studio class. One way we continue to refine our transformation is through our STEAM Team K–12, which meets formally several times a year to build and ensure that we maintain our vertical alignment; thus, our program continues to evolve.

We have learned many lessons, and listed below are the most important ones (Rondinelli & Owens, 2017, p. 26).

Figure 1.1. South Fayette Middle School students. Photo Credit: Aileen Owens, 2017.

Figure 1.2. Students demonstrating robotics to visitors. (Owens, 2017).

- Adopt a mindset for innovation. Create an understanding and acceptance of the importance of the iterative process. One example is using after-school incubator projects to test ideas before full-scale implementation.

- Articulate a strong vision. Embed this vision into practice through the district's operational plan and ongoing themes each year.

- Involve the board and community. Provide stakeholders with the opportunity to understand the vision in order to support ongoing work.

- Rethink your system. Share and borrow existing models and then remake them to fit your circumstances.

- Build and nurture a team. Support and sustain innovation with an emphasis on vertically aligned curriculum. Remake existing staff positions and create new positions. Creating a position such as the director of technology and innovation is critical for continuous improvement and for connecting education to the changing world. Be prepared to invest in professional development, including activities never previously attempted.

- Embed project-based learning experiences. Use project-based learning to provide a catalyst for real world, engaging learning experiences, particularly when partnering with businesses and professionals.

- Communicate the vision. Use unique ways to share, such as through district briefings that benefit students and staff and partnerships that establish and showcase a collaborative environment.

- Develop after school programs. Provide connected learning experiences while simultaneously building the curriculum.

- Don't go it alone. Cultivate partnerships from experts in the field. You will be surprised by how many universities and businesses will open their doors to you and provide talent and resources. You will find the support you need.

- Focus on your students. Listen to their advice. Engage them in the process. Use student focus groups and interviews as part of the iterative process. The students have the answers you are seeking.

▪ ▪ ▪ ▪ ▪

San Francisco Unified is piloting a push-in model for computer science and coding. The district does not mandate that schools teach coding at the expense of another subject; rather, the district will provide 20 hours of CS instruction to preK–5 students and 40 hours to middle school students each year. Park City, Utah, realized they needed to include coding and robotics in their schools. They are working on integrating this into the schools, but first they determined it was important for them to solve logistical challenges such as staffing, scheduling, professional development, and even the curriculum itself had to be ironed out in a hurry.

Most of the schools who are interested in infusing STEM into their curriculum and students' experiences struggle to simultaneously include the "A for arts" to build a STEAM program. Todd LaVogue works at an arts-based school that focuses on instrumental music but also offers vocal, dance, and visual arts; he has the enviable position of integrating technology into this rich curriculum.

 **SPOTLIGHT 1.2**

Fostering Computational Thinking from the Ground Floor

The Conservatory School, North Palm Beach, Florida

Todd LaVogue (@ToddLaVogue), Design, Innovation and Technology Specialist

I teach at a Title I public school focused on music education. In preparing our students with the skills needed to be successful learners, I have the opportunity daily to help teachers with their curriculum by infusing technology where appropriate to teach content from kindergarten through eighth grade in new and exciting ways in my classroom that has been named "The Ground Floor Collective." We already have the "A" in our curriculum; my role is to add more of the STEM.

Through grant writing by myself and my administration, my classroom has numerous educational technology tools one might wish for in a classroom. What makes my role exciting is working with teachers and learners each day to support their curricular goals. I teach coding and, more importantly, computational thinking. I accomplish this in a variety of ways. Sometimes we use directional note cards to demonstrate pathways; at other times we use programming languages and robotics. Through the use of robotics, we learn forms of coding to help our educational technology tools accomplish our goals of solving a problem while getting from point A to point B.

We focus on soft skills in the Ground Floor Collective: collaboration, communication, negotiation, creative problem-solving, cognitive flexibility, emotional intelligence, and critical thinking.

We have created underwater realms as well as models of our solar system, and we coded robots to journey through these environments while we learned along the way. We have used robots to help us recreate famous voyages of discovery and tell stories about explorers such as Juan Ponce de León. We have used loose parts and low-tech coding to retell the story of a Civil War figure as we mapped their life and how this event changed the course of their history.

We also spend significant time in the Ground Floor Collective just making. Soft skills can be developed through a pile of cardboard and some duct tape. We spend time creating original products through lessons on user-centered design, and we create prototypes for these designs with cardboard.

My pinned tweet on my twitter account (@ToddLaVogue) is a quote from Plato: "Don't train a child by force or harshness but guide them to it by what excites their mind." This quote is my philosophy. I do not expect kids to learn the way I teach; I expect to teach the way they learn. This philosophy and remaining a lifelong learner have made me the best possible teacher for my students, and they deserve nothing less.

■ ■ ■ ■ ■

The Cincinnati Public Schools (CPS) partnered to bring STEM-related curriculum into the public schools in perhaps a first-of-its-kind adventure. Not many schools or learners have the opportunity to see sharks in their own classroom!

SPOTLIGHT 1.3

WAVE Foundation (@WAVEfoundation5)

Newport Aquarium (@newportaquarium), Newport, Kentucky

Scott Wingate, Executive Director

The Welfare of Aquatic Animals through Advocacy, Volunteerism, and Education Foundation (WAVE) at Newport Aquarium, Newport, Kentucky, has partnered with Cincinnati Public Schools (CPS) and through the generous support of the Louis & Louise Nippert Charitable Foundation to create the Living Curriculum Initiative (LCI). This type of program is built to inspire curiosity and bring science to life in elementary school classrooms. The LCI features traveling aquariums with live sharks, brought into classrooms, to elicit students' natural curiosity and facilitate understanding of the scientific process. The LCI is based on the QCER (Question, Claim, Evidence, Reasoning) inquiry process, which allows students to guide their own learning from observing the live shark to asking a testable question and gathering their own evidence. Students then identify their claims and the reasoning required to support this investigation. The classroom series culminates in student-led presentations about what knowledge they created through their investigation. The collaboration of informal educators along with formal CPS classroom teachers has created a program focused on student achievement and state standards, but with the excitement and curiosity that live animals can bring to science.

The LCI was created to allow students to engage with live animals to develop higher-order thinking skills and enhance student achievement on science proficiency tests. The LCI is a three-year program that includes three visits per year totaling nine interactions with the students (nine contact hours). Beginning in third grade, students engage with the animals using the QCER process. Each year, students will gain more autonomy with the scientific process, becoming responsible for their own experimental procedure and data collection. Fifth grade will bring another level of scientific thought into the program by having students interact with local species and consider what actions they can take to contribute to local conservation for these animals. WAVE has only completed the first year of this program as of 2017, but the students, CPS, and WAVE are excited to continue this partnership focused on student success. Erin Shultz, Community

Outreach Coordinator for WAVE Foundation said, "The mission of this program is to teach students the scientific process in a way that is engaging and accessible to all students and to connect them at a young age with the conservation of our natural resources" (personal communication, 2017). This can certainly be seen

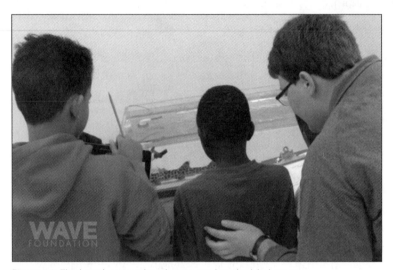

Figure 1.3. Third-graders recording data on coral catshark behaviors.

in the student work.

In the first three years of the LCI, WAVE will work with students from 16 elementary schools within Cincinnati Public Schools. One of these schools has taken the LCI programming and incorporated it into nearly every aspect of the students' learning. After the three-week experience that the third grade students shared, their teachers have referred back to this in many other ways (*experience-resonance*). Students created charts to show what they know (K), what they wonder (W), and what they learned (L) before and after each visit (KWL Chart). They gathered this information to write informative essays about the coral cat shark after the LCI program was completed. They will also be reading about another species of shark in order to compare and contrast the two species, then create illustrations for a book about these animals. One of these third-grade teachers said her "students were listening and asking pertinent questions" and that LCI gave students the "ability to interact with a live animal, observe, and think critically" (personal communication, 2017). This experience will be a focal point for these students, increasing their confidence and desire to participate in scientific thinking. Scott Wingate, WAVE Foundation's Executive Director, said, "Through the Living Curriculum Initiative students are learning the scientific process in a way that will affect their view of science for a lifetime."

Figure 1.4. Traveling Shark Cart from the WAVE Foundation, Newport Aquarium.

■ ■ ■ ■ ■

Robotics and coding, within the STEM and STEAM initiatives, have become universal throughout educational entities around the globe. For example, "Fifth- and sixth-grade students from the Gems Modern Academy in Dubai have invented a robot that tracks the sun's movement and adjusts solar panels throughout the day, allowing the panels to capture the maximum amount of sunlight (and energy)" (Sebugwaawo, 2017, n.p.).

Student teams participating in the 2017 *FIRST* Global Robotics Games, an international competition with entrants from 160 countries, are addressing the water crisis by developing solutions to store drinkable water, filter contaminated water, and find new sources of clean water (Freeman et al., 2017). The San Juan School District, San Juan Island, Washington, made a commitment to STEM education through its STEM center (stemsji.wordpress.com), which is operated in collaboration with the University of Washington. Its goal is that every learner have the opportunity to experience its curriculum, which includes courses in materials engineering and computer-aided drafting (CAD); robotics; remotely operated vehicles (ROVs); quadcopters to cover land, air, and sea; and video game design and programming. The district has also considered new ways to earn credit for what students learn, acknowledging it is outdated to think that students can only earn credit by sitting in a class for 90 hours.

SPOTLIGHT 1.4

Blending Coding, Robotics, and Community Development in Carnegie Mellon's CREATE Lab (@cmucreatelab)

Carnegie Mellon University, Pittsburgh, Pennsylvania

Dror Yaron (@dror_yaron), Director of Outreach

The Community Robotics, Education and Technology Empowerment Lab (CREATE Lab) at Carnegie Mellon University's Robotics Institute explores socially meaningful innovation and deployment of robotic technologies. It is a "technology breeding ground" that incorporates engineers, computer scientists, artists, educators, and innovators who strive to "empower citizens to chart their technology future" and improve their "community's prospects for quality of life" (cmucreatelab.org). The projects developed here are implemented throughout the Pittsburgh area, in schools, and to a broader network of satellite schools and universities. The goal is to spin off these projects to become self-sustaining products.

A key focus of the CREATE Lab's efforts in education is to cultivate "technology fluency": the confidence to author or creatively configure technology in the pursuit of individual and collective goals. In the context of education, technologically fluent students apply tech tools to study, communicate, and address issues of direct concern. Technologically fluent educators use technology in contextually relevant ways across content areas, leverage it to grow their practice, and integrate tech in a way that supports identification and nurturing of diverse student talents and the creation of multiple learning pathways.

The CREATE Lab is committed to technology empowerment in underserved communities. The lab partners with universities and other organizations serving educators to establish CREATE Lab Satellites. The Satellites support local educators in promoting technology fluency and empower learners to author/leverage technology for social good.

The CREATE Lab Satellite Network includes nine universities in four states, and it brings technology fluency to communities in locally relevant ways. For further details about the CREATE Lab's motivation and vision, please see the white paper at bit.ly/clwpaper.

Some projects out of the CREATE Lab (full list and more details at cmucreatelab.org):

Message from Me: *Technology in the service of a better dinner table conversation.*

Children ages 3–5 are developing language, social, and other crucial life skills during the day but, because of their limited ability to recollect and communicate, are unable to fully express what they did "at school" to their parents. Using this app on tablets at childcare centers, young children record their daily experiences through pictures and speech and send them to their parents' cell phones or email. This age-appropriate adaptation of existing technologies allows young children to practice their communication skills and build their self-confidence by talking about their day, their accomplishments, and their discoveries. Message from Me (messagefromme.org) enhances parent-child conversations and involves families in the educational experience of their children.

Children's Innovation Project: *Technology as raw material.*

Developed at the CREATE Lab by Melissa Butler and Jeremy Boyle, then spun out on its own, Children's Innovation Project (cippgh.org) embraces innovation as *finding something new inside something known*. This frame for innovation allows a slow space for children to find small, authentic discoveries and reflect on themselves in relation to the materials they explore. An approach of technology as raw material further supports children's innovation as it nudges children to work deeply at technology as they explore with Circuit Blocks (a kit of components designed for young hands), electronic toys, and other devices and components.

The project does not attach value to technology itself, and it approaches technology as a means to learning, not an end. Through a focus on the language-logic systems of technology, children gain access to the thinking of technology, instead of just using the stuff of technology.

Arts & Bots: *Robotics as an expressive tool*

Students combine craft materials and robotic components (Hummingbird Robotics Kit; hummingbirdkit.com) to build their own robotic creations, and they animate them to tell a story or express an idea using visual-programming tools, or by writing code. Arts & Bots (cmucreatelab.org/projects/Arts_&_Bots) supports interdisciplinary learning by integrating robotics and computer science into nontechnical subjects, including English, social studies, math, music, physical education, and more. This helps engage students, who may not self-identify as technologically inclined, with robotics and computer science as a creative tool, a vehicle for communicating their thinking, and not as a focal point.

Teaching a nontechnical subject in this new way allows a teacher to notice and foster student talents that may not be evident in a traditional setting. The initial target audience was middle school girls, but the project now engages all genders from intermediate grades through high school.

Flutter: *Seeding tech confidence*

Feedback from CREATE Lab partners about the need to engage elementary school students with technology earlier on yielded the development of Flutter, a circuit board system similar to the Hummingbird Robotics Kit. With the Hummingbird, students animate their robots using code or visual programming; with Flutter (cmucreatelab.org/projects/Flutter), students choreograph their robot's behavior by defining the relationship between input and output in a feedback loop. Students build robotic sculptures to represent physical conditions and changes in their environment such as soil moisture in a flower pot, air quality in the classroom, light levels in the school, and temperature outside. Feedback loops are an essential part of many technological innovations, from the thermostat to self-driving cars.

Finch: *Foster diverse participation in computer science*

The Finch is a small robot designed to increase and sustain diverse participation in computer science studies by providing students a tangible and physical representation of their code: the robot can be programmed to move about, light up, change colors, and make sounds. The Finch is loaded with sensors, so the inputs for the program students write can also be connected to the physical world, responding to light, temperature, obstacles, and the robot's orientation in space.

The Finch (finchrobot.com) was developed to catalyze a wide range of computer science learning experiences, from an entry into the basics of computational thinking all the way to writing richly interactive programs. It has support for more than a dozen programming languages, including environments appropriate for students as young as five years old.

GigaPan: *A robot for building empathy*

An earthly adaptation of NASA's Mars Rover imaging technology, GigaPan helps bring distant communities and peoples together through images that have so much detail that they are, themselves, the objects of exploration, discovery, and wonder. The GigaPan robot and website (gigapan.com) allow learners to document, annotate, and explore in outstanding detail their own environment and the environment of peers from across the globe (or across the street). Using a robotic camera mount, point and shoot camera, stitching software, interactive online platform, and large-scale prints, GigaPan is enabling people to explore, experience, and share each other's world.

With more than 100,000 gigapixel panoramas to explore online, students, educators, and community members can find interactive images related to their interests and area of inquiry.

Earth Time: *Democratizing big data*

Earth Time (earthtime.org) is a zoomable, terapixel-scale animation: a time-lapse animation of satellite imagery of Earth over several decades, combined with a library of global data visualization layers. This tool was developed in collaboration with Google and a growing group of institutions and experts providing massive data collections on climate, health, immigration, urbanization, and more. The vision for this project is for school children and world leaders to have access to the same massive data and interactive tools for visualization, exploration, and sensemaking. Earth Time has been shared at World Economic Forum gatherings with world and industry leaders to raise awareness of issues and inform action. It is also shared in schools and universities, to support data-driven discovery, inquiry, and advocacy.

∎ ∎ ∎ ∎ ∎

Many new programs and materials are available to support the teaching of coding and the development of robotics. One recent entry is the BBC micro:bit, which is a tiny handheld programmable computer. They have small LED lights that are capable of flashing messages, a built-in compass, and motion detectors, plus they are able to be hooked up to other devices through cables or Bluetooth technology (goo.gl/DjUQFy). They were given to every learner in Year 7 or equivalent (approximately 12 years old) across the UK in 2016 for free. They can be used to accomplish all sorts of things like power cameras, write words in lights, choose playlists, or control musical instruments.

Sitka School District (SSD) is a relatively small but mighty district; with its six schools and approximately 1,250 students, it represents an innovative district. On a recent visit, students were gaining incredible experiences in digital age hard and soft skills. Cindy Duncan is a second grade teacher with a philosophy that includes teaching young children coding. She begins the year by introducing the student to Ozobots and builds it into literacy through stories. During the first week of class, she used a story common to most children, *The Gingerbread Man*, and taught dyads of children how to develop the story characters as part of the Ozobot coding.

According to recent research, 90% of students said the micro:bit showed them that anyone can code; 86% of students said the micro:bit made computer science more interesting; 70% more girls said they would choose computing as a school subject after using the micro:bit, and 85% of teachers agreed it has made ICT/computer science more enjoyable for their students (Sentance et al., 2017). The micro:bit has projects that move beyond just computer science but include design technology, physics and even art and music classes.

SPOTLIGHT 1.5

Beginning Early with Coding and Robotics

Sitka School District, Sitka, Alaska

Cindy Duncan (@DuncanSSD), Second Grade Teacher

I teach coding and robotics because as an educator it is my job to recognize that my students are digital age students; they are global innovators, thinkers, and problem-solvers. I need to help them develop the skills they will need to be successful in the world they will grow and work in. One way I can do that is through programing.

Computer science and programing is a basic skill in our students' lives and future. We can't leave them behind because we feel unqualified or intimidated. The exponential growth of technological development can be overwhelming, but we need to move away from a teacher-centered approach. In my student-led classroom I am not the expert; rather, I am the facilitator of their learning. I provide my students with devoted time to program, and I value the work they do. I use my students' interests to show them they can be creators and not just consumers of educational information and projects. By incorporating the education edition of the super popular sandbox game, Minecraft, I have increased attendance, motivation, and traditional subject knowledge, but my students are learning to code and program with a purpose. Even at the early age of seven, many of my students' coding skills exceed mine. This is not an issue for any of us, because the students are the center of their learning. My role is to help students develop a desire for further knowledge, to make learning irresistible and valued.

I understand that not all my students will grow to actually write code as a profession, but it is teaching them so much more. Students are learning critical and computational thinking as well as problem-solving skills that transcend actual coding skills. I tell my students they are the writers of their code and they are the ones who understand it better than anyone else; thus, it is up to them to persevere and problem-solve. It creates habits of the mind that they can apply to every aspect of life. There are no limits to what they can achieve. It's about my students taking ownership of their growth and flourishing.

My favorite moments are when my students exceed all expectations, even their own! The results have been so amazing that I wanted to reach more students, so I started offering after-school coding to at-risk youth, and I started mentoring and collaborating with other educators around the globe. Coding and robotics help my students develop a culture of learning that will benefit them throughout their lives.

■ ■ ■ ■ ■

In the SSD middle school, Amanda Duvall believes that coding and robotics offer a way to more than digital age knowledge; she sees them as a way to change the nature of teaching and learning. She tells her students, "I don't know this but we're learning it together. You may learn it faster and that is okay" (personal communication, 2017). Mrs. Duvall also serves as chair of the SSD technology committee. She explained that she starts her learners on the road to coding by introducing them to the "Code-a-piller" to help them understand the basic concepts involved in coding, and then moves them into more complex challenges. All sixth grade students take an introduction to technology class in which multiple opportunities are given for learners to gain knowledge and get excited about their learning.

Sitka does not stop there! The Career and Technical Education (CTE) program is actually an incredible makerspace; it is well-equipped with digital fabrication materials, a plasma cutter, small engines, and also includes woodworking and other traditional CTE programs. Because Alaska is deeply committed to its culture and heritage, the Sitka School District started a unique program that stresses the integration of arts, culture, and technology. To support these goals, the CTE lab brings in local artists to encourage the students to blend their art and culture into their projects. In addition, the high school offers a strand that brings together robotics, forensics, applied physics, cyber security, engineering, CAD, and more. High school students also have the option to learn Python as a programming language. After-school clubs allow students to specialize in their areas of greatest interest. For example, they have the opportunity to participate in the FIRST LEGO League, which is an international challenge program that introduces students ages 9–14 to a scientific and real-world challenge for teams to focus on and research. (For more on how the Sitka School District implements a unique approach to innovation, please see Dr. Wegner's spotlight in Chapter 8).

Coding is also very popular in after-school clubs. Tom Bijesse is the national training manager for Code Club in New Zealand, which is part of an international organization currently supporting more than 10,000 clubs in 100 countries. The goal of Code Club is to support volunteers and educators who run free coding clubs for young learners, ages 9–13, who build and share their ideas, learning along the way. The international mission is that "all children should have the opportunity to learn to code, no matter who they are or where they come from." Tom explained that they also host free teacher training courses, and although the technology industry has clear issues with gender diversity, Code Clubs enroll a more balanced number of girls and boys. The clubs are funded through governments, private companies, foundations, and others. According to their website (codeclub.org.uk),

> Our projects are easy to follow, step-by-step guides which help young people learn Scratch, HTML & CSS, and Python by making games, animations, and websites. The projects gradually introduce coding concepts to allow young people to build their knowledge incrementally, which also means there's no need for the adult running the session to be a computing expert (CodeClub, n.d.).

Interestingly, the Code Club and the Raspberry PI Foundation have joined together to further promote the idea of coding for all. The Raspberry Pi Foundation is an educational charity organization that manufactures tiny, affordable, programmable computers. The organization seeks to increase young people's knowledge of computers and computer programming. Raspberry Pi products are often incorporated into robotics, coding, and other STEM integration experiences.

A small school outside Auckland, New Zealand, is also doing many things to ensure their students have the opportunities that other learners have.

 **SPOTLIGHT 1.6**

One School's Make Club

Taupaki School, New Zealand (@TaupakiSchool)

Paula Hogg, (@diana_prince_ww) Deputy Board Chairperson

Paula Hogg serves multiple roles in the Taupaki School; she is a former student, a parent, and Deputy Board Chairperson on the Board of Trustees. She has been on the board since 2009. New Zealand has an interesting system for self-governance of schools in that each school organizes and makes decisions for itself. To accomplish this, each school has a Board of Trustees, which is an elected body charged to ensure the school complies with all directives from the NZ Ministry of Education and government, but also sets the school's strategic goals, core values, and vision. The self-governing school model allows for a school's vision to be co-constructed with the community to best serve their needs. Thus, the special character of each school community can be actualized through each school's envisioned future. Mrs. Hogg explained that the board must be focused on the future and on guaranteeing that the students of the school are ready for their futures.

To that end, she helped start a maker club that encompasses coding, robotics, and other STEAM activities; they often mash up art with technology. For example, recently the learners were creating a "Len Lye"–inspired interactive art sculpture (which included learning about engineering concepts). This club is open to everyone in the community: the students, of course, but also teachers, parents, grandparents, and community members. The learners drive many of the things they do, and many of these do not need a special place in which to do them. In fact, most of the time the club is held in a classroom unless a large group is expected. One of the strong beliefs is that anyone can lead a project or teach about something they know; during one robotics session, one of the grade 6 students (10 years old) gave the demonstration to all. Parents also share their knowledge; one showed the learners how to make an analogue sprite for a game. Mrs. Hogg explained how projects evolve:

> The learners choose what they want to make in the sessions (unless it is a group activity like building a hovercraft). Probably the best example is when they decided they wanted to make an interactive rubbish bin unit for the school because they were seeing lots of litter on the grounds, and caring for our environment is a big part of our vision and core values. We provide the materials and do a demonstration/example, then people make their own creations. For example, we show students how to use Scratch or Tinkercad, but then they will all design and make different games or different 3-D printed objects—the students control where they take their learning. We are a guide and support. Another example is e-textiles. We show them the basics of how to make a circuit, but they design and make whatever they want to. People can work independently

if they want to as well. For example, we had a father and son working on building a robot together while we were learning how to make a tabletop arcade machine. Make Club belongs to the people in it, so they drive the learning and direction. (personal communication, 2017)

The school, though rather rural and small (about 260 students), is nonetheless offering other opportunities for learners. The board and leadership team made the decision that all students must have access to a device. Students use these devices to create and express learning in ways that are meaningful to them. For example, one student decided to design a heart in Tinkercad and then print it in 3-D to show what they had learned about hearts. Other students created a slide show. Students also blog about their learning, and all their learning is uploaded to a parent portal which students take their parents through in student-led conferences.

This school also has a technology center that provides learning experiences in food, hard materials, and design technology to their grade 7 and 8 students and others in the surrounding area. The school also has a robotics group and a rocketry group.

The Make Club is also timely as the New Zealand Government began its Network for Learning program to make sure that every school has high-speed access, and its Digital Technology Policy will be implemented during the 2018–2019 school year.

■ ■ ■ ■ ■

The goal of infusing STEM/STEAM and computer science into our educational system is not limited to K–12 learners. The U.S. Department of Education's Office of Innovation and Improvement has launched an important initiative for educators and families to promote early STEM education. It has funded some projects but challenged other organizations to donate or find resources to develop a large number of projects to broaden access to early STEM resources and promotions and to help prepare educators to support these projects. For example, Sesame Workshop will develop a course for educators called Make Believe with Math. The Grable Foundation will invest $1 million to encourage early STEM learning through the development of robust, hands-on activities for young children; for early educators to incorporate technology into their practice; and for the early learning field to move forward in its understanding of the constructive role STEM topics can play for young learners. The National Science Teachers Association (NSTA) is creating the NSTA Initiative for Learners 0–5, a streamlined array of NSTA resources—many of them at no cost—to preschool and elementary school educators, parents, and childcare providers that will engage our youngest learners in STEM. A professional development organization, Teaching Institute for Excellence in STEM (TIES) will bring Early Childhood Fab Labs to schools, childcare programs, museums, and other settings serving young learners. In addition, it will bring the Early Childhood Fab Lab to Head Start programs throughout the country. TIES will prototype these Labs in two Head Start programs with the intent to build a scalable model that would enable all Head Start programs to be able to have Early Childhood Fab Labs.

University and K–12 Interactions

McDonald (2016) conducted a review of the literature on STEM teaching and detailed results in the area of professional development. She concluded that the majority of research on professional development in STEM disciplines has been concentrated on science and mathematics; the findings support that it has been beneficial to teachers, but most especially for primary educators who frequently lack depth of science content knowledge.

Bozkurt Altan and Ercan (2016) conducted a study on providing professional development on STEM to science teachers and found an increase in their appreciation and interest in teaching an integrated approach to STEM in their science classes. They concluded that "in-service training programs should be developed for teachers to raise their awareness of the necessity of STEM education and to enhance their competencies in planning, implementation and evaluation of an instructional process suitable for this approach" (p. 103). Burrows (2015) found a similar outcome when she investigated a professional development model to introduce teachers to STEM concepts, and in particular to introduce astronomy as part of the STEM curriculum. She concluded,

> The faculty/PD teams emphasized the value of all of the participants in every possible situation and this led to an increase in the K–12 teachers' perception of themselves—an increased self-efficacy—using astronomy content and creating partnerships as a contributing member of the team. (p. 35)

Educators are continuously being handed new standards to meet and new skills to evaluate as part of their professional responsibilities. We know that this often requires new learning or upscaling of knowledge and skills; this is exactly what has happened with the Next Generation Science Standards (NGSS) that require weaving of engineering principles into many aspects of the science curriculum. Two professors recently created a project to support middle school teachers and learners in meeting these standards. Read about it in Spotlight 1.7 below.

SPOTLIGHT 1.7

I-Engineering—Engineering for Sustainable Communities by Youth and with Youth

Professors Angela Calabrese Barton (Michigan State University) and Edna Tan (@Mlgetcity) (University of North Carolina, Greensboro)

Through an NSF-funded grant, these two educators have identified middle school teachers who then go through a deeply immersive experience in which they watch learners in an informal STEM program (for more information about this, please see Spotlight 7.1). The teachers have the chance to work with the materials and, more importantly, to see how community engagement can drive identification of authentic challenges and lead students to investigate solutions. Drs. Tan and Calabrese Barton identified three main dimensions of their work that they think can help teachers to shape their classrooms:

* Knowledge and practices

* Recognition by others for what one knows and can do

* Agency to use what one knows to make a difference

They describe the focus of their 12 units as:

...energy engineering for sustainable community units with middle school students and teachers. The units support youth in designing solutions to challenges that matter to their local community. Youth develop expertise in renewable energy systems, circuitry, engineering practices, and community ethnography. Through this work, the I-Engineering

Figure 1.5. Engineering design process.

team has developed and collected resources that will support others in teaching engineering for sustainable communities and in ways that support youth in developing STEM knowledge and practices, and engaging in productive identity work in engineering, capable of making a difference in the world. (engineeriam.org/?page_id=180)

Their design process is shown in Figure 1.5.

One example demonstrates the power of engineering, solving real problems, and using a powerful design model. After interviewing eighth grade students regarding their views on school, one young woman was struck by comments about the types of events that result in a "silent lunch" penalty. It seems that students who are unable to rapidly pull out the correct book, or a pen, may be assigned this punishment! This sixth grade young lady, June, was determined to find a way to "light up" the inside of a desk, so that items could be quickly located to avert an unwelcome and, to the students, unjust punishment. June

Figure 1.6. Light-up desk. Photo Credit: Dr. Edna Tan.

innovated a portable light-up desk system where a parallel copper-tape circuit was laid on two stiff cardboard pieces measured and constructed so that they can be folded and opened up against one length and breadth of the student desk (Figure 1.6). Her system featured four white LED lights, first powered by coin cell batteries during the prototyping. After community feedback, June then switched the power source from coin-cell batteries to a hand-crank generator that can now be taped to one of the legs of the desk, to address sustainability in her design.

When reflecting on her innovation, June commented: "I want [people] to think about me as a really smart girl and for my product, I want them to think that it really works." Six months after the I-Engineering unit, June's sixth grade science teacher, Ms. D, said:

> June's definitely empowered and proud. She took much in pride in her idea coming into fruition. She came back at the beginning of the year to see if her prototype still worked and she was so proud that I still had her light-up desk intact and was able to show it to my new set of sixth-graders. She's coming back to fix some lights that are not working, and she can't wait to do that, she's actually asked to get out of science class to do so (personal communication).

■ ■ ■ ■ ■

Dr. Steve Terrell (Nova Southeastern University) describes below another example of a school-university partnership to boost STEM interest and knowledge, which he is spearheading with Dr. Deirdre Krause (Nova Southeastern University) and Dr. Bruce Campbell (Palm Beach State College).

SPOTLIGHT 1.8

Increasing the STEM Awareness of Sixth Grade, Minority Females in West Palm Beach, Florida

Steve Terrell, Professor, Graduate School of Computer and Information Science, Nova Southeastern University

In the information sciences programs at our university, it is common to find classrooms where 70% to 80% of the students are male. In trying to understand this, we found the same phenomenon reported at numerous universities throughout the U.S. Many researchers and educators believe that this disparity begins when young female students, primarily in their middle school years, become less interested in the science, technology, engineering, and math (STEM) fields, with many feeling that these topics are "subjects that boys like." With that in mind, we are conducting a small, grant-funded study to learn if we can increase awareness and interest in the STEM fields by developing an after-school program for sixth grade female students. We focus particularly on minority, lower-socioeconomic students, as we have discovered that the phenomenon of "girls do this, and boys do that" is even more prevalent within these groups of students.

In order to begin our project, we contacted administrators at a middle school in downtown West Palm Beach, Florida. After we explained to the principal that we wanted to create a twice-monthly after-school club for these students, he readily agreed to participate and identified two female sixth grade science teachers who were eager to become involved. In order to "bring the program to life," we developed partnerships with the STEM program in the Palm Beach County school system, the South Florida Science Museum, and other science-focused organizations within the community. The teachers recruited 25 young females to participate in the first session, delivered by the local science museum, where they were introduced to the physical changes of matter using a "chilling" program about liquid nitrogen. That program, titled "Nitromania," was followed two weeks later by "Go Girl," where students were introduced to the work of Florence Nightingale and Marie Curie by using stethoscopes to measure their resting and active heart rates, and creating models of molecules using miniature marshmallows and toothpicks to help them understand the ideas of molecular structure. The most recent session—demonstrating Newton's law of equal and opposite reaction by launching air-propelled rockets in the school's courtyard was the most exciting yet!

It is obvious, after only a few sessions, that the young females' interest and awareness of science has been piqued; the excitement on their faces, as well as on the faces of their teachers, is a testament to that! We are looking forward to sessions focusing on electricity and the work of Thomas Edison, the ideas behind ROYGBIV (an acronym for the sequence of hues commonly described as making up a rainbow: red, orange, yellow, green, blue, indigo, and violet) and the mysteries of the electromagnetic spectrum, and developing an even better understanding of Newton's Laws of Motion by, in the words of the scientists we're working with by, "having FUN as we push, pull, and get the job done!"

■ ■ ■ ■ ■

Summary

This chapter has focused on the efforts and energy in teaching STEM as an integrated approach to science, technology, engineering, and mathematics, plus adding the "A" for arts into the curriculum. It has explored the idea of teaching coding to all age learners and of assisting these students in creating authentic robots using their coding skills. It offered a variety of examples in these topics as they are being practiced in schools today. Educators who employ the ideas of STEM, robotics, and coding will be incorporating the following ISTE standards for students and for themselves as educators.

ISTE STUDENT STANDARDS ADDRESSED IN THIS CHAPTER

Standard 1: **Empowered Learner**	Students leverage technology to take an active role in choosing, achieving and demonstrating competency in their learning goals, informed by the learning sciences.
Standard 3: **Knowledge Constructor**	Students critically curate a variety of resources using digital tools to construct knowledge, produce creative artifacts and make meaningful learning experiences for themselves and others.
Standard 4: **Innovative Designer**	Students use a variety of technologies within a design process to identify and solve problems by creating new, useful or imaginative solutions.
Standard 5: **Computational Thinker**	Students develop and employ strategies for understanding and solving problems in ways that leverage the power of technological methods to develop and test solutions.

ISTE EDUCATOR STANDARDS ADDRESSED IN THIS CHAPTER

Standard 2: **Leader**	Educators seek out opportunities for leadership to support student empowerment and success and to improve teaching and learning.
Standard 5: **Designer**	Educators design authentic, learner-driven activities and environments that recognize and accommodate learner variability.
Standard 6: **Facilitator**	Educators facilitate learning with technology to support student achievement of the 2016 ISTE Standards for Students.
Standard 7: **Analyst**	Educators understand and use data to drive their instruction and support students in achieving their learning goals.

Questions and Reflections

- What are some ideas from this chapter that might help you enhance the STEM or STEAM focus in your classroom, school, district, or community?

- What might you need to learn in order to be comfortable introducing coding or robotics to your learners? Is there a way you might get that professional development?

- Depending on the content area(s) you teach, can you think of ways that coding and robotics might fit into your lessons?

- Could you collect data on the interest level toward coding and robotics of your learners? Could the learners collect those data themselves? If the data were collected, could your learners present them to the school leadership and parents?

- Are there opportunities for clubs, or interest groups, within the school day to implement students' interests?

Further Resources to Get Started

Open Educational Resources (Free)

New York City Department of Education Professional Development Opportunities (cs4all.nyc/2016/12/12/pd-offerings) Resources for the Computer Science for All initiative to support professional development for educators so that every learner receives instruction in computer science.

8 Free Tools That Teach Kids How to Code by Sarah K. White (www.cio.com/article/2955336/it-skills-training/8-free-tools-that-teach-kids-how-to-code.html) Easy to use tools to support coding for children.

6 Tips for Teaching Kids to Code by Al Sweigart (opensource.com/life/15/6/6-tips-teaching-kids-code) These tips support every teacher in helping learners, and teachers.

Guide to Teaching Kids to Code (www.edsurge.com/research/guides/teaching-kids-to-code) This guidebook helps every teacher in including coding into lessons.

5 Reasons to Teach Kids to Code (www.kodable.com/infographic) The reasons presented will assist in preparing parents and others in starting coding.

i.am.FIRST: Science is Rock and Roll (www.youtube.com/watch?v=BohT20oUy4M&feature=youtu.be) An amazing video of learners' love of STEM.

My Robot is Better Than Your Robot (www.youtube.com/watch?v=vYuOKb3gO7E&feature=youtu.be) A video that engages and encourages robotics in school.

Further Resources (For Purchase)

The 17 Best STEM Toys That Teach Kids to Code (for Toddlers to Teens)
(www.workingmother.com/stem-toys-teach-kids-to-code) These toys are excellent
for sharing with families that want to encourage coding.

11 Toys to Teach Kids Coding and Engineering
(uncubed.com/daily/11-toys-to-teach-kids-coding-engineering-and-more) This is
another set of toys that are useful for beginning coders.

Books That May Be of Interest

Fultz, C., & Sitzler-Frazier, R. (2016). *Robotics programming and math: Introductory guide for teachers and students.* New York, NY: CreateSpace Independent Publishing Platform.

Payne, B. (2015). *Teach your kids to code: A parent-friendly guide to Python programming.* New York, NY: No Starch Press.

Woodcock, J. (2015). *Coding games in Scratch.* New York, NY: DK Children.

CHAPTER 2

Makerspaces and the Maker Movement

I am convinced that the best learning takes place when the learner takes charge.

—Seymour Papert

To invent, you need a good imagination and a pile of junk.

—Thomas Edison

In This Chapter:

- What is the maker movement?

- What do we know about the maker movement?

- Where are makerspaces being implemented?

- How can I get started?

What Are Makerspaces and the Maker Movement?

There is a great deal of discussion these days about **making** and the maker movement! It brings together many of the ideas that educators have known about forever; perhaps it is best stated that it is fundamental to what it means to be human, which requires that we create, develop, and invent (Hatch, 2014). According to Gerstein (2016), makerspaces and the maker movement include:

- Hands-on, experiential learning, with learners being engaged intellectually, emotionally, socially, and physically.

- Participation in and engagement with authentic tasks.

- An integrated and interdisciplinary focus that often combines STEM, as well as art and language arts.

- Learner choice and decision making within the learning process.

- Personalized learning based on unique interests and passions.

- Learner-centric meaning-making based on constructivist principles.

- A focus on the process of creating, innovating, and learning; the process is as, or even more, important than the product. (p. 14)

The entire movement has a wide variety of definitions, which seems appropriate given the nature of this wave. Any space is expected to also meet the definition of the Association for Experiential Learning, including "success, failure, adventure, risk-taking and uncertainty, because the outcomes of experience cannot totally be predicted" (Association for Experiential Learning, n.d., n.p.).

> The Maker Movement refers to the recent wave of tech-inspired, do-it-yourself (DIY) innovation sweeping the globe. Participants in this movement, known as makers, take advantage of cheap, powerful, easy-to-use tools, as well as easier access to knowledge, capital, and markets to create new physical objects. This revolutionary change in how hardware is innovated and manufactured has great potential to change the future of computing, particularly for girls and women, a group traditionally underrepresented in Science, Technology, Engineering, and Math (STEM) fields. (Intel, 2014, p. 7)

In fact, Davee, Regalla, and Chang (2015) conducted a survey of more than 50 makerspace groups and reported 45 different titles for their spaces; these included sandboxes, studios, labs, learning environments, workshops, camps, and more. The literature is replete with verbs to describe the types of activities conducted in makerspaces including *craft, design, manufacture, tinker, engineer, fabricate,* and *repair with authentic materials.* What they conclude, however, is that "makerspaces come in all shapes and sizes, but they all serve as a gathering point for tools, projects, mentors, and expertise. A collection of tools does not define a makerspace. Rather, we define it by what it enables: making" (p. 3).

What Do We Know About Makerspaces and Making?

Many educators involved in this movement would agree on some common themes one would find in a makerspace. Makerspaces are "places where learners have the opportunity to explore their own interests, to tinker, create, invent, and build ..." (Fleming, 2015, p. 2) using a wide variety of physical and digital tools and materials. Makerspaces are located in community centers, libraries, museums, schools, and other formal and informal settings. Halverson and Sheridan (2014) describe the maker movement as "the growing number of people who are engaged in the creative production of artifacts in their daily lives and who find physical and digital forums to share their processes and products with others" (Halverson & Sheridan, 2014, p. 496). This movement has influenced K–12 education as schools have rebranded shop classes as makerspaces and sought to incorporate making activities to support science, technology, engineering, and math (STEM) initiatives (Clapp, Ross, Oxman Ryan, & Tishman, 2016).

Educators, potential funders, and policy makers also need to know what makerspaces may afford regarding the future of STEM and STEAM education in the coming decades. Although Martinez and Stager (2013) made a compelling case for the maker movement, in-depth examples of how this movement has developed in the past few years are needed as models for how others might take up this movement.

The integration of making activities into educational contexts is not a new idea. More than 20 years ago, Seymour Papert (1991) introduced the theory of constructionism, which suggests that learning is facilitated through the construction and sharing of physical artifacts. His definition of this term provides evidence of the direction he proposed:

> The word constructionism is a mnemonic for two aspects of the theory of science education underlying this project. From constructivist theories of psychology, we take a view of learning as a reconstruction rather than as a transmission of knowledge. Then we extend the idea of manipulative materials to the idea that learning is most effective when part of an activity the learner experiences as constructing a meaningful product. (Papert, 1986, p. 2)

Now, technological innovations over the past few years, such as 3-D printers, have brought about an increased interest in these types of activities. In 2014, President Obama recognized the maker movement with the establishment of a National Day of Making. One of the hallmarks of this movement is the democratization of access to equipment and tools, spread through a wide variety of organizations and individuals. According to Peppler and Bender (2013), "The grassroots energy behind this movement can be a model for how to successfully scale and spread future educational innovations across diverse locations and populations" (p. 23). In fact, they suggest not waiting until a perfect makerspace is set up; rather, they encourage asking for donations, and just seeking all sorts of recycled items or "donations of used or unwanted materials from local companies" (p. 26). Stager (2014), a proponent of constructionism and making, concurs:

> Even if you don't have access to expensive (but increasingly affordable) hardware, every classroom can become a makerspace where kids and teachers learn together through direct experience with an assortment of high- and low-tech materials. The potential range, power, complexity, and beauty of projects have never been greater thanks to new tools, materials, and ingenuity. (p. 44)

What Types of Makerspaces Exist?

Makerspaces in K–12 schools are relatively new entities and not a lot is known about them. What is available for educators interested in developing makerspaces includes advice about how to configure these spaces and materials that should be purchased to stock them (e.g., Burke, 2014; Fleming, 2018; Preddy, 2013). Three different models of the implementation have emerged and schools have adopted, or adapted, these to fit their space and needs.

Dedicated Makerspaces

One option for schools has been to identify a dedicated space to the notion of making. Since space can be at a premium, often schools will put all the maker materials, tools, and equipment into one, sometimes quite limited, space. Libraries are popular for housing makerspaces; the Singapore American School (SAS) has divided its campus into age/grade areas and has placed its age appropriate makerspaces in each of its four libraries (personal communication, 2017). Often spaces are reimagined from their original purpose into makerspaces. For example, the Elizabeth Forward School District, in Pennsylvania, repurposed one wing of its middle school and dubbed it the "Dream Factory." Superintendent Bart Rocca described the intentional focus of this change as a way to meet the needs of his students and his community (personal communication, 2015).

In his small district, he realized that many students left the community after graduation to seek good jobs, thus he was committed to make sure they had skills and experiences to help them.

Distributed Makerspaces

Other schools have conceptualized the nature of the maker movement in diverse ways and have decided to install different types of materials in multiple places throughout a school. For example, classrooms in Monticello High School (part of the Albemarle County School District) in Charlottesville, Virginia, have access to a library learning commons with 3-D printers and options for computer programming, a "genius bar" where students can give IT support to their peers, a recording studio, materials and tools for making in classrooms, and even the use of the cafeteria as a dance studio and rehearsal space (Harris, 2013). "It's a place to gather, to collaborate, to study, to read, whatever it is they want to do," said Chad Ratliff, the assistant director of instructional programs at Albemarle County Public Schools (cited in Harris, 2013). Students can drop in before or after school, when they have free time, or during lunch.

At Opal Charter School, located in the Portland Children's Museum, the philosophy and guiding principles "are inspired and influenced by the early childhood schools of Reggio Emilia, Italy; research in the field of neuroscience, and constructivist practices in the U.S. and beyond. They support an instructional approach based on listening and relationships" (Opal Charter School, 2018, n.p.). Each classroom is equipped with a small studio space (an *atelier* or workshop); it also has a wide variety of other materials. At Lighthouse Community Charter School in Oakland, California, a dedicated "Creativity Lab" space serves as a center for the school; however, to distribute the concepts and abilities to all students, older students created miniature makerspaces for the kindergarten classes. "Our kindergarten classes *make* year-round. They use hand tools (like handsaws, hammers, and drills) to make their own toys and furniture. They make puppets with hot glue. They build scribble machines, sew, program computerized cars, and so on" (Perlis, 2015, n.p.).

Mobile Making

Sometimes, regardless of intention, it is not possible to have designated spaces at all. However, that has not stopped many creative educators from seeking a solution to this challenge. Gierdowski and Reis (2015) documented their university's efforts to create access to composition and writing tools; through a university grant to one residence hall, they came up with the idea of a mobile lab that would be unique to the goals and context. Thus, unlike other university makerspaces that have technical staff available, theirs would need to specifically fit their needs. They said, "The MobileMaker needed to be designed so that it could be used even if no support staff was available so as not to limit user access" (p. 485). Since this mobile makerspace needed to be left in the halls, it had to be designed with lockable cabinets to hold all the equipment. It also had to be sturdy enough to move to other residences, if needed. This is one example that offers excellent insight to problem solving, to ensure access with safety, and yet to support a project useful in multiple ways.

Still other mobile makerspaces were designed to solve different problems. Vanderbilt Children's Hospital wanted a makerspace that could be wheeled into patients' rooms, with all the equipment visible and inviting (Echegaray, 2015). Their cart (shown in Figure 2.1) includes a 3-D printer, microcontrollers, and other supplies of interest to children.

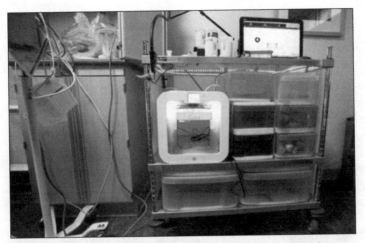

Figure 2.1. Mobile makerspace. Photo Credit: Joe Howell (news.vanderbilt.edu/2015/02/05/mobile-makerspace-provides-patients-tools-to-create-inspire).

"We wanted to see how we could support 21st century skills while also supporting patient care," said Gokul Krishnan, who is the founder of the mobile makerspace at Children's Hospital, also known as Project M@CH. "Makerspaces foster collaboration and creativity. This is designed by patients for patients." (Echegaray, 2015, n.p.)

Vehicle-based makerspaces are another form of mobile makerspaces. For example, the Geekbus is a retrofitted bus that brings 3-D printers, robots, electronics, and other maker tools for hands-on exploring to schools and other organizations in the San Antonio, Texas, area. Geekbus is operated by the nonprofit SASTEMIC (the STEM Connectory, which is aimed at connecting education, business, industry, and military to bolster the local STEM economy). Its goal is to encourage students to study the STEM fields (sastemic.org/geekbus). Reminiscent of the old bookmobile model, the Geekbus spreads the idea that the maker movement was founded on: democratization of access to new and interesting learning opportunities.

How Are Educators Implementing Makerspaces?

Schools around the world are embracing the notion of making that we have described. In fact, the authors of the 2017 Horizon Report (Freeman et al., 2017) estimate that the "time to adoption" is less than one year; they state that "Educators are leveraging maker activities to engage learners in creative, higher-order problem-solving through design, construction, and iteration" (p. 40). As Halverson and Sheridan (2014) reported, there are a "growing number of people who are engaged in the creative production of artifacts in their daily lives and who find physical and digital forums to share their processes and products with others" (p. 496).

The Ormondale Elementary School, in Portola Valley, California, developed a STEM lab/makerspace a few years ago, to help prepare and engage all students. Its website (ormondale.pvsd.net/academics/s_t_e_m) provides as its mission, "In this place we will EXPLORE, CREATE, PLAY and COLLABORATE." All students have the ability to use the STEM/lab/makerspace during their lunch period or during scheduled class periods; in the lab they are able to engage in a variety of activities of their choosing. This lab includes authentic materials: old toasters, hard drives, and more! The students learn what is inside everyday things. Some build, others gravitate take things apart at the "Take Apart Table." All manner of materials and tools can be found there, including a 3-D printer, iPads, and more. "The Maker Space is really about creating interesting projects and opportunities with whatever materials we have on hand." The beauty of the STEM Lab/Maker Space is, according to the school's website, "the spontaneous collaborative nature of many of the projects, and the complete creative freedom of it." The open-ended exploration allows students to persist in creating a project over days or weeks and serves as a great resource. (Ormondale School, n.d.).

The Singapore American School is an institution that has embraced appropriate use of technology on several levels. Its philosophy and plans are described in Spotlight 2.1.

SPOTLIGHT 2.1

Technology Integration in Singapore

Singapore American School, Singapore

Jason Cone, Chief Innovation Officer

Singapore American School (SAS) has a large campus with different build-ings, cafeterias, and libraries for their early learning center, elementary school, middle school, and high school. Technology is "meaningfully integrated" into all these spaces, and it is a 1:1 school. SAS is appropriately proud of its "world class educational technology specialists" who assist teachers in integration of the technologies available, including makerspaces in each of the grade-level build-ings and libraries. Students in middle school attend a boot camp; high school students have AP classes in computer science, engineering science, and robotics. They also offer engaging electives on "mobile app development, graphic design, and game design." All the students have the opportunity to engage in "making" in age-appropriate spaces. In addition, extracurricular activities include coding, robotics, and even a space lab where high school students design, build, and code a project to be launched to the International Space Station.

The SAS educational tech team works with librarians, coaches, teachers, and curriculum specialists to find opportunities to integrate coding, computational thinking, making, and design in authentic and relevant ways. They coordinate with science teachers to offer STEM-aligned learning experiences for all students. The ed tech team supports all teachers and students in pedagogy that is aligned to an inquiry approach.

SAS educational technology coaches and librarians have customized our digital citizenship curriculum and approach based on commonsense media. Coaches and librarians work with teachers to design and deliver lessons on digital resil-ience and safe, responsible, and balanced use of technology. The SAS educational tech team works with administrators to engage with parents and community members on the challenging issues of parenting in the digital age.

■ ■ ■ ■ ■

Teacher Education and Makerspaces

Bullock and Sator (2015) suggest that the maker movement may affect teacher preparation in positive ways. They note, "Maker pedagogy is an approach to working with teacher candidates drawing from principles in the maker movement that in our view represents a potentially useful way forward in engaging teacher candidates in thinking about curriculum and working with students" (p. 60).

 SPOTLIGHT 2.2

SELF Design Studio

University of North Carolina, Greensboro (@uncgself)

Matt Fisher (@mattfisher718), Assistant Director

Through a series of excellent and timely events, the School of Education at University of North Carolina at Greensboro has created the SELF Design Studio that is revolutionizing preservice education, as well as helping seven local schools to create their own makerspaces. The studio, described as a STEAM education laboratory, provides the School of Education students with state-of-the-art tools such as 3-D printers, a laser engraver, circuitry invention kits, computer graphic applications, virtual- and augmented-reality tools, robotics, and arts and crafts supplies.

The space began with a grant in 2014, and then the School of Education was awarded a large T4 grant (a Teacher Quality grant) through the U.S. Department of Education. This funding allowed the studio to work with local schools (four elementary, two middle schools, and one high school) to employ coaches to work in the schools and to assist the schools in establishing their own STEAM labs, and to have a full-time assistant director in the studio, Matt Fisher.

Mr. Fisher embraced this position with enthusiasm and a spirit of inclusion. He has ensured that faculty in all areas of the School of Education have the opportunity to include their students in working with him in the studio to further their course learning goals and to introduce their students to the possibilities of open-ended activities and student-centered learning. For example, the Philosophy of Education students design a physical "representation of their philosophy of education." In another project, future teachers of deaf or hard-of-hearing students, who are learning American Sign Language (ASL), are presented with an image of a monster. In a video, they use ASL to describe their monster to another student, who then has to create that monster using polymer clay. The lab has also given out mini-grants to faculty members who have ideas they would like to try in the studio. The Design Studio also sponsors summer camps for students of local schools, and teachers from the seven schools have the opportunity to participate in those camps as instructors and learners.

Mr. Fisher's goals do not stop there. He has networked with many regional organizations and provides outreach to the greater Greensboro community through public events such as the National Folk Festival, makerfaires, and educational workshops and exploration activities. Additionally, undergraduate preservice students act as Makers in Residence for a few hours each week. In this role, they work as ambassadors and recruiters for the studio at open house events, including workshops for UNCG students and community members, and at regional makerfaires. They also introduce the School of Education students to ways to integrate new technologies (e.g., 3-D printers, robots, and art/engineering building projects in curriculum).

The schools that are part of this T4 grant are similarly adapting the design studios into their curriculum goals. Students learn to use LEGO Story Starters kits, littleBits, Cubelets, and a wide variety of other tools. One coach explained that her job was to work with teachers to help them integrate these tools into their classes, rather than add one more required activity. The principal of McLeansville Elementary School, Shervawn Sockwell, took a creative approach to an early-release day. She explained that the limited hours of school often creates a challenge for teachers who may need to reteach important material or deal with early lunch periods. So, she started a ClubHouse opportunity; teachers identified topics they wished to work on with learners, and the students were able to select the one that most interested them. In an observation, we witnessed several educators who took advantage of the materials in the makerspace lab. Over the course of four opportunities, one group will learn to model and print a 3-D artifact that will solve a real-world problem. Others (some as young as first grade) were learning to create stories using LEGO Story Starter or invent and program robots to accomplish tasks they define.

In the spring of 2017, the SELF Design Studio worked with the Kiser Middle School Meteorology Club and N.C. Near Space to launch a high-altitude balloon into the stratosphere, more than 100,000 feet above the earth's surface. With the help of UNCG student and preservice educator Eric Winkelman, and N.C. Near Space's Paul Lowell, Kiser students began designing their payload, contemplating what to send to the stratosphere. Ideas ranged from Hot Cheetos to a bacon shell, to see if it would cook from exposure to solar radiation. Finally, they decided on a raw egg, creating the world's highest egg-drop experiment, and they also sent along a small toy tiger, Kiser's mascot. In Mr. Fisher's words:

> It's been an amazingly fun journey and opportunity to be able to build the SELF Design Studio from the ground up. When I started, I knew literally nothing about the maker movement and design thinking. I remember going to the North Carolina Makerfaire and having my jaw drop upon seeing a group of middle schoolers who created a banana piano with a Makey Makey and Raspberry Pi. At the time, I swore it was either witchcraft or magic! Now, after four years of creating and inventing with our UNC students, I am always psyched to have opportunities to encourage students to create their own little piece of magic. Whether it's using the laser engraver to create a custom "journey box" for a social studies project or a fortune-telling robot with a Makey Makey and Scratch, no two days are ever the same. I am thankful for my past experiences as a middle school teacher and an artist, as they have prepared me well to help our preservice teachers see the possibilities that lie in front of them on their journey to becoming professional educators. Over the next few years, I am looking forward to beginning a research project that will focus on our Makers in Residence. We will be studying how their experience in the studio has affected their motivation and confidence to integrate new technologies and activities meaningfully into their teaching practice.

■ ■ ■ ■ ■

Dr. George Meadows, professor at University of Mary Washington, has a passion for science education and environmental studies, as well as for preparing future educators to be the best teachers possible. A few years ago, he wanted to incorporate the new Next Generation Science Standards (NGSS), and engineering into his classes. What began with a freshman seminar on makerspaces turned into an evolving and growing development! The university started a STEM lab/makerspace in the library, and he also found funding to start one in the College of Education. Soon a public library asked for assistance in developing one, and then a principal at a local school requested similar help. Now there are STEM labs/makerspaces in several Virginia counties, in libraries, schools, and even an environmental nonprofit organization, Friends of the Rappahannock River (one of the most endangered rivers in the U.S.). One outstanding benefit of this has been the creation of excellent practicum locations for Dr. Meadows' students. They have the opportunity to help others in the use of equipment and materials while learning about their possibilities in education. According to Dr. Meadows, these STEM labs can be defined as a place to "design, build, and test solutions to authentic problems" (personal communication, October, 2017).

Dr. Janette Hughes is the Canada Research Chair, Technology & Pedagogy, in the Faculty of Education at the University of Ontario Institute of Technology. She is the Director of the STEAM-3D Maker Lab. The Ontario Ministry of Education funds a project titled Science 3D: Discovery, Design, & Development, which has funded schools to participate during the 2016–2017 school year, and the project was extended to 2017–2018; during these two years there were 20 school districts participating.

The Ontario Ministry of Education, the Council of Directors of Education (CODE), and Dr. Hughes selected the school districts' school based on Ontario demographics (i.e., public/Catholic, French/English, rural/urban, north/south/east/west). From there, the director of each school district selected the specific school, and then the principal of the school selected the teachers. Each school was given $30,000 to purchase maker materials, tools, and equipment to establish a makerspace in the school. Teachers were committed to professional development sessions (two in Dr. Hughes' lab and two on site at the school), and they could also agree to be participants in her research, which included surveys, interviews, and focus groups.

Dr. Hughes has a unique perspective on personalized learning, which she calls a "passion-based learning." She said,

> Rather than using the makerspace like we've traditionally used the computer lab, i.e., come to the lab and everyone is working on the same program, the maker activities have centered on student interests. In an inquiry-based approach, they identify the topic, problem, or issue they want to explore

and then use the makerspace tools, equipment, and materials to work on that. Rather than everyone building the same product, students are given the freedom to play, imagine, tinker, design, code, and build what they want. This approach has required a shift in mindset for many teachers, who are accustomed to being the ones who drive the lessons and activities. (personal communication, 2017)

Informal Education and the Maker Movement

Happily, the notion of making is not confined to public schools (see Chapter 7 for further discussion of blending of formal and informal educational spaces). "Public libraries have embraced this movement by developing various makerspace programs, ranging from artists in residence workshops, digital design studios, and meet-spaces (Willett, 2016, p. 313). By reviewing the library discussions of makerspaces, Willett found that another "key theme underlying the makerspace movement in public libraries is learning, particularly learning practices that are informal, participatory, and collaborative" (p. 316).

Abram and Dysert (2014) described ways in which libraries and museums are using the technology to provide access to their collections to millions.

> Some libraries have developed incubators for businesses based on their collections and offered the ability to use test kitchens, graphic and video software, and more. These included woodworking, cooking, animation studios, 3-D scanning and printing, making apps and games, video production, Arduino and Raspberry Pi robotics, and LEGO from DUPLO through CAD-CAM-aided LEGO design and robotics" (p. 11).

Museums are also becoming more innovative; for example, Richard Hulser from Los Angeles County showed how dinosaur fossil parts can be scanned and printed in 3-D for study and display. The ArtScience Museum in Singapore (goo.gl/MBXQyj) explores creative processes at the heart of art, science, technology, and culture, and their roles in shaping society. They pride themselves on being a living, breathing embodiment of the ArtScience theme. Through programs of exhibitions, events, performances, and education activities, the museum strives to illuminate the processes at the heart of art and science and their far-reaching influence in the world we live in.

Figure 2.2. Exhibit in ArtScience Museum of Singapore (Source: science.edu.sg/aboutus/PublishingImages/KidsSTOP/KidsSTOPmap.jpg)

Another Exemplary Museum

The Children's Museum of Pittsburgh has been a leader in the creation and spread of making for children. In addition, they have fostered the spread of this concept. "Making Spaces: Expanding Maker Education Across the Nation is a partnership between Google, Maker Ed, and Children's Museum of Pittsburgh, which aims to develop a national strategy to sustainably integrate making into schools across the country." The museum's website (makeshoppgh.com/2017/04/06/making-spaces) describes the project further.

> Making Spaces employs an innovative model by providing schools with maker education expertise from a nearby museum, library, school district or community organization, known as a "hub." Ten hubs across the country, of which the Children's Museum is one, each collaborate with 5–10 schools to help them launch crowdfunding campaigns to raise funds for their makerspaces, as well as provide guidance to help each school hone their approach to implementing maker education. The Museum will also provide the schools with professional development to support educators in creating

productive makerspaces and programs, as well as a toolkit on crowdfunding campaigns based on lessons learned through their pilot program. (Children's Museum of Pittsburgh, 2014)

The Children's Museum of Pittsburgh has been recognized as a leader in the field of makerspaces and making. Its core values include a commitment to good design principles, use of only authentic materials, and support for diversity. Its vision statement is, "We provide the highest quality exhibits and programs for learning and play. We are a partner and a resource for people who work with or on behalf of children" (pittsburghkids.org/about/fact-sheet). The museum has shown itself to be a collaborator, a catalyst for innovative projects, and the developer of school-museum interactions, both short-term and long-term, with educational entities.

Perhaps one of the most recognizable implementations of distributed makerspaces can be seen in the Children's Museum of Pittsburgh. This museum has put making throughout the entire museum, including the art studios, play areas, and a MAKESHOP that includes crafts, sewing, electronics, construction, and design. Jane Werner, Executive Director, and Lisa Brahms elaborate below.

SPOTLIGHT 2.3

MAKESHOP

Children's Museum of Pittsburgh, Pennsylvania

Jane Werner and Lisa Brahms

The Children's Museum has been at the forefront of local, regional, and national efforts around the research and practice of maker education. Developed in partnership with Carnegie Mellon University's Entertainment Technology Center (ETC) and the University of Pittsburgh's Center for Learning in Out of School Environments (UPCLOSE), MAKESHOP is a permanent, 1,800-square-foot exhibit space that provides a rich, supportive informal learning environment for children and families to engage in authentic making experiences with the *real stuff*—materials, tools, processes, and ideas—of making. Since opening in 2011, MAKESHOP, both in theory and practice has blossomed beyond the museum's walls, and itself become a national model for the design of learning-rich making experiences. MAKESHOP has collaborated with numerous community centers, schools, and teachers to create and sustain learning opportunities for diverse audiences throughout our region.

Working at the intersection of learning research and practice, the museum and our partners have furthered internal as well as field-wide conversations about making as a learning process, within museums and libraries (e.g., Brahms, Carrigan, Reich, & Wardrip, 2017; Brahms & Wardrip, 2015; Brahms & Wardrip, 2014; Brahms & Werner, 2013; Sheridan et al., 2014), as well as the integration of making into more formal learning contexts such as classrooms and school culture (e.g., Brahms & Wardrip, 2014; Brahms & Wardrip, 2016a; Brahms & Wardrip, 2016b; Brahms & Wardrip, 2016). This has included four federally funded learning research studies; the organization and hosting of three national convenings; and the development and dissemination of *Making + Learning in Museums and Libraries: A Practitioner's Guide and Framework*, a research-driven framework and suite of resources designed to build the capacity of libraries and museums to create and sustain effective makerspaces and programs for learning, developed in collaboration with the Institute of Museum and Library Services.

Among the many projects the museum has undertaken with regard to making and education, perhaps the most internally influential has been our development of a practice-based approach to identify, describe, and evaluate learning within and across the museum and its community efforts. Using an iterative design-based professional learning model, our team of researchers and practitioners collaboratively focuses on the behaviors—the actions and interactions of learners as they engage in learning processes—rather than on the end results of their experience. Viewing learning in this way, the learner and the learning experience are at the center of design. Together, we have empirically identified the Learning Practices of Making (see Table 1), which are observable forms of engagement that we design to support through maker-based learning experiences (Brahms & Wardrip, 2014; Brahms & Wardrip, 2015; Brahms & Wardrip, 2016a). Researchers, educators, and designers iteratively document and discuss evidence of learning, and they design, evaluate, and modify experiences to better support children and families' engagement and growth in these collaboratively derived learning practices.

Through this work, our museum community has jointly developed a common language for learning through making that is rooted in research, yet practice-based. This common language and process now guides discussions about making as a learning process by providing a lens for conceptualizing, supporting, evaluating, and assessing learning within MAKESHOP and across the museum, through design.

TABLE 1. MAKESHOP LEARNING PRACTICES OF MAKING

LEARNING PRACTICE	PRACTICE DESCRIPTION
Inquire	Learners' openness and curious approach to the possibilities of the context through exploration and questioning of its material properties.
Tinker	Learners' purposeful play, testing, risk taking, and evaluation of the properties of materials, tools, and processes.
Seek & Share Resources	Learners' identification, pursuit/recruitment, and sharing of expertise with others; includes collaboration and recognition of one's own not-knowing and desire to learn.
Hack & Repurpose	Learners' harnessing and salvaging of materials, tools, and processes to modify, enhance, or create a new product or process; includes disassociating object property from familiar use.
Express Intention	Learners' discovery, evolution, and refinement of personal identity and interest areas through determination of short- and long-term goals; includes learners' responsive choice, negotiation, and pursuit of goals alone and with others.
Develop Fluency	Learners' development of comfort and competence with diverse tools, materials, and processes; developing craft.
Simplify to Complexify	Learners' demonstration of understanding of materials and processes by connecting and combining component elements to make new meaning.

■ ■ ■ ■ ■

California Tinkering Afterschool Network (CTAN) is a research-practice partnership involving after-school directors, researchers, and facilitators with the informal learning institutions Exploratorium, Discovery Cube, and Techbridge. CTAN is a member of the Research + Practice Collaboratory and is supported by the National Science Foundation (nsf.gov) and the S.D. Bechtel, Jr. Foundation (sdbjrfoundation. org). The program itself is an after-school tinkering program, reaching low-income and underserved communities. According to their website, their fundamental focus is to promote STEM-rich tinkering: "Young people develop their understanding and interest in scientific phenomena, like circuitry, while engaging them in scientific and engineering practices such as designing, building, testing, and revising battery-operated Scribbling Machines" (California Tinkering Afterschool Program, 2017). This program is an excellent example of a making partnership that brings together formal and informal learning spaces, communities, STEM professionals, and government agencies. It is an excellent example of a large-scale partnership. Several brief descriptions of makerspaces connected to this network, specifically in informal learning spaces, are available online (see maked.org; remakelearning.org).

Fitting Making into Your School: Getting Started

Pocock (2016) suggests that the maker movement embodies and promotes multiple goals at one time: communication of technical details, lifelong learning, development of engineering knowledge for problem-solving, work on multidisciplinary teams, and working to design with realistic constraints.

Gary Stager and Sylvia Martinez have a great approach to lesson planning for maker education; instead of teacher-led and cookie-cutter curricula for best results in constructionism, Stager suggests "Anytime an adult feels it necessary to intervene in an educational transaction, they should take a deep breath and ask, 'Is there some way I can do less and grant more authority, responsibility, or agency to the learner?'" (Stager, 2012). Good prompts are simple enough for kids to understand, vague enough to allow a diverse and open array of solutions, and immune to standardized testing (Martinez & Stager, 2013).

The maker movement offers "new approaches to instruction, one in which teachers give up control and understand that they need not be the single vessel that delivers the instruction of skills" (Fleming, 2016, p. 19). Fleming (2018) suggests seven attributes for a great makerspace, but also warns that there are no cookie-cutter answers. Each should be unique to fit the needs and interests of the audience. Those seven attributes are that it must be personalized, deep, empowering, equitable, differentiated, intentional, and inspiring. She is particularly passionate about allowing the learners to determine what they want to make.

In addition to empowering students to lead their own project, it is equally important that students have necessary skills before they begin creating. According to Bevan, Petrich, and Wilkinson (2015), classrooms may need to alternate between step-by-step fabrication, or assembly tasks, and inventing or creating what they wish to do while tinkering. It will be important for safety and successful making that they know how to use the equipment.

It is also important to document student learning; although typical standardized tests will not assess exactly the types of skills and knowledge that students do gain, it will be essential to have some ability to understand that learning. One way to do this is with a formative set of agree-disagree statements to understand any common misconceptions; throughout the units, these statements can be revised, with a summative assessment after the experiences have been completed (Keeley, 2015). Keeley states, "Students are learning while at the same time the teacher is gathering valuable information about their thinking that will inform instruction and provide feedback to students on their learning" (p. 3).

Oliver (2016b) suggests, "A variety of strategies can be undertaken to sustain a makerspace in terms of attracting participants, community volunteers and expertise, and donations of supplies and cash" (p. 213). "We are seeing a greater self-efficacy in the students who use the makerspace, but the space might just attract students with greater design self- confidence" (Linsey, cited in Pocock, 2016, p. 36). Educators can also find information online (see resources at the end of this chapter), and there are some suggested lessons and activities published in books (e.g., Gabrielson, 2013; Preddy, 2013) and online (tinkerlab.com).

Summary

This chapter has focused on the relatively recent but robust energy around maker-spaces and the maker movement. This effort has spread to students around the globe, in classrooms, schools, museums, and on mobile carts. It offered a variety of examples in each of these contexts, and suggested ways for educators to begin bringing making into their curriculum. Educators who employ the ideas of making and makerspaces will be incorporating the following ISTE standards for students and for themselves as educators.

ISTE STUDENT STANDARDS ADDRESSED IN THIS CHAPTER

Standard 1: Empowered Learner	Students leverage technology to take an active role in choosing, achieving and demonstrating competency in their learning goals, informed by the learning sciences.
Standard 3: Knowledge Constructor	Students critically curate a variety of resources using digital tools to construct knowledge, produce creative artifacts and make meaningful learning experiences for themselves and others.
Standard 4: Innovative Designer	Students use a variety of technologies within a design process to identify and solve problems by creating new, useful or imaginative solutions.

ISTE EDUCATOR STANDARDS ADDRESSED IN THIS CHAPTER

Standard 5: Designer	Educators design authentic, learner-driven activities and environments that recognize and accommodate learner variability.
Standard 6: Facilitator	Educators facilitate learning with technology to support student achievement of the 2016 ISTE Standards for Students.

Questions and Reflections

- Is my classroom, school, district, or community ready to consider developing for expanding makerspaces? If so, to whom should this be targeted?

- Identify the benefits you see in moving forward with this concept.

- What resources might be available? (Partnering with others? Working with local businesses? Potential grants?)

- Who are the stakeholders to bring into this plan?

- What roadblocks might be standing in your way?

- Create a letter to your school board, or local newspaper, describing the rationale for developing one or more makerspaces in your classroom, school, or district.

Further Resources to Get Started

Open Educational Resources (Free)

Design Thinking for Educators
(designthinkingforeducators.com) Download a design handbook/toolkit that encourages educators to develop their own design thinking and provides ways to introduce it into their lessons.

Exploratorium
(www.exploratorium.edu/education/california-tinkering-afterschool-network) Find out more about the California tinkering afterschool network.

Learning from Toy Makers in the Field to Inform Teaching Engineering Design in the Classroom
(www.asee.org/public/conferences/56/papers/12915/view) This report offers information on bringing engineering principles into the classroom.

MakeHers: Engaging girls and women in technology through making, creating, and inventing
(www.intel.com/content/www/us/en/technology-in-education/making-her-future-report.html) This article provides suggestions specifically to encourage girls to engage with STEM and making.

The weird, wild world of citizen science is already here
(www.wired.com/2014/05/the-weird-wild-world-ofcitizen-science-is-already-here) This article provides examples of authentic science activities.

Science Museum of Minnesota: Building and sustaining a thriving maker hub
(makered.org/wp-content/uploads/2014/12/Building-and-Sustaining-a-Thriving-Maker-Hub.pdf) Examples to assist in developing an innovative makerspace.

Skills Canada Alberta
These three publications provide detailed instructions and information for encouraging making and student centered learning.

- Taking Making into the Classroom
  (innovativelearningcentre.ca/about/ilc-publications)

- MakerDay Toolkit 1
  (issuu.com/ubcedo/docs/mar27makerdaytoolkit)

- MakerDay Toolkit 2
  (issuu.com/ubcedo/docs/makerdaytoolkitver2revisemay31e)

Books That May Be of Interest

Burke, J. J. (2014). *Makerspaces: A practical guide for librarians.* Lanham, MD: Rowman & Littlefield Publishers.

Honey, M., & Kanter, D. E. (Eds.). (2013). *Design, make, play: Growing the next generation of STEM innovators.* New York, NY: Routledge.

Martinez, S. L., & Stager, G. S. (2013). *Invent to learn: Making, tinkering, and engineering in the classroom.* Torrance, CA: Constructing Modern Knowledge Press.

Thornburg, D., Thornburg, N., & Armstrong, S. (2014). *The invent to learn guide to 3D printing in the classroom: Recipes for success.* Torrance, CA: Constructing Modern Knowledge Press.

Wagner, T. (2012). *Creating innovators: The making of young people who will change the world.* New York, NY: Scribner.

CHAPTER 3

Gamification and Digital Game-Based Learning

If someone offers you an amazing opportunity but you are not sure you can do it, say yes—then learn how to do it later!

—Richard Branson

Motivation is such a huge part in what ends up differentiating student outcomes. Everyone has the ability to do fantastic work at a high school level. It's just, without the right teacher and the right motivation, you don't always get there.

—Bill Gates

In This Chapter:

- What is the foundation of gamification and digital game-based learning?

- How does game-based learning align with the digital age classroom?

- What examples exist of educators and learners using digital game-based learning?

- In what ways can you begin to explore using digital game-based learning in your educational environment?

What Do We Know About Gamification?

Game theory, a term previously coined in the economic sector, uses gaming reward systems, social interactivity, problem-solving strategies, and challenges and competition models in a nongaming environment (Azriel, Erthal, & Starr 2005; Ehrhardt, 2008; Gros, 2007). Over the past several years, an increased interest in the application of game theory within the field of education has evolved. It is safe to say that almost every person—educator, parent, learner—has played games in his or her life; these might include tabletop board games, outdoor tag, single-player app games, or advanced digital role-playing games. From kindergarten through high school, innovative educators use various aspects of game theory to promote participation and learning in their classrooms. Specifically, within the language arts curriculum, educators develop and implement multimodal, game-based learning activities to enhance student motivation, reading comprehension, and vocabulary. *Digital game-based learning (DGBL)* can be used as a tool to develop content knowledge, learning strategies, motivation, social interactivity, creativity, and innovation; improve group dynamics; and prepare students for the digital age workforce (Bratitsis, Dourda, Griva, & Papadopoulou, 2014; Chin & Tsuei, 2014; Fernández-Manjón Sancho, Fuentes-Fernández, & Moreno-Ger, 2009). The literature on digital game-based learning is emerging and has yet to fully capture the potential benefits and implementation techniques of game achievement, critical thinking, reading comprehension, and learning motivation in the classroom.

Foundations of Game-Based Learning

The use of game theory in the classroom is still new; to date, the most common use of game theory is in the business world to bolster customer product consumption and employee morale (Azriel et al., 2005; Ehrhardt, 2008). Game theory did not really exist as a unique field until John von Neumann published a paper in 1928 (Tucker & Luce, 1959). He was a mathematics professor at Princeton University who sought to quantify the actions a player makes in a game that lead to a positive outcome (Dixit & Nalebuff, 2008). von Neumann (von Neumann & Morgenstern, 1947) primarily studied games that resulted as zero-sum games, wherein one player's successes result in another player's failures. von Neumann also studied alternate forms of competition through collaboration where one player's decisions in a game result in positive outcomes for themselves and other players (Dixit & Nalebuff,

2008). Business owners adopted this gaming framework as a new coding for business transactions to motivate their employees and promote business sales. Employees were given incentives to motivate their production in the form of monetary or activity rewards (Deterding, Dixon, Khaled, & Nacke, 2011). From the goals of business to promote their product and encourage motivation, educators, who frequently may see disengagement in class and lack of motivation to complete tasks, have begun to adopt the practice of gamification.

Gamification

The term *gamification* was first used to encourage electronics manufacturers to improve their production using gaming tactics (Tulloch, 2014). The term, therefore, describes the process of using gaming mechanics in a nongaming context (Deterding et al., 2011). Mechanisms such as leaderboards, challenges, levels, badges, points, and rewards are frequently used by businesses to engage employees to bolster morale and production and certainly to stimulate customers to remain loyal (Tulloch, 2014). In the classroom setting, many teachers have integrated gamification practices insofar as the class itself becomes a game.

Game-Based Learning

Entering this multitude of innovative education practices, digital game-based learning (DGBL) gives educators a new platform to capture student engagement and facilitate learning in a way that mirrors student engagement outside the school environment (Chin & Tsuei, 2014; Sanford & Madill, 2007). Unlike gamification, game-based learning relates to the use of games to enhance the learning experience (Tulloch, 2014). Founded on game theory, which holds that people are intrinsically motivated by competition, achievement, status, and collaboration, DGBL activities are designed in a way that is similar to the daily social media activities that students encounter in their typical world: chat rooms, video games, film scripts, online blogs, graphic novels or comic books, text messages, and tweets (Azriel et al., 2005; Sanford & Madill, 2007).

Educators, of course, have been using games in the classroom for years, as they strive to engage students in meaningful and complex skill acquisition. Gee (2005,

2008), who is a strong proponent of incorporating video games in modern education classrooms, explains that video games and other digital games are at their core educational experiences. In the digital arena, game-based learning arises from the belief that if teachers can make learning as engaging and motivating as a video game, students will be more willing to learn rigorous material (Eseryel, Law, Ifenthaler, Ge, & Miller, 2014; Gee, 2005). Players have to learn the rules of the game, which are oftentimes not fully explained at the beginning of the game, and maneuver their way through complex narratives to attain a preset goal, or in many cases, an unknown resolution to an authentic problem. When tied to the educational curriculum, game-based learning acts as a powerful learning tool because it engages students in their gaming milieu (Eseryel et al., 2014; Gee, 2005). Digital game-based learning provides students a unique, immersive experience that allows ample opportunities to frame learning experiences in terms of goals, apply previous knowledge for problem-solving, participate in social interactions, and provide and receive immediate feedback on their learning experiences (Gee, 2008). Using digital game-based learning strategies and platforms in conjunction with gamification techniques enriches the classroom experience and bolsters student learning and motivation (ClassCraft, 2014; Gee, 2005, 2008; Tulloch, 2014).

Of course, it is important to remember that gamification can occur in nondigital formats, with leaderboards, team competitions, and other activities. Schools have used competitions among grades (who can read the most books in the summer, for example); however, this chapter does focus on the ways in which digital technologies have changed the nature of gamification in our schools today.

Game-Based Learning Aligned with the Digital Age Classroom

Students in the digital age are voracious consumers of visual media; they seek entertainment from television screens and community interactivity from social media, and find comradery by participating in online gaming (Sancho et al., 2009; Sanford & Madill, 2007). As a result, we have seen a true shift in educational technology and pedagogy to a digital educational thrust in order to meet the changing needs and interests of current students (Eseryel et al., 2014; Gros, 2007; Sancho et al., 2009). We have progressed from the teacher standing behind the wooden podium, to purposefully circulating around the room, facilitating learning, and guiding students through their thought processes (Jong & Shang, 2015). Instead of vigilantly trying to stamp out gaming, teachers support learning goals for their students with digital game-based learning opportunities. The portable digital platform has made research and learning more accessible, immediate, and integrated within traditional curriculum (Gros, 2007; Prensky(a), 2001b; Sancho et al, 2009). Digital textbooks incorporate enhanced visual, audio, and video components to promote comprehension among diverse learners (Morgan, 2014; Sanford & Madill, 2007). The 2017 Horizon Report classified gaming and gamification as a *digital strategy* and stated,

> Digital strategies are not so much technologies as they are ways of using devices and software to enrich teaching and learning, whether inside or outside the classroom. Effective digital strategies can be used in both formal and informal learning; what makes them interesting is that they transcend conventional ideas to create something that feels new, meaningful, and 21st century. (Freeman et al., 2017, p. 38)

Tools for Formative and Summative Assessment

We know that digital games are frequently used for motivation, enhanced engagement, and persistence in learning (Burguillo, 2010; Dickey, 2007; Divjak, & Tomic, 2011; Esryel et al., 2014); however, many educators also use them for assessment. The A-GAMES project (Analyzing Games for Assessment in Math, ELA/Social Studies, and Science), which is a joint project between the University of Michigan and New York University, has been studying how teachers actually use digital games for assessment (Fishman, Riconscente, Snider, Tsai, & Plass, 2014). "Our objective in A-GAMES is to illuminate how teachers understand and make use of game features that support formative assessment" (p. 3).

In a recent study, Fishman et al. (2014) found that "The most frequent uses of games are to cover content mandated by state/national or local/district standards. In comparison, fewer teachers use games at least weekly to teach supplemental content" (p. 4). Additionally, 34% of those surveyed stated that they use the games at least weekly for formative assessment. One key finding, with implications for professional development and educator preparation is that "Teachers who use digital games to make instructional decisions on a daily basis are more than twice as likely to check for motivation and engagement during formative assessment than teachers who rarely use games to make instructional decisions" (p. 5). They also found that "Teachers who use digital games daily to document student progress are much more likely to use information from formative assessment on a daily basis to find or create alternative instructional strategies for a particular topic" (p. 5) and those who use digital games more frequently are those who are inclined to use the feedback to track students' progress.

How Are Educators Implementing Gamification?

Gamification systems such as ClassCraft (2014) add an interactive, digital game layer on top of the existing course structure. Through the ClassCraft software, students are able to select and customize their own characters, which act as their avatars in the game (ClassCraft, 2014). Students may play individually or as part of a team, earning experience points and rewards based on classroom behaviors and use of class knowledge—they can alternately lose experience points and receive consequences if they misbehave in class (ClassCraft, 2014). Packaged within the game quests, students are learning and demonstrating course objectives, previously only assessed through traditional academic assessments. In the advent of the digital age, gamification platforms also include digital game-based learning activities, such as interactive online quizzes and academic quests.

Zieger and Farber (2012) conducted a study looking at whether seventh grade students, involved in studying the Constitutional Convention, would be able to transfer their traditional face-to-face cooperative strategies to an online multiuser virtual environment (MUVE) setting, and also whether they might become more civic-minded. The study found that "The virtual environment did provide an authentic setting for students to practice the civic lessons they learned academically. Student involvement in a participatory culture translated to an increased tendency to be civic-minded" (Zieger & Farber, 2012, p. 393).

An interesting attempt to narrow the achievement and readiness gap is being implemented through an innovative program in middle and high schools serving economically disadvantaged students in several U.S. states. The Globaloria program offers a game design intervention that aims to introduce innovative STEM curriculum, in which students develop functioning interactive web games by the end of the school year, with a goal to teach others about their chosen social-impact topic, often from their own lives. Minnigerode and Reynolds (2013) studied two students who were engaging in a collaborative game design within a formal elective game design class. They concluded that "on the whole, the team members demonstrated high levels of engagement with their chosen topic of dropout prevention, illustrated by their behavior, final accomplishment, and an analysis of their game" (p. 290).

It is important to think about what each game requires and how learners must be able to engage with it, and having supporting knowledge of what and how to play it. Weppel, Bishop, and Munoz-Avila (2012) worked with a program called MyRulerMaker, which strives to introduce middle school learners to artificial intelligence and computer programming. This program interfaces with IBM's CodeRuler (goo.gl/2qXYzU; the program is now called "developerworks" at ibm.com/developerworks) and the overarching goal is to defeat an opposing army and steal a flag, which requires programming in Java. However, the program is not immediately intuitive, and these researchers investigated if interrupting play to provide scaffolding was useful or disruptive to the students. They found that "more prescriptive support (regardless of intrusiveness) may have provided the students with the confidence and self-efficacy they needed to stay engaged. Levels of intrusiveness may have been less important because students seemed to seek out the support they needed" (p. 373).

An excellent example of gamification of an extremely complex issue is The World Peace Game. Educator John Hunter developed the World Peace Game, which offers a deep and elaborate political simulation that invites young students to explore a world not unlike our own, consisting of four or five prominent nations. As student teams direct each country, learners are encouraged to explore the global community and learn the nature of the complex relationships between nations, addressing social, economic, and philosophical issues.

In the White Bear Lake Area School, a third grade teacher, Mr. Pai, has been using game-based educational activities to make learning fun, but also to improve student achievement. He introduced the use of Nintendo DS, among other technology, into his daily curriculum. Students practiced math and language through the use of computer and video games. In just 18 weeks, his class went from below third grade level to the middle of fourth grade level. He states that he "continues to explore and use digital tools" (personal communication, 2017).

According to Thompson (2014), the popular online game Minecraft can help students learn to read. The game works similar to an infinite set of programmable LEGO blocks, and it is a way to instill spatial reasoning, math, and logic (see Cindy Duncan's Spotlight 1.5 in Chapter 1). Yet, in his review of its use, he is convinced that it presents "a culture of literacy" (Thompson, 2014, n.p.). The game does not have extensive instructions; thus, new players must find ways to learn about the rules and the best ways to play and win, and this often involves reading. There are of course YouTube videos of games and players, but there are many "how-to texts at Minecraft wikis and 'walk through' sites written by gamers for gamers" (Thompson, 2014). There are also guides and handbooks, which of course require reading. He also reported on one study by a literacy researcher at Sam Houston State University. "She monitored several 10th grade students at school and at home and saw that they read only 10 minutes a day in English class—but an astonishing 70 minutes at home as they boned up on games" (Thompson, 2014). One parent and educator stated that Minecraft also "teaches them about different materials, food, resource management, project planning, teamwork (if they use multiplayer), problem-solving, responsibility, and accountability for their animals" (Milanesi, 2017).

Thompson concluded, "I'm praising Minecraft, but nearly all games have this effect. The lesson here is the same one John Dewey instructed us in a century ago: To get kids reading and writing, give them a real-world task they care about. These days that's games" (2014, n.p.).

It is important to recognize that gamification, while fun, can also tackle very serious issues. As a timely example, consider the experiences of immigrants. The National Endowment of the Humanities (NEH) has supported and funded digital games, including Mission US: City of Immigrants (mission-us.org/pages/landing-mission-4), a game about the immigrant experience. Learners play as Lena Brodsky, a Jewish immigrant in 1907 New York. Taking on this persona adds an element of empathy as students realize how difficult it can be to assimilate to a new country. There are also games about the revolutionary war, escape from slavery, the Great Depression, and more; each game includes an educator guide.

Other options for using gamification to address complex issues includes Papers, Please (papers-please.en.softonic.com), a serious game about being a border patrol agent checking passports in a fictional Communist nation in 1982.

Educator Preparation and Professional Development Use

Many educators are learning about gamification and digital game-based learning through their teacher preparation programs, or through professional development opportunities at their schools, or that they seek out. Matthew Farber has become an expert in the use of digital game-based learning and describes his experiences. His latest book (Farber, 2018) will be especially helpful to all educators interested in the topic.

SPOTLIGHT 3.1

How Games Can Be the Centerpiece of a Lesson

Matthew Farber (@MatthewFarber), University of Northern Colorado

The Tribe is an affinity group of likeminded game-based learning practitioners that includes teachers, academics, and game designers. As a member of this community of practice, I sought to understand how my colleagues use games for the systems of their classrooms. This led me to study their methods, with the intent of parsing out important lessons learned, and to share best practices in game-based learning.

The Tribe is composed of connected learning practitioners who meet at conferences and online and play games together, as well as openly share ideas. They do not assess student play; instead, they measure learning transfer through the creation of their own assessment strategies, which are typically reflection-on-action practices such as exit ticket questions or journal writing (Schön, 1983). Rather than fetishize gamification approaches (e.g., the use of digital badges and leaderboards to create a reward-based engagement model), The Tribe embraces play theory modalities, setting up affordances that enable students to move through a personalized zone of proximal development, from novice to master, via game mechanics (Vygotsky, 1978). Their classrooms are also gameful, displaying an embrace of self-determination theory: students have a sense of "competence, autonomy, and relatedness" (Deci & Ryan, 2000, p. 57). The Tribe represents the interaction of expert teaching and high-quality gaming.

Best practices in using educational technology often means that technology is used as a tool for learning—not as the focal point of class instruction. For example, when making a green screen video, students insert different locations in the background of videos; the application used (e.g., DoInk or WeVideo) should not matter. The learning goal is to create an authentic learning experience, not to become proficient in a particular technology.

Adapting video games to meet a teacher's specific curricular objectives can run contrary to the educational game market, which can fetishize teacher dashboards that report personalized analytics on student game achievement. For the most part, these teachers do not wholesale adopt games to teach specific skills, such as typing; instead, they adapt games to fit the learning goals and targets. For example, professor Chris Haskell began with the digital rocket simulation game, which is intended to teach physics and rocketry. But Haskell (2015) had his students play in two teams, using two computers, role-playing as the U.S. and the Soviet Union. Students took on roles, like spies and media, to simulate the Cold War space race. Here, Haskell adapted and appropriated a STEM game to be used other than the designers may have originally thought possible. Haskell calls this *contextual transposition*, "when you take an environment intended for one thing and you co-opt it to be for what you want it to be" (Farber, 2018).

Much like close reading and analyzing a novel, members of The Tribe use the systems in story-driven games to be the centerpiece of lessons (Farber, 2018). In this sense, video games are read like *digital texts*, which can "provide students with mediated experiences" (Shaffer, Nash, & Ruis, 2015, p. 10). Let's take Tribe member Steve Isaacs (@mr_issacs). A video game and development middle school teacher in New Jersey (and ISTE's 2016 award winner for Outstanding Teacher), Isaacs has his students play the classic video game Oregon Trail. Then, like a book club, students analyze the experience, including the game's goals, the narrative elements, and the core mechanics or actions of play. Next, his students write and publish game reviews on blogs. Finally, his students play the Oregon Trail map on Minecraft: Education Edition, making their own versions by modifying or "modding" and hacking the game.

Isaacs, like many game-based learning experts I studied, uses video games as the hub of his lessons, much like a teacher would use traditional media, such as books or film. Oregon Trail is a model—a centerpiece for Isaacs' instruction, all surrounded by the authentic and meaningful assessments he designed.

■ ■ ■ ■ ■

Other institutions are also working to help teachers learn how to use games, as it is clear this is necessary. "Well-designed games provide scaffolding and motivation for a player to learn skills and apply knowledge in service of meeting specified goals … However, how games are implemented in classrooms affects the learning and engagement outcomes and therefore their efficacy," reported Rosenheck, Gordon-Messer, Clarke-Midura, & Klopfer (2016, p. 33). For example, the University of South Australia's Connect program is offering professional development for secondary school teachers and students across the country that helps them develop engaging projects that incorporate tools such as 3-D printing and electronic games while exposing them to career choices (unisa.edu.au/UniSA-Connect). Curtin University has developed a challenge-based learning game within a global context, which is an extension of problem-based, project-based, and contextual teaching and learning in higher education. It supports global collaborative team problem-solving experiences (academicexperts.org/conf/site/2017/papers/51013)

Fitting Gamification into Your School: Getting Started

There are many ways to get started. One way you might try to introduce gamification to your class community is through competition by teams, rather than individuals, so that rewards go to collaborative teams. You might set a goal that is reachable; for example, perhaps the class can earn an extra recess if a certain percentage passes a test or completes their work on time. This supports the idea that students are mastering material, and students are more likely to help each other.

One way to support gamification is through badging. Gibson, Coleman, and Irving (2016) present three primary roles of using digital badges to support learning:

bringing *visibility* and *transparency* to learning, teaching and assessment; *revealing meaningful, identifiable and detailed aspects of learning* for all stakeholders; and providing *a new mechanism to recognize skills, experience and knowledge* through an open, transferable, stackable technology framework. (p. 115)

Another option might be to gamify homework, which can encourage persistence and responsibility. How about a treasure hunt? Quests? Or perhaps you will choose to try all of the above. Acedo (2017) suggests, "Gamification uses game elements such as challenges, feedback, levels, creativity, and rewards to motivate students to learn, and master concepts," and he offers these 10 ideas to gamify specific parts of your teaching:

1. Make Students Co-Designers

2. Allow Second Chances. And Third.

3. Provide Instant Feedback

4. Make Progress Visible

5. Create Challenges or Quests Instead of Homework and Projects

6. Give Students Voice and Choice

7. Offer Individual Badges and Rewards

8. Have Students Design a Classwide Skills and Achievement System

9. Implement Educational Technology

10. Embrace Failure; Emphasize Practice

Thus, some educators may gamify in individual areas, and others may choose to tackle the entire classroom milieu. Heidi Lihou is a sixth grade social studies teacher at Sitka School District's Blatchley Middle School; she attended a conference and that experience changed her educational pedagogy and practice as she began to gamify her entire classroom.

SPOTLIGHT 3.1

Gamification works!

Sitka School District, Sitka, Alaska

Heidi Lihou, Teacher, Sixth Grade Social Studies

I am lucky to have the opportunity to teach about my passion—ancient civilizations! I have also been able to incorporate this passion with a second love of mine—games. Two years ago, I was looking for something to revitalize myself and my classroom. I attended a Schoology workshop presented by Beth Box, a Florida middle school civics teacher who had gamified her entire class. I left her presentation feeling inspired and armed with examples and practical knowledge. I went home and spent the entire summer designing my gamified classroom. I created a scenario in which the world as we know it had been destroyed by a black hole, instigated by CERN (the European Organization for Nuclear Research). This resulted in the bending of time and space so that an emperor from China might be walking down 5th Avenue in New York with peasants from the French Revolution! Today's countries were wiped out. It was time for a new empire to emerge and rule the world! This wove geography and history together with challenges to encourage students' inquiry and engagement.

Students have the opportunity to earn experience points (XP) as they complete class assignments. These XP allow students to "level up." They begin as Hunter Gatherers, move up to be Farmers, and so on. Eventually students can become a Master of Time and Space, the highest level. Students can also earn achievement points (AP) by demonstrating mastery of key concepts and standards on assessments. These AP are used as currency in my game. I use Schoology to create an electronic store. Students can purchase virtual villages, buildings, technology, Wonders of the World, etc. Students also love the ability to attack or burgle other students' villages. Of course, I offer defensive walls and anti-theft systems to thwart such attacks. An electronic leaderboard updates live as well, thanks to Google Docs.

The students love the way this works and get quite caught up in learning the history and geography as they are engaged in progressing through the game. The only response from families has been positive since the learners enjoy this so much. Two things really support this adventure: first, it is important to have a good learning management system (LMS), as there are many things to keep track of and to organize. Second, it is essential to have a supportive administration. Although Sitka is not yet a 1:1 district, the administration gave me a cart of laptops for my classroom and we use them almost every day.

If you are considering gamification yourself, my advice is to do it! Spend a few minutes investigating those teachers who have gamified their classrooms; many of them have published their ideas, tips, strategies, and examples. You don't have to travel this road alone, nor start from scratch. Be organized and deliberate in your planning as well. This will save you time and energy in the future. And most of all—have fun! You and your students will not regret it.

■ ■ ■ ■ ■

Summary

This chapter presented the concept of gamification, which includes using games for engaging students in content materials. It can also be used as a strategy to make a game out of an entire classroom. The educators who use gamification report that while students do engage in deeper learning for longer periods of time, it is their enthusiasm for learning that is most striking to them. The chapter suggested ways to begin small, by gaming small parts of the learning environment and places to learn more about the topic. Educators who employ the ideas of game-based learning and gamification will be incorporating the following ISTE standards for students and for themselves as educators.

ISTE STUDENT STANDARDS ADDRESSED IN THIS CHAPTER

Standard 1: **Empowered Learner**	Students leverage technology to take an active role in choosing, achieving and demonstrating competency in their learning goals, informed by the learning sciences.
Standard 4: **Innovative Designer**	Students use a variety of technologies within a design process to identify and solve problems by creating new, useful or imaginative solutions.
Standard 5: **Computational Thinker**	Students develop and employ strategies for understanding and solving problems in ways that leverage the power of technological methods to develop and test solutions.
Standard 6: **Creative Communicator**	Students communicate clearly and express themselves creatively for a variety of purposes using the platforms, tools, styles, formats and digital media appropriate to their goals.

ISTE EDUCATOR STANDARDS ADDRESSED IN THIS CHAPTER

Standard 1: Learner	Educators continually improve their practice by learning from and with others and exploring proven and promising practices that leverage technology to improve student learning.
Standard 5: Designer	Educators design authentic, learner-driven activities and environments that recognize and accommodate learner variability.
Standard 6: Facilitator	Educators facilitate learning with technology to support student achievement of the 2016 ISTE Standards for Students.
Standard 7: Analyst	Educators understand and use data to drive their instruction and support students in achieving their learning goals.

Questions and Reflections

- Is the idea of gamification something you think could improve students' enthusiasm and persistence for learning?

- What are some of the concerns you have about implementing this digital strategy in your classroom, school, district, or community?

- Are there local resources or individuals who might assist or inform your school or colleagues about gamification?

- What safeguards are necessary to protect privacy within a gamified classroom?

- Can you identify one area where your grade- or subject-level teachers might work together to gamify an assignment or a project? Is there something the entire school might work toward together?

Further Resources to Get Started

Open Educational Resources (Free)

Wikispaces
(gamifi-ed.wikispaces.com) This article offers an introduction and overview of gamification.

The Arab-Israeli Conflict Game

(aic.conflix.org) This free game provides authentic problem solving and practice in politics.

Taleblazer

(taleblazer.org) Find interesting games for your students.

PBS LearningMedia

(www.pbslearningmedia.org) Provides resources for the classroom.

Education Arcade

(education.mit.edu) A rich site from MIT that includes dozens of games for learners of all ages.

Gaming Can Make a Better World

(www.ted.com/talks/jane_mcgonigal_gaming_can_make_a_better_world) An excellent TED talk about gamification by Jane McGonigal.

The Ultimate Guide to Gamifying Your Classroom

(www.edudemic.com/ultimate-guide-gamifying-classroom) This offers ideas and support for introducing gamification into your classroom or school.

Further Resources (For Purchase)

Globaloria

(globaloria.com) Power up any brain with excellent computer science courses for grades K–12 and engage all students in computer science education.

Top Hat

(tophat.com/blog/gamification-education-class) This site offers support and assistance for gamifying your curriculum.

BrainPOP

(www.brainpop.com) A commercial system to support learning games.

World of Warcraft

(worldofwarcraft.com/en-us) This is one of the most popular games and offers a chance to teach strategy and collaboration to students.

CHAPTER 4

Digital Citizenship

A lie can travel half way round the world while the truth is putting its shoes on.

—Mark Twain

Never doubt that a small group of thoughtful committed citizens can change the world; indeed it is the only thing that ever has.

—Margaret Mead

In This Chapter:

- What is known about digital citizenship and efforts to address this topic in educational contexts?

- What examples exist on the importance of teaching about digital citizenship?

- In what ways is digital citizenship being taught in K–12 and postsecondary education?

What Do We Know About Digital Citizenship?

Digital citizenship refers to guiding students in the appropriate, responsible use of technology. This concept includes a multitude of topics, but overall most educators, parents, and organizations agree that a structure is required to teach everyone about how to act regarding technology (Ribble & Bailey, 2007). Digital citizenship addresses appropriate ways to interact with others and use technology, but it also includes potential negative impacts on students and communities, such as cyberbullying, digital footprints, sexting, privacy and copyright violations, and the newer phenomenon of digital addiction. "The indelibility of a digital footprint has implications unprecedented in society, particularly for youth. Giving young people the tools and ethical code to make good choices is vital" (Dotterer, Hedges, & Parker, 2016, p. 59).

Ribble (2012) identified several elements of digital citizenship, and the most pertinent to this discussion are:

Digital Communication: understanding global communication options, when each is appropriate and selecting the most effective tools.

Digital Literacy: learning and teaching about the use of digital technologies.

Digital Etiquette: electronic standards of conduct or procedure.

Digital Law: having an awareness of rules and understanding responsibility for digital actions and deeds.

Digital Rights and Responsibilities: understanding the requirements and freedoms extended to everyone in a digital world.

Digital Security (self-protection): electronic precautions to protect personal information and guarantee safety. (p. 149)

Digital citizenship is increasingly recognized as an essential aspect of P–12 education. The 2010 Online Safety and Technology Working Group (OSTWG; tinyurl.com/2fuqldd), developed by the National Telecommunications and Information Administration (NTIA), released its report titled, *Youth Safety on a Living Internet.* It advocated that educators "in the process of teaching regular subjects, teach the constructive, mindful use of social media enabled by digital citizenship and new media literacy training." Based on these recommendations, the NTIA identified digital citizenship in P–12 education as a national priority (Ribble, 2012, p. 149). The emphasis on digital citizenship has been to protect students from harm and promote appropriate use of technology. Educators can help students understand the potential risks and dangers in a digital world, learn how to keep themselves and their personal information safe, and foster constructive digital relationships. "Teaching digital citizenship keeps young people and their futures safer and allows positive communications and relationships to grow out of social media connections. It also helps cultivate an appreciation of power over others and an ethos of, "Do no harm," (Dotterer, Hedges, & Parker, 2016, p. 59).

With growing awareness of the importance of including digital citizenship as an integral part of the curriculum, school districts are addressing the development of safe, responsible technology users by designing a digital citizenship curriculum, providing ongoing professional development, and including parents and community members in the digital citizenship conversation. A digital citizenship curriculum may be part of an overall literacy or technology program and is usually woven into all curricular areas. For example, in 2011 the Lewisville Independent School District, in Texas began with "a strategic design plan integrating digital citizenship across the curriculum" (Stout, 2017, p. 15).

Providing ongoing professional development for teachers and administrators in an ever-changing digital world is considered critical for a successful digital citizenship program. For example, "In 2012 the New York City (NYC) Department of Education created social media guidelines for staff" as well as the role of digital literacy and citizenship director to "help ensure that staff, students and their families engage responsibly online." In addition, through partnerships with CommonSense Education (commonsense.org/education) and EVERFI (everfi.com), an education technology company, they offer teachers digital citizenship classes throughout the year (Ullman, 2017, p. 19).

Bringing parents into the conversation early, as well as helping them understand and guide appropriate technology use at home, has been identified as a vital aspect of digital citizenship education. "A good digital citizenship curriculum encourages parents to become active participants in teaching and understanding how digital citizenship can help their children engage safely" (Dotterer, Hedges, & Parker, 2016, p. 62). A growing number of school districts offer parents education about digital citizenship, which may include parent events, posting information on school websites, and having students create appropriate technology use materials to share at home.

In addition, schools can provide parents with information about websites, such as Google's Be Internet Awesome family link (tinyurl.com/ya5qlaed), which offers guidelines and resources to help parents discuss and monitor home technology use, or the U.S. government's Admongo site (consumer.ftc.gov/Admongo/parents.html), which provides parents with resources to help children discern the information of digital commerce and decide what information is true and what is not.

After 20 years of efforts on behalf of digital safety, the organization NetFamilyNews (netfamilynews.org) has summarized several major conclusions. According to Collier (2017), generalizations are just that and may be completely misleading because of the ever-changing nature of the use of social media. Second, she has concluded that children's social media use "is the exposure of their deepest needs: deep connection and to be heard and accepted by people they love or care about" (n.p.). Next, Collier has posited that privacy has many different meanings, in terms of children developing their sense of privacy from adults, as well as creating their own sense of self, and any efforts for digital safety must include the children themselves in developing rules for safety. More importantly, she maintains that all rules are "individual, situational, and contextual." Collier concludes that the United Nations Convention on the Rights of the Child (commonly abbreviated as the CRC or UNCRC), which seeks to protect children but also to strongly protect their rights, is recognized as leading this important work. It created a human rights treaty that sets out the civil, political, economic, social, health, and cultural rights of children, which includes digital rights. Livingstone and Third (2017) summarized this work:

> Rights-based approaches to children's digital media practices are gaining attention as a framework for research, policy and initiatives that can balance children's need for protection online with their capacity to maximize the opportunities and benefits of connectivity. But what does it mean to bring the concepts of the digital, rights and the child into dialogue? (2017, p. 1461)

Responsible Use Policy

Digital citizenship curriculums typically include adoption of an Appropriate Use (AUP) or Responsible Use Policy (RUP), to guide student use of technology and address potential negative aspects of digital communications, particularly cyberbullying. A well-crafted AUP developed with input from students, parents, teachers, staff, and administration creates a framework for discussing online behavior (Bolkan, 2014). At one time, many school districts implemented AUPs; however, recently schools are choosing instead to adopt RUPs; the difference is rather important as this new model suggests that individuals take responsibility for their actions. According to the Renton, Washington, school district, "A RUP is a policy that treats the student as a person who is responsible for their own ethical and appropriate use of the internet and their devices" (rentonschools.us/Page/2458). Equally innovative are Global Digital Citizen agreements, which can be found on the Global Digital Citizen Foundation website (tinyurl.com/y8d225mf).

Privacy

Cortez (2017b) recently described the importance of protecting the privacy of all students. She explained the two guiding documents that govern this aspect: the Family Education Rights and Privacy Act (FERPA), which "keeps parents apprised of how their children's information is being used and gives them control over much of what is shared;" and the Children's Online Privacy Protection Act (COPPA), which "requires makers of websites, online services and apps to notify parents and get consent before collecting information on children under the age of 13" (n.d.).

She goes on to explain that schools can only allow access to student information when it is directly related to a student's education, and only in limited areas. It is necessary for teachers and school leaders to understand both of these laws.

Cyberbullying

According to the U.S. government, "Cyberbullying is bullying that takes place using electronic technology. Electronic technology includes devices and equipment such as cell phones, computers, and tablets as well as communication tools including social media sites, text messages, chat, and websites" (stopbullying.gov, n.d.). The 2014–2015 School Crime Supplement (National Center for Education Statistics, 2016) indicates that, nationwide, about 21% of students ages 12–18 have experienced bullying. The 2015 Youth Risk Behavior Surveillance System (Centers for Disease

Control and Prevention, 2016) also indicates that an estimated 16% of high school students were bullied electronically in the 12 months prior to the survey.

Teen suicides related to cyberbullying have also been reported. According to the Centers for Disease Control and Prevention (CDC), "Suicide was the second leading cause of death among youth ages 10–24 in 2015. While most youth who are involved in bullying do not engage in suicide-related behaviors, those who have been bullied or who bully others are more likely to report suicidal thoughts and suicide attempts." (Stone & Mercado-Crespo, 2017).

Trolley and Hanel (2010) suggest that cyberbullying is often more hurtful because it is anonymous, under the radar, less likely to have adult intervention, and can involve hundreds of people (p. 35). The National Education Association has offered suggestions, too (nea.org/home/schools-and-online-socil-networking.html). The National Crime Prevention Council has created a source for information about cyberbullying and how to prevent it (ncpc.org/topics/cyberbullying). Google has initiated a free course for educators and others, regarding digital citizenship (tinyurl.com/y84tcrc7). The course includes five interactive units:

- Teaching students about internet safety and privacy, including setting strong passwords and privacy settings

- Staying safe on the go by securing your mobile device and avoiding harmful downloads on your smartphone

- Savvy searching, to help students evaluate the credibility of online sources of information

- Staying safe from phishing and other scams

- Managing online reputation, including protecting sensitive information

Counterspeech

Several organizations work to defuse and eliminate hate speech and bullying in social media; perhaps the most effective is termed *counterspeech*, which Dr. Susan Benesch defines as "a direct response to hateful or dangerous speech." She and her colleagues conducted a qualitative study (Benesch, Ruths, Dillon, Mohammad

Saleem, & Wright, 2017) to investigate counterspeech as it is practiced spontaneously on Twitter. From their work, they offer suggestions that are useful for all learners, from K–12 to postsecondary education.

First, they suggest providing a warning that outlines the consequences of specific behaviors. This might include raising awareness of what might happen through the hate speech, or as alumni of the University of Illinois at Champaign-Urbana did, warn students that current and future employers would be able to see their tweets. Second, they recommend shaming and labeling the speech as hateful or inappropriate. Next, they suggest empathy, that is, changing the tone of a hateful conversation, as an effective way of ending the exchange. They also recommend humor, which they have observed can "shift the dynamics of communication, de-escalate conflict, and draw much more attention to a message than it would otherwise garner" (p. 5).

Examples of Digital Citizenship Activities

The Mesa Arizona School District created and curated a wide variety of videos (www.mpsaz.org/edtech/resources/cybersavvy/youtube/#Elementary) for elementary and secondary students, as well as one for parents. These videos provide an introduction to being safe online, but also raise issues about cyberbullying. Dr. Myers and his team have created an incredibly rich set of activities to promote and teach about digital citizenship, which includes internet safety, personal information, digital footprint and reputation, netiquette, cyberbullying, and other topics of importance. These resources are curated by one of the 24 certified educators who work in the educational technology department. Each grade has specific resources, most of which are free for anyone's use. In addition, each seventh grade student takes a required class that includes more information on digital citizenship. To support the goal of creating good digital citizens, they have developed "Digital Citizen Certificates" and have expanded the reach of the training to include parents and teachers. Parents can learn about a wide variety of topics, including technology use and digital citizenship, offered online or face-to-face, through its Parent University. Educators have several education technology courses that they can complete on their own time, including information on digital citizenship. Through these courses, they are able to earn recertification hours to satisfy Arizona's educator requirements.

Figure 4.1. Think-before-you-post poster (goo.gl/LXg6Hs).

The Evergreen Public Schools, Vancouver, Washington, has a strong commitment to teaching everyone about digital citizenship. According to Chris McMurray (@LearnLeadGrow), Assistant Superintendent,

> Digital citizenship is a cornerstone of technology integration. Culturally, and philosophically, we believe that students must learn safe, responsible use and interaction with digital tools and ecosystems. The Common Sense Media curricular resource is required for every student, and it is also used by schools to educate families about responsible and safe use of technology. Because students will be using many common digital tools, such as YouTube, for learning, it is critical that they be equipped to make appropriate decisions about use. Beyond the curricular resource, schools are embedding digital citizenship in daily activity, policies, and procedures. (personal communication, 2017)

Stout (2017) discussed her district, the Lewisville Independent School District in Texas, and stated, "A core value of our district is making students responsible users and creators of digital information" (p. 15). Delaney (2014, n p.) reports,

As the stakes of online content grow, schools around the globe have built increasingly comprehensive digital citizenship programs aimed at helping students—and teachers, staff and parents—to stay safe, be wise consumers, respect intellectual property, communicate effectively and think critically on the internet.

Barbara Brown, chief technology officer at Lewisville ISD (cited in Delaney, 2014, n.p.) said, "They need to realize that their digital footprints will follow them their entire lives."

Strategies such as the poster shown in Figure 4.1 are found in classrooms, media centers, and around schools to help remind students of their responsibility!

SPOTLIGHT 4.1

Teaching Digital Citizenship with *Wonder*

Angela Hartman, Hutto Independent School District, Hutto Texas

In 2012, R. J. Palacio wrote a book titled *Wonder*, and it began a global phenomenon that has had an impact on bullying in general, cyberbullying, and digital citizenship. The middle grade novel tells the story, from multiple perspectives of a young man named Auggie Pullman who was born with severe craniofacial anomalies. He underwent multiple surgeries and was homeschooled, until he enters fifth grade in a private school. The book illustrates how he is treated because of the way he looks. This book encourages students to "choose kind" as a matter of proactive decision making, and schools have adopted this as yearlong projects, ideas, and themes to promote the lessons from the book. Library media specialists have joined in celebrating this young man's story.

One library media specialist, Angela Hartman of the Hutto Independent School District in Hutto, Texas, was so engaged by this book that she decided to bring the book and activities to her entire community. First, she wrote a grant to purchase 800 copies of the book in English and Spanish, so that every campus of the district and community members could read it. She explained,

Wonder was read at all campuses by most grade levels. Teachers were able to choose if and how they wanted to participate. Some classes read it together with a set of books. Some teachers read one copy aloud and some classes listened to the audio recording. We had copies available for checkout in each library and we had "floating" copies that students, staff, and others could read, sign their name in, and pass on to a friend or family member. *Wonder* provided a connection at campuses between students of all ages and all abilities. We all loved Auggie and loved to talk about the book. (Hartman, 2016)

Hartman also introduced the book to the entire community—the school board, the mayor, public employees, and school district employees. The community even held a Wonder 5K walk/run to raise money for the Children's Craniofacial Association to help children like Auggie. She concluded, "I believe that, as teachers, one of our most important jobs is to teach to the heart of kids. Reading and discussing *Wonder* has helped us cultivate empathy, a trait that is crucial to getting along and having a peaceful world" (personal communication, 2017). She added that they are negotiating to rent out an entire theater for a showing of the upcoming movie (personal communication, 2017)!

■ ■ ■ ■ ■

The University of Michigan School of Education embraces the idea of digital citizenship for its student interns (Slaton, 2016). Each year, Professor Liz Kolb of the University of Michigan School of Education leads a team of University of Michigan teaching interns through Common Sense's Digital Citizenship Curriculum, teaching the students such concepts as formulating strong passwords, standing up to cyberbullies, and identifying harmful posts. The teaching interns facilitate activities and discussions on digital safety and responsibility and create opportunities for teachers to learn how to talk about digital citizenship. The goal is to teach middle school students how to be wise digital citizens. Spotlight 4.2 shares what they do.

SPOTLIGHT 4.2

Teaching Digital Citizenship

Dr. Liz Kolb, University of Michigan

Sixth Grade: Safety

The sixth grade students focus on digital safety and security, with the goal to understand these key concepts: safe vs. risky, privacy, security, identity, footprints, phishing, positive vs. negative, predator, catfishing, and Creative Commons and copyright. They develop comics or cartoons to share what they are learning. They end the unit knowing about strong passwords, what to do when confronted by a stranger or uncomfortable conversations, and how to use Creative Commons copyright rules when finding media to use or share.

Seventh Grade: Identity

The seventh grade students begin middle school by learning how to critically evaluate websites for bias and reliability, with the goal of understanding these key concepts: bias, website evaluation, deep web, reliable sources, and Creative Commons and copyright. These students create posters to demonstrate what they've learned about being media literate in a digital world: how to find and evaluate reliable and authoritative sources online; how to evaluate a webpage, blog post, or social media post for bias; how to understand the difference between the general internet and the deep web and how to use the deep web for finding reliable information; and how to be sensitive regarding gender, ethnic, and racial stereotypes. Students create infographics on how and why to create a positive digital identity.

Eighth Grade: Empathy

Eighth grade students develop public service announcements (PSAs) around the concept of empathy, with a focus on these key concepts: cyberbullying, identity, footprints, reputation, upstander, bystander, hate speech, harassment, flaming, catfishing, deceiving, empathy, and Creative Commons and copyright. They learn what it means to walk in someone else's shoes (be empathetic), become an upstander when they see others being treated poorly online, as well as to differentiate between an upstander, a bystander, and a cyberbully. They also learn the consequences of being a cyberbully or contributing to negative behavior online, and they use Creative Commons copyright when searching for media to reuse, modify, or remix online.

Of great interest is the response of the student interns. According to Dr. Kolb, "Ninety percent of the teaching interns have said this project experience was an exceptional or extremely useful way to learn about their own digital citizenship skill as well as learn how to teach and talk to students about digital citizenship" (personal communication, 2017). Some of their comments include:

> "The digital citizenship project was one of the most important projects that I worked on, because it allowed me to see the outcome of what I taught throughout the three days. I was fully prepared to teach the guidelines of what it means to be a digital citizen. We literally spent so much time on designing the lesson plans to best fit sixth-graders so they can learn and use the information in their daily lives. Listening to students' thoughts and ideas was one of the parts that I really enjoyed. Watching their enthusiasm to win the game filled me with joy and showed how huge an impact we left on them."

> "I really enjoyed our digital citizenship field experience. I actually think that it has been one of my favorite field experiences we have had so far. The students were so authentic and funny, and their comics were hilarious! One group that we worked with made a comic about giving out their password to a ghost who hacks their computer and makes it act glitchy. Another group had a character put their personal information online and was abducted by aliens. I didn't know what to expect, but I thought that storyboard was highly effective. The site was especially effective for students who were co-using the computer and having to discuss the plot and citizenship aspects of their comic."

> "I really enjoyed working with the middle schoolers and I was surprised by how engaged they were in the activities and how willing they were to offer their opinions on everything!"

■ ■ ■ ■ ■

Fitting Digital Citizenship into Your School: Getting Started

Resources to support educators' goals in teaching about digital citizenship, privacy, and bullying are everywhere. Common Sense Education has created many ways to introduce and educate learners about digital citizenship, safety online, and prevention of bullying. Most impressively, it has developed a digital passport for learners in grades 3–5 (commonsense.org/education/digital-passport); students earn their passport through a variety of engaging games that address key issues facing kids in today's digital world. The skills include digital safety, respect, and community. The games include videos, offline activities, and provide educators with rich reporting of students' experiences (as individuals and as groups).

Media Literacy Now (medialiteracynow.org/about-us) is an organization focused on improving schools' recognition of its responsibility to teach students about media, privacy, source authenticity, and protection of all learners. It has helped many states to pass rules and regulations requiring media literacy in schools and to bring these issues to public attention. The National Association for Media Literacy Educators (namle.net) is another professional education group that offers resources to support the inclusion of these topics into the curriculum. Ultimately, however, it falls to teachers to find ways to make this an important aspect of their assignments and activities.

Three businessmen determined that if consumers could provide feedback to companies, they could also provide feedback and rate media sources. They developed an organization, Tribeworthy, to build an interactive community of critical thinkers called "Crowd Contested Media" (Fesler & Palmieri, 2017). Crowdsourcing critical media literacy became a way to connect their tribe of users with their desire for "trustworthy" sources and focus on people evaluating media and sharing it as part of their mission. Students have begun posting their evaluations of media sources, after careful investigation, and some middle school educators have begun using political advertisements to teach about propaganda (middleweb.com/28053/teaching-about-propaganda-using-political-ads).

PACER (pacer.org/bullying/nbpm) supports National Bullying Prevention Month each October, and offers free resources for young children, others for teens, and an online toolkit for educators. It also offers materials for parents, peers, and others interested in this topic.

Another option for getting started is demonstrated by an organization in Utah, where individuals have come together to tackle this issue as a challenge larger than one district or one city can solve. Read more in Spotlight 4.3.

SPOTLIGHT 4.3

EPIK

EPIK Deliberate Digital (@DigCitSummit), Salt Lake City, Utah

Jann Garbett (@UseTech4Good), Founder

EPIK Deliberate Digital, based in Salt Lake City, Utah, is a nonprofit that was founded in 2014 with a simple mission: to facilitate cross-sector conversations (whole-village conversations, if you will) and community collaborations around digital citizenship. EPIK's founder, Jan Garbett, had many years' experience in the nonprofit world and had seen both the benefits and limitations of any one organization trying to tackle an issue or opportunity. While serving as the president of a different nonprofit, Garbett learned about a model for collaborative community change called collective impact (see fsg.org, tamarackcommunity.ca, or collectiveimpactforum.org). Garbett was motivated to create a nonprofit that could help bring multiple organizations and individuals together to combine expertise, reduce redundancy, and combine learning in the spirit of collective impact. (See EPIK's website for examples of community meetings that EPIK has facilitated: epik.org/category/meeting-reports).

In its first year and a half, EPIK held multiple cross-sector community meetings to open conversations about the risks and benefits of the internet and to help organizations and individuals connect with each other. One community partner, a legislator, invited EPIK to consult on a bill that began as a filtering bill and ended up being the nation's first digital citizenship bill (HB213, 2015). The bill mandates that digital citizenship education options for parents and students be addressed by a local school community council, itself a microcosm of a cross-sector team of parents, teachers, and administrators. To help support influencers in Utah, EPIK created DigCitUtah (digcitutah.com) for parents, teachers, administrators, and others who are looking for more resources around facets of digital citizenship. Two hundred resources were curated and organized into categories for ease of navigation.

Figure 4.2. In 2017, a unique summit expanded conversations around learners and digital citizenship.

DigCitUtah also invites school community councils to consider working with youth in schools to create positive digital citizenship projects. EPIK also invites parents to do the same. So often when adults talk to children about the Internet, they focus on the don'ts. But long before children own devices of their own, they also need mentoring and side-by-side experiences around how to use technology deliberately to learn, to build relationships, and to help others.

This vision of co-creating a culture that both helps protect children and engages them in side-by-side learning around positive digital citizenship has become EPIK's passion.

In collaboration with Marialice Curran, cofounder of the Digital Citizenship Summit (digcitsummit.com) and founder of the Digital Citizenship Institute, EPIK hosted the third annual DigCitSummit in Provo, Utah, in 2017. Adults and youth discussed digital citizenship and how to create a more positive digital citizenship culture that helps kids avoid the negative and use technology in positive ways. The summit engaged participants in roundtable discussions and workshops and offered a free #UseTech4Good Youth Extravaganza for the community, as well as several free community breakout sessions. For more information about the results of the 2017 Summit, visit DigCitSummit2017.com, or follow the Twitter hashtags #digcitsummit and #UseTech4Good.

■ ■ ■ ■ ■

Summary

This chapter has focused on the concept of digital citizenship, which encompasses many topics that support the appropriate use of all technologies, including protection, privacy, behavior, and bullying. It presented background on the topic, and also provided information regarding the ways in which schools are assisting their students, and their families, in understanding and dealing with these issues. Educators who employ the ideas and goals of digital citizenship will be incorporating the following ISTE standards for students and for themselves as educators.

ISTE STUDENT STANDARDS ADDRESSED IN THIS CHAPTER

Standard 1: Empowered Learner	Students leverage technology to take an active role in choosing, achieving and demonstrating competency in their learning goals, informed by the learning sciences.
Standard 2: Digital Citizen	Students recognize the rights, responsibilities and opportunities of living, learning and working in an interconnected digital world, and they act and model in ways that are safe, legal and ethical.
Standard 7: Global Collaborator	Students use digital tools to broaden their perspectives and enrich their learning by collaborating with others and working effectively in teams locally and globally.

ISTE EDUCATOR STANDARDS ADDRESSED IN THIS CHAPTER

Standard 3: Citizen	Educators inspire students to positively contribute to and responsibly participate in the digital world.
Standard 4: Collaborator	Educators dedicate time to collaborate with both colleagues and students to improve practice, discover and share resources and ideas, and solve problems.
Standard 5: Designer	Educators design authentic, learner-driven activities and environments that recognize and accommodate learner variability.

Questions and Reflections

- What is your classroom, school, district, or community currently doing to teach about digital citizenship? If you were able to add one more intentional activity in this area, what would it be?

- Does your classroom, school, district, or community have an Acceptable Use Policy? Could this be transformed into a Responsible Use Policy? What do you see as the benefit of this?

- What systems are in place to protect learners' privacy? Are there ways you can identify to expand this protection?

- What is the current effort to prevent or expose bullying in your school? In what ways might the culture against bullying be expanded and deepened?

- What role do parents play in assisting the educational environment in preventing bullying? Could this be expanded?

Further Resources to Get Started

Open Educational Resources (Free)

Edutopia

(www.edutopia.org/blog/film-festival-digital-citizenship) Edutopia offers frequent articles about digital citizenship, but also has this five-minute film festival on digital citizenship.

Google Training Modules for Educators
(edutrainingcenter.withgoogle.com/digital_citizenship/preview) These modules will help educators understand and teach about digital citizenship.

Global Digital Citizenship Foundation
(solutionfluency.com/en/downloadables/gdc-agreements) Sample agreements on technology use.

Scarlett Digital Citizenship Project
(scarlettdigitalcitizenshipproject.weebly.com/resources-for-families.html) Multiple resources to assist families and teachers in supporting students' understanding of citizenship.

Common Sense Education
(www.commonsense.org/education/toolkits; code.org/curriculum/course3/20/ Teacher; www.commonsense.org/education/scope-and-sequence) Toolkits and lesson plans to teach about digital citizenship.

Edudemic
(www.edudemic.com/teachers-guide-digital-citizenship) This guide will be useful for professional development and PLN conversations, as well as implementing a useful education plan.

Digital Citizenship Institute
(digitalcitizenship.net) Information for families and educators on using all digital tools responsibly.

The Net Safety Collaborative offers social media helpline for schools!
(angel.co/the-net-safety-collaborative) This group will assist with helping schools and teachers understand their responsibility and identifying appropriate responses to challenging situations.

Dangerous Speech
(dangerousspeech.org/considerations-for-successful-counterspeech) Information on promoting counterspeech to avoid bullying and hate speech.

Teachhub
(www.teachhub.com/how-teach-digital-citizenship) Free lessons on digital citizenship for all grades.

PBS Kids Webonauts

(pbskids.org/webonauts/about) Lessons to encourage appropriate use of the web.

Digital Education Revolution

(www.digitalcitizenship.nsw.edu.au/index.htm) Multiple resources to assist teachers, learners, and families.

Media Education Lab

(mediaeducationlab.com/curriculum/materials) These materials help integrated digital citizenship policies and lessons into the curriculum.

Michael Gorman

(www.k12blueprint.com/blog/michael-gorman/10-digital-citizenship-resources-web-classroom-part-3) These resources provide useful tools for the classroom.

U.S. Federal Trade Commission

(www.consumer.ftc.gov/topics/protecting-kids-online) Lessons and videos to assist in talking with learners about safety online.

Further Resources (For Purchase)

BrainPop Citizenship

(www.brainpop.com/technology/digitalcitizenship) Brainpop offers many lessons, videos, and other curricular activities on digital citizenship.

Nearpod

(nearpod.com/digital-citizenship) Interactive lessons on digital citizenship; some features are free.

Global Digital Citizenship Agreements

(solutionfluency.com/en/downloadables/gdc-agreements) The agreements are free; they also sell options and solutions.

Violence Prevention Works

(www.violencepreventionworks.org/public/olweus_bullying_prevention_program.page) Resources, surveys, lessons, and recommendations to prevent or end bullying.

CHAPTER 5

Pedagogical Changes: Project-Based Learning and Personalized Learning

Tell me and I forget, teach me and I remember, involve me and I learn.

—Benjamin Franklin

Everybody is a genius. But if you judge a fish by its ability to climb a tree, it will live its whole life believing that it is stupid.

—Albert Einstein

In This Chapter:

- What is the foundation of project-based learning (PBL)?

- How does PBL align with the digital age classroom?

- How does personalized learning (PL) support the PBL learning environment?

- What are teacher and student roles in a PBL/PL environment?

- How are schools successfully integrating a PBL approach supported with technology?

- How can I get started?

What Is the Foundation of Project-Based Learning?

Educators work hard to consider the ways classroom practice can better prepare our diverse digital age learners for a workforce where many of the job opportunities available after graduation do not currently exist. With cutting-edge technology changing so rapidly, it is easy to get focused on the interesting and engaging tools that our students can use to complete their work. While many digital tools and trends in education can be fleeting in their significance, often we look to the tools of the past that have withstood the test of time.

Project-based learning (PBL) has maintained an unwavering role in curricular approaches since its introduction, in 1918, by William Heard Kilpatrick, an educational philosopher and student of Dewey (Knoll, 2010). Dubbed "The Project Method," Kilpatrick believed that the work of children in school should be purposeful and align with genuine experiences encountered in life. At its core, a *project* should have a concept or idea that is personally meaningful and relates to an authentic life experience. In addition, Kilpatrick emphasized that it is critical that the work have real-world applications to those engaged in the project (Kilpatrick, 1918).

Integrating personalized learning (PL) experiences into a PBL environment allows teachers to differentiate experiences by adapting aspects and roles within a project to meet the academic needs and learning styles of individual students. In addition, projects provide opportunities for students to master skills that are specific to their learning goals, while working in cooperative learning environments with more skillful peers. With a well-chosen project, both PBL and PL are personally meaningful for the students, which leads to individual and team empowerment and engagement.

PBL for the Digital Age Classroom

While PBL, in various forms, has been a part of the education field over the past 100 years, it is the emphasis on preparing students with digital age work skills that has brought it back to the forefront of classrooms as a way of bridging learning with life outside the school campus. PBL supports students developing communication, collaboration, and critical thinking skills that are needed whether they pursue either a college or career path after graduation (Gómez-Pablos, del Pozo, & Muñoz-Repiso, 2016). PBL's student-centered, hands-on approach to learning requires participants to work effectively as a team to address multifaceted, real-world topics that are meaningful within their community. Since the topics addressed in a project will vary based on current events and the interests of the community of learners, the diverse approaches students take to investigate the many facets of each topic often require creative problem solving by those engaged in the inquiry process (Buck Institute for Education, 2013). Most importantly, productive PBL lessons support students in the construction of new knowledge, the acquisition of new technical skills, and the awareness of how to extend the use of these skills as they learn through discovery and prepare for college and careers outside the K–12 system.

Teacher and Student Roles in a PBL Classroom

In a PBL approach to curriculum, the teacher's role shifts from one of lesson planning, delivery, and resource gathering to that of a facilitator who guides the inquiry process and scaffolds the learning experiences to meet individual needs of all students. Teachers ensure that tasks address appropriate grade-level content standards across content areas and are academically rigorous, while developing an action plan to implement and evaluate the tasks throughout the project (Ravitz & Blazevski, 2014). From the outset, teachers guide students as a team to develop detailed plans that will guide their inquiry, build a bank of resources, self-evaluate throughout the project, and prepare for a final presentation (The Buck Institute for Education, 2013).

PBL also supports the technical skills of the tech-savvy generation of digital natives (Prensky, 2001a) who are fluent in the use of technology to communicate and prefer to be actively engaged in the learning process. Although incorporating technological tools and online resources can often feel overwhelming, the use of digital resources can strengthen student interactive experiences, facilitate more complex thinking about challenging topics among peer groups, and often streamline the assessment of student progress for teachers (Beckett et al., 2016). With the increasing field of online programs and applications available, students can use the internet to remove physical barriers to connect with external resources, as well as to improve collaboration and sharing opportunities between students, peers, and teachers. Teachers can mine a seemingly endless bank of materials and resources to reduce planning and research time, as well as assess and monitor individual and group progress (Gómez-Pablos, del Pozo, & Muñoz-Repiso, 2016).

Students use Voice over Internet Protocol (VoIP) technology such as Skype or FaceTime to gain direct access to experts working in the field of interest to learn more about their cutting-edge work, gain a deeper understanding of the topic they are studying, and pose questions they may have on a specific topic related to their project. Students also engage with VoIP tools to collaborate on ideas with peers interested in similar topics who may be located at a school across town or around the globe. Students can also follow the blogs of experts to connect with and learn from leaders in the field of study, as well as create their own blogs to share their thinking and engage in critical thinking with their peers and teachers.

Robust and successful projects have the following characteristics: they do not have one answer; they present authentic problems; group members take on well-defined roles in the process; they include multiple benchmarks through the (typical) four-week project; and they offer students the opportunity to make decisions about how to present and represent their learning. In STEM-related projects, students use simulations to understand complex topics such as long-term effects of deforestation or what might be the most effective way to design a new highway exit ramp based on current traffic patterns. In projects such as these, technology can ease the manipulation of measurements and expedite the manipulation of data so that students may, for example, consider the best way to build a 3-D model that might help determine the necessary pitch of the earth surrounding the school building to correct the problem of a basement that has a history of taking on water (Darling-Hamilton, Zielezinski, & Goldman, 2014). In addition, students can gain access to a treasure trove of information necessary to research topics through free and reliable public resources, such as the many Smithsonian Museums, to discover topics on art history, natural history, astrophysics, or space exploration, or take a virtual tour of one of the many facilities across the country or close to home.

Once students have completed research and collected the necessary information to complete their inquiry, technology tools such as multimedia presentations can be created using local software and online resources to display their findings. Basic tools such as PowerPoint and Publisher allow students to create supportive resources to share with the community at large. Tools such as iMovie and YouTube are examples of ways for students to create documentaries detailing the information they collected, gather oral histories from multigenerational families, or create video reports to visually represent their findings and demonstrate understanding of the topics explored. Podcasts and vodcasts can be created to document interviews with experts and members of the learning group to capture key information that allows students to revisit critical information, as well as using the platform to share these ideas with others in a final presentation (Darling-Hamilton, Zielezinski, & Goldman, 2014).

The variety of digital tools available are endless and new ones arrive on the scene daily, but it is important that the novelty of tools does not overtake the meaningfulness of the work. What is most important when using a PBL approach to curriculum is the value gained from capitalizing not only on student interest and engagement, but also the limitless possibilities it offers for teachers to differentiate and personalize learning for each student.

Whereas rich projects often emanate from an inquiry or experience that is directly meaningful to the community of learners, there is a natural connection in using this approach to personalize the learning experiences embedded within a project. A well-developed project allows all learners to participate equally by assuming different roles, conducting independent inquiries, creating individual artifacts, and completing individualized assessments that target their specific goals. However, just using the PBL approach does not ensure learning will be personalized for each student; yet, there is an inherent relationship that offers itself to these two student-centered methodologies that when combined could heighten learning for all members of the community.

Personalized Learning

Similar to PBL, personalized learning (PL) is not a new trend. However, it is the resurgence of these two methodologies that is allowing teachers to reconsider how they will meet the needs of learners who must strengthen their leadership, communication, and collaboration skills in addition to building academic content knowledge. By providing opportunities to develop all these skills, we better prepare our students to embrace the challenges of the rapidly evolving employment opportunities they will face in the digital age, as well as help create more informed and engaged citizens of the world.

The RAND report (Pane, Steiner, Baird, Hamilton, & Pane, 2017) defines PL as an approach that

> prioritizes a clear understanding of the needs and goals of each individual student and the tailoring of instruction to address those needs and goals. These needs and goals, and progress toward them, are highly visible and easily accessible to teachers as well as students and their families, are frequently discussed among these parties, and are updated accordingly. (p. 6)

The report credits the work of Benjamin Bloom that connected the significant academic growth of students who received personal engagement with a tutor as compared to those receiving instruction through whole-group engagement. In 2011, VanLehn conducted a meta-analysis comparing the effects of human tutoring vs. computer-based tutoring experiences. His study not only supported Bloom's research from 1984, it further revealed overall that student growth was equally impressive regardless of whether tutoring was provided by a human or a computer program (VanLehn, 2011).

As access to technology and digital tools is becoming more affordable for schools, educators are finding it easier to individualize learning content and lesson pacing and to personalize assessment of each student. PL is on the minds and in the rich conversations of many in education looking for ways to meet the individual needs of their students to help each reach their potential. However, PL is also in a plethora of marketing brochures of organizations and publishers claiming to have the program guaranteed to simplify teachers' lives, while meeting the needs of all learners. It is with this reality in mind that educators are using a discerning eye to search for authentic ways to meet the individual needs of all students and to embrace personalized learning "as a practice, not a product" (Feldstein & Hill, 2016, p. 26).

The International Association for K–12 Online Learning (iNACOL) conducted a survey of thousands of educators to better understand current pedagogical approaches in the field of education (Abel, 2016). Through their responses, educators stated that one of the key foundations for PL is the ability to differentiate for each student to address any potential gaps in understanding or skill development. In addition, curriculum and assessment must be developed to enhance student agency, provide flexible pacing of instruction with immediate feedback and intervention supports, incorporate personalized learning plans, and provide varied assessments that are performance-based and demonstrate the knowledge and skills students have attained (Abel, 2016; Basye, 2016).

The call to personalize the learning experiences of each student creates a tall order for educators who are continuously requested to make sure to individualize goals, assignments, assessments, and learning environments to meet the needs, personal interest, and career aspirations of each student. Because the PL approach positions the student at the center of all learning experiences, teachers are looking to technology to ensure they are working within a collaborative framework to empower students to take ownership of their learning, while ensuring that the students are meeting academic milestones and attaining the critical knowledge necessary to be successful (Alliance for Excellent Education, 2017).

According to Bray and McClaskey (2014), making the shift from a traditional learning environment to one that works to vary instruction based on students' individual needs can look different depending upon each unique circumstance. Often the shift comes in stages, where initially students develop some choices in the learning experiences they receive from the teacher, then gradually move to experiences where teacher and student work together as co-creators of the material and topics. In the final step, the community has developed a relationship where students partner with teachers to consider the content and pacing that is personally meaningful and academically significant, in an environment that extends beyond the classroom walls.

The partnership between these two engaging approaches blends the best of all learning experiences and opportunities for students in digital age classrooms, while creating a challenge for teachers to find balance. Technology allows teachers to create flexible and customizable assignments that can be individualized while also meeting the needs of many by differentiating the pacing, performance tasks, and assessments of each student. When teachers personalize learning, students have more access to the content and more ownership in the project. While each student may have different roles as they collaborate on a project, "a PL approach grounds teachers in student needs as they work toward authentic products" (Wolking, 2016, n.p.).

How Are These Two Educational Pedagogies Being Used?

Neither of these approaches is new to the field of education, but the use of technology has certainly transformed students' ability to access resources and use more sophisticated tools allowing for more meaningful and engaging experiences. Marysville School District, outside Columbus, Ohio, partnered with KnowledgeWorks to develop a districtwide framework of PL that included competency-based curriculum to meet the needs of all K–12 students in the district. In addition, a STEM-focused early-college program provided opportunities for college-bound high school students.

SPOTLIGHT 5.1

Committed to Personalized Learning

Navin Elementary School, Marysville, Ohio

Lynette Lewis (@navinelementary), Principal

At Navin Elementary, we have been working to embed personalized learning into our professional practices for the past two years and, although we are still a work in progress, we continue to grow every day. As we started our journey, we shared a vision/mission and five simple rules, which have anchored our learning and our commitment to our students along the way.

Our Vision and Mission

At Navin, we truly believe that "Our Kids Will Change the World" in big ways and small ways, and we need to prepare them to make their mark on our world.

Our staff, from the custodian to the principal, and everyone in-between, follows the following five simple rules:

1. Love your kids!

2. Love them more when they're difficult.

3. Love them the most when they push you away.

4. Every child that walks through our doors belongs to *all* of us.

5. Every child deserves our best every single day.

Personalized learning has multiple components that interweave to provide an individualized learning experience for each child. Growth mindset is the foundation. This includes helping students to understand how they can grow their brains through practice and set their minds to accomplish their goals. The components are:

Vision & Identity: school climate, culture; your message to the world

Standard Operating Procedures: SOPs (made in collaboration with students)

Flexible Seating: options for students to work where they're most comfortable

Voice & Choice: students have a say in how and what they learn

Personal Learning Profiles: helps students to understand how they learn best

Universal Design for Learning: UDL; removing barriers so every child can learn and reach mastery

If you enter a classroom at Navin, you will see students actively involved in learning tasks and problem-solving. They may be bouncing on an exercise ball or standing at a table to work. Some students choose to work independently and some choose to work with others. They may prefer to read about a subject or watch a video or research it on the computer. As students work, they will be demonstrating our Habits of Mind. The room will be organized to allow for various types of activities. The teacher may be teaching the whole group, a small group, or conferencing with one student. Students may be leading a lesson for peers.

But the most noticeable thing that has resulted from personalizing learning at Navin are the high levels of student engagement, hope, and agency, which has been a direct result of implementing high-quality, focused student-centered practices. As our superintendent, Diane Mankins, is often heard to say, "Which one of our students *doesn't* deserve this?" At Navin, we believe they *all* do. And this will enable them to go out and "Change the World."

■ ■ ■ ■ ■

In *Building a Vision for All Students*, Robin Kanaan, Director of Teaching and Learning for KnowledgeWorks explained, "One of the exciting things we're seeing in Marysville is a shift in teacher roles. They're moving away from owning everything that happens in the classroom to opening up to more student voice and choice" (KnowledgeWorks, 2017, p. 3). Hillary Weiser, kindergarten teacher for Marysville

Schools, shared that with the implementation of PL, students have taken more of an ownership role for their learning and within their classroom. "I've let the kids take charge of their learning. They know what they need to learn, and it's up to them how they get there. It's their choice. This room is theirs" (KnowledgeWorks, 2017, p. 6).

PL is one of the primary initiatives at Evergreen Public School District, one of the largest districts in the state of Washington. Through their approach, the district has placed an emphasis on ensuring that all members of the learning community, teachers and students, have access to both the hardware and software necessary to support their important work. Chris McMurray, Assistant Superintendent, shared how they go about personalizing learning experiences for each of the students they serve.

SPOTLIGHT 5.2

Essential Elements for Authentic Learning

Evergreen Public School District, Vancouver, Washington

Chris McMurray, (@LearnLeadGrow) Assistant Superintendent

In our system, teachers are learning designers. They plan explicitly, using a workshop model, to create experiences that integrate multiple content areas and give students hands-on application of skills and practices with voice and choice. We developed a framework of essential elements that set a floor and definition for personalization, and articulated a range of applications in each. The Essentials encompass best practice in areas identified by best practice, as well as those identified by business and community partners as being critical skills for success in the workplace. Teachers use the Essentials document as both a planning tool to inform their units and experiences and as a metric for students and teachers to use to monitor progress and design around large project-based units that contain multiple makes.

The units are designed to set multiple entry points, remove artificial ceilings, and promote student agency in determining the path their learning will take to reach the targets. This means that students are exercising creativity and critical thinking, for example, in the context of their learning, to deepen understanding and application. Authentic experiences connect student interest in an area of inquiry around a common real-world problem, often connected to a community organization, business partner, or other relevant agency. Technology is leveraged where appropriate to facilitate information input, processing, collaboration, and output, using a range of resources available in our digital learning system.

■ ■ ■ ■ ■

Part of what makes a PBL project so successful is the personal connections students make to professionals in the field they have chosen to investigate. While it is possible for students to reach out to experts locally, often to get firsthand information from those in the field, technology provides the opportunity to engage in a dialogue and get specific answers to their questions. Lynn Ojeda, Principal at Plano ISD Academy High School (PAHS), underscores the critical nature of technology to bridge conversation and to participate in presentations that are not able to occur in a face-to-face situation. "It is their window to the world in terms of accessing other people that helps us raise the authenticity of their learning as well as provide them expertise that enhances their learning in a powerful way" (personal communication, 2017).

Access to long-distance communication tools has allowed students in many PBL environments to have unprecedented access to experts working in far-reaching fields of study. This access connects students with professionals across thousands of miles and helps establish intercontinental projects, such as the following project where students in Hong Kong are designing and building a hospital for children in Kenya.

One school set about to create itself as an environment that focuses on skills such as problem-solving, teamwork, creativity, innovation, cultural awareness, and resilience; it placed second worldwide in a global competition for "21st Century School of the Year" in 2014 and was also a finalist in the 2015 Global Innovation Awards competition. Based in Hong Kong, The Harbour School (THS) is a "primary and secondary international school that recognizes children as complex individuals with differing needs, goals, personalities, and backgrounds and thus takes a customized approach to learning" (www.ths.edu.hk/about-the-school). Drs. Craig and Jadis Blurton, who have always had a belief in education for all learners, started THS in 2007 and have seen it grow in recognition as a center of educational excellence. They state, "We have created an environment that provides a comprehensive, integrated education building on a strong foundation of core skills to develop a global cultural literacy in science, history, technology and the arts in an atmosphere of kindness, flexibility, respect and individualism."

SPOTLIGHT 5.3

Problem-Solving in Hong Kong

The Harbour School, Hong Kong

Craig and Jadis Blurton, (@harbourschoolHK)
Founders/Head of School and Managing Director, respectively

The Harbour School high school students are currently working to design and build a school for the only public children's hospital in Kenya. This involves everything from fundraising and budgeting to designing the physical site, imagining an appropriate flexible curriculum, and ultimately hiring staff. It's not a little project. The challenge is further complicated not only by medical issues of the prospective students but also by the fact that some will be short-term while others might be in the school for years. In order for the THS students to reach their goal, they have to first meet with experts in fundraising, architecture, and education; produce a detailed plan; and then jump from design to actual production. But there are real children depending on them, with a real problem that is impossible to ignore. THS students are not working for a grade—they are working for something far more important.

In the spring of 2017, middle school students at THS designed and built a furniture unit for subsidized housing in Hong Kong that solved many of the problems faced by residents. Halfway through construction, they found out that they had been given the wrong size for the units. It would have been easy to give up at that point, or to continue with the wrong size for a grade, but the students were solving a real problem for real people, some of whom they had met and interviewed for the project. So, in a real "back to the drawing board" moment, they redesigned and rebuilt the unit, doubling down and staying after school when necessary. The result was a complete construction, which the students exhibited with passion and pride. They had powered through adversity for a purpose, one that was real and relevant to them.

The Harbour School attempts to teach children to notice problems large and small, and to feel empowered to solve them. They have submitted policy papers on children's rights to the Hong Kong government and created a prosthetic leg for a three-legged dog in the neighborhood. When the government decided to build an incinerator on a small island close to the city, one student in the fifth grade worried that the new incinerator would affect the quality of the water around it. He and his friends approached the crew of the Black Dolphin (the school's 50-foot sailboat) to take measurements of the water before construction, and they have made voyages every six months to track changes. Another group of younger primary school students designed and built a remotely operated vehicle to measure plastic in the ocean. After the oil spill near Bangladesh, one eight-year-old student found a picture of a child her age attempting to clean water that seemed to be "all brown." She gathered a team of kids to explore ways to help, and they created a do-it-yourself fluorospectrometer to send to schools in Bangladesh. And other students at the primary school have written and coproduced rock videos to address issues such as cage homes, refugees, ocean plastic, and Earth Hour.

Of course, each of these projects has promoted learning of necessary subject matter, and of course the students have collaborated, created, discussed, and thought deeply about the issues. But even more importantly, the students at THS are learning a way of responding to life that is proactive and powerful. They are not the passive recipients of education, practicing for a future in which they may be involved. They are learning that everyone is involved now.

Figure 5.1. On board the Black Dolphin, the school's "outdoor classroom," fifth grade students measure water characteristics near the site of a proposed new incinerator. Photo Credit: Craig Blurton.

Figure 5.2. Working together in the school's makerspace, middle school students rethink and reinvent the interior design for Hong Kong's subsidized housing units, attempting to address the problems that they have learned about by interviewing the inhabitants.

Figure 5.3. Students build a full-size functional prototype housing unit to test the features they designed and incorporated into the improved living quarters.

■ ■ ■ ■ ■

Kathy Wright, principal of Hughes High School (HHS) in the Cincinnati Public School District, shared that PBL is a framework for their curriculum that is focused on changing the outcomes for their students. While teachers have always been strong leaders at HHS, using the PBL approach created the shift in classroom dynamics where teachers took on more of the role of facilitator and allowed students to take a lead role in their education. "This approach has developed agency with our students, allowing them to lead and become advocates for their own learning" (Wright, personal communication, 2017). Wright said she notices, as students develop agency, they are more confident to visit her office and request a meeting when they have concerns or an idea they would like to implement for activities like community service or homecoming dances.

Last year, a group of eight students in grade 11 requested a meeting to create a project to plan extracurricular activities for their senior year. They came prepared with a plan for fundraising and activities and the principal provided the space and time for a two-hour meeting where they planned the entire year including activities, role assignments, timelines, contacts, and costs. From their exposure to so many projects in the classroom, they understood how to create a project plan, how to consider all stakeholders, and who to involve for support outside their core group. With this information carefully documented, they were able to apply the PBL framework to a project they created, one that was meaningful to them, and they understood the final step of getting approval from the key stakeholder, which was the principal, Ms. Wright. They began with a bake sale as the fall fundraiser and followed their plan, moving forward through each step to reach their goal. "This is where we are winning. This does not get measured on a test, but I have confidence that those kids, the ones that embrace that learning and take those skills with them, will be a success. It is a wonderful win for our kids; and who wouldn't want that for their kids?" (Wright, personal communication, 2017).

Sometimes a school is created with a particular philosophy in the forefront; that philosophy serves as a lens through which all decisions are made. Spring Street International School serves a local community of learners that uses the unique opportunities its location provides as a backdrop for the PBL approach. The following two Spotlights demonstrate how two teachers experience the power of project-based learning, and what it means for the students they serve.

SPOTLIGHT 5.4

Place-Based Learning

Spring Street International School, Friday Harbor, Washington

Timothy Dwyer (@TeacherTimDwyer), Science and Mathematics Teacher

Spring Street International School (SSIS) is an independent day and boarding school in the San Juan Islands of northwest Washington state. The school's progressive philosophy is grounded in its faculty developing a personal understanding of each student's particular strengths and tailoring teaching methods to reach different students. Teachers here pride themselves on teaching students and not classes. With approximately 110 students in grades 5–12 located in a rural town, the school's small class sizes (10–26 students) and close connection with its community promote explorations in project-based learning.

Recognizing that the careers that students are ultimately preparing to lead may not be invented yet, the school actively searches for methods and opportunities to promote creativity, problem-solving, reasoning, and resilience across disciplines. The class schedule incorporates a two-hour double-period every week to accommodate field trips, laboratory work, and other collaborative projects, because group work makes it safer for students to take risks, fail, revise, and ultimately succeed. The school understands that project work—when it is purpose-driven and open-ended—encourages goal development, perseverance, and self-reflection.

The school capitalizes on its location on an island in the Salish Sea by providing teachers with the freedom and opportunity to ground their teachings in a strong sense of place. For middle school humanities students, this takes the form of a three-act performance inspired by journals from 19th-century explorers, written and performed by students. High school sculpture students build cedar strip canoes under the guidance of Native American artisans. For seventh grade students of science, bathymetric maps drawn from canoe-based depth soundings in a local pond inform an understanding of island glacial history. Ninth grade students of mathematics work with archaeologists from the island's National Historical Park to set up site surveys looking for evidence of an old school house. Eleventh grade students of environmental systems develop their understanding of "systems thinking" while trouble-shooting the hydroponic gardens they recently designed and constructed.

Spring Street International School's program reflects its deeply held understanding that learning happens best when it connects to real life. Beyond the classroom, every May the academic year pauses for three weeks to allow students to explore internships with local businesses, agencies, and organizations, as well as to accommodate group travel domestically and internationally. The broad suite of experiences each student graduates with reinforces the philosophy that learning is a lifelong endeavor, one capable of providing great joy and promoting endless opportunity.

■ ■ ■ ■ ■

SPOTLIGHT 5.5

Teaching Science with Real-World Experiences

Spring Street International School, Friday Harbor, Washington

Sharon Massey, Science Teacher

Sharon Massey, eighth grade science teacher at SSIS, shares her experience working with students to embrace the natural beauty that surrounds them while engaging in real-world work. One example was when her eighth grade science class studied oceanography, which included bathymetry, the study of underwater topography. One of the questions with which they began the unit was: How do scientists map the ocean floor? Her students embarked on an authentic project where they learned about measuring grids and high- and low-resolution maps by making models of the seafloor in cardboard boxes.

The project became more meaningful when the class decided to take the skills they learned in the classroom out to a local pond. Using a boat and a weighted line, students begin measuring depth at key points in the pond, directed by team members on the shore. The students recorded the depths and used the data to create a bathymetry map of the pond—uncharted waters as the class was thrilled to discover. The results are shown in Figure 5.4.

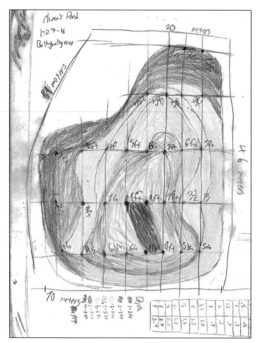

Figure 5.4. Student-created bathymetry map of depths of the pond. Photo Credit: Sharon Massey.

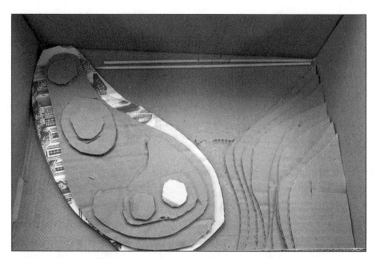

Figure 5.5. Students' rendering of the pond depths in relief. Photo Credit: Sharon Massey.

Ms. Massey shared, "My philosophy is, 'Nature is our best teacher.' When students know a place, they love that place and when they love that place they will take care of that place. The patterns of stewardship we instill now, students will take with them wherever they go. My students know the island intimately by sight, sound, smell, and feel" (personal communication, 2017).

■ ■ ■ ■ ■

Riley Johnson, Principal of New Technology High School (NTHS) in Napa, California, which began as a PBL school in 1996, shared that while technology supports their work, it is more important to find a way to "marry the pedagogy with the right tool." Riley explained, "There is not a recipe or a formula to ensure success, but there are some tools and structures that will help formulate a path to increase student outcomes. We take the approach that PBL as a mindset and a lifestyle, rather than a way to deliver instruction" (personal communication, 2017). Freshmen entering NTHS take required courses such as Adobe Suite and Introduction to Computer Science to develop a foundation with fundamental technology for the work they will be doing through the end of their senior year.

While technology is available for students and is frequently used to communicate and chronicle the phases of their projects, teachers at the Minnesota New Country School (MNCS) in Henderson, Minnesota, have made an effort to not let it overshadow the authentic project work students are conducting or to deflect from the importance of their hands-on learning experience. MNCS is located in the Minnesota River Valley and, based on its more rural setting, finds many projects have an outdoor or nature-centric emphasis.

SPOTLIGHT 5.6

Student Ownership of Learning

Minnesota New Country School, Henderson, Minnesota

School Advisors: Kelsie Halvorsen, Kiersten Dahl-Shetka, Sirena Woyt, Dean Lind, and Paul Jaeger

The Minnesota New Country School is a K–12 learning community, with the mission to guide students toward self-actualization. To achieve this, we operate as a teacher powered school that practices project-based learning to nurture whole and healthy lifelong learners. Through project work, students are presented with opportunities to learn about what they want to learn and challenged to make the things they believe need to exist in the world. Students at MNCS are empowered to direct their learning endeavors, and our goals are for them, by the time they graduate, to know how to learn anything they want and be able to execute projects that matter to them. It takes some doing for students to arrive at that place, and we guide the process by gradually transferring agency to them as they move through their career at MNCS.

Starting in the primary elementary, advisors (our term for teachers) introduce the project-based process through teacher-led projects. At the intermediate elementary level, projects begin to be more student-directed, with guidance from their advisors. When students transition to our secondary school (grades 7 through 12), more time is allotted to develop their project work. At this stage, the job of the advisor is to understand the students in their advisory. Some students will need help framing an idea they have, creating a plan of action for a project, or getting unstuck on a difficult phase of a project. Some students will require little help at all. The advisor reads their students, listens to them with care, and figures out if and how they might need assistance. It is common for our middle-level students, as well as students arriving to MNCS from another setting, to need extra attention with designing and completing their project work. As students progress to the upper levels of our secondary school, the goal is to move them to a place where they fully direct their learning.

For anyone trying to find their footing with project-based learning, we like to ask them about something that is or is not happening in their community that could be improved. Two years ago, a student leaned into this prompt and ended up pouring more than 500 hours into creating a project that benefitted the community. One of our students had fallen in love with mountain biking the summer leading into his senior year. However, there were a couple issues with that passion: 1) There are no mountains in Minnesota, and 2) there were no rugged bike trails in or around our community.

The Ney Nature Center is situated on a bluff overlooking the Minnesota River Valley. This student started spending time there. He studied maps of the Ney Nature Center and noticed a portion of it was mostly unused. He examined the typography of one particular area and got a feel for the lay of the land. A picture in his mind began to form of a trail that would allow him to share his passion for mountain biking with our community. He committed to making the trail exist for his capstone senior project and created a team to engage in the work.

To set this project in motion, he knew he would need to get approval to construct the trail from the board of the Ney Nature Center. For that to happen, he and his team needed to cast a persuasive vision of their idea and demonstrate they understood how to engineer a functional biking trail. Essentially, they needed help. They worked with their advisor to reach out to people who had built trails before and found trail builders willing to share their expertise. They learned about design and grade and how to construct a trail that endures. After several revisions, the board accepted their pitch to engineer a biking trail in Henderson.

With that hurdle cleared, it was time to put a shoulder behind their idea. The trail they envisioned was to be a one-mile loop. To make that loop a reality, they needed to rally people behind their cause to build the trail. With massive help from students, community groups, and local experts, they made a trail that exceeded the original vision by half a mile. Two years later, people continue to use the trail. It is an asset to our community and an example of what student-directed, project-based learning can look like.

For 24 years, staff at Minnesota New Country School have been making a bet that students will own their learning if given the chance. And when they take that chance, we believe something honest and beautiful will come out of it. It is a risky bet to make at times, and we are dependent on students to make our learning community interesting. Sometimes we lose the bet, but we intend to make it for as long as we are able. We have cast our lot with our students and use project-based learning as a vehicle for granting students more agency in their learning adventures. Any success we have had has been born from taking them, their ideas, and their crazy dreams, seriously.

▪ ▪ ▪ ▪ ▪

Lake Washington Girls Middle School takes pride in providing a place where students are empowered to become independent leaders, critical thinkers, and learn more about themselves as citizens. Through a more personalized learning experience, students gain from smaller class sizes and a close-knit community. Ms. O'Boyle explained their philosophy.

SPOTLIGHT 5.7

Teaching STEAM with Design Thinking

Lake Washington Middle School, Kirkland, Washington

Becky O'Boyle, (@LWGMS) Director of Institutional Advancement

This small girls' school, located near Seattle, prepares 108 young women to become leaders, take their next steps to high school, and pursue their passions. The school provides financial support to approximately 30% of its students.

STEAM (science, technology, engineering, arts, and mathematics) undergirds a great deal of the school's curriculum. The lead mathematics teacher collaborates with other teachers, and art is threaded through everything. The focus is on the design thinking process. Ms. O'Boyle explained, "3-D printing is a bit passé. Now the students want hands-on, which includes hydraulics, power tools, and more."

Lake Washington is not a 1:1 school, but sets of Chromebooks are available. The technology is not a focus; rather, it is just a tool to support project-based learning. The students learn it to accomplish their goals. For example, eighth grade students design and create a social justice documentary film festival, in groups of three. This six-week project is part of their humanities content and includes action research as part of the goal.

The seventh grade class creates a science fair, in which the school brings in experts to help review their results. These students have developed exciting projects such as testing runoff water in Lake Washington or looking for ways to harness energy. The school considers the whole learner; students can earn a green belt in karate; can learn about robotics and coding; and take art, music, poetry, and drama.

According to Ms. O'Boyle, "I think we rely too much on assessment, and the way they're assessed thwarts creativity and curiosity. We have to rethink how we assess and teachers teach to the test. They spend so much time on that."

■ ■ ■ ■ ■

Learning Management Systems

An LMS can be an instrumental tool to best use technology to manage a project. An LMS is an online software tool that allows educators to administer and deliver content and track progress through assessment tools and discussion boards. It allows students to keep track of and share collaborative documents, complete and turn in assignments, and use discussion boards and chat pods to collaborate with peers. Most schools interviewed shared the importance of using an LMS to help maintain a common area for students and teachers to house information, assignments, discussion boards for teams, and all pertinent resources for a project. An LMS helps instructors, students, and administrators collect and track all key information used when engaged in a project. "Our deep study of LMSs was critical in learning how to effectively leverage the tool to understand how to better serve individual students as well as how to use and adjust groups, and help teacher collaborates (Wright, 2017). Of course, there is a steep learning curve initially, but ultimately the LMS is an important tool to manage and monitor all the components of a project. Although it can be overwhelming initially, the students were not daunted: "They were not intimidated, they were waiting for us to catch up" (Wright, personal communication, 2017).

Summary

Educators have always been mindful of ways to better serve students to prepare them for life beyond the classroom. However, using the paradigm developed with a 20th century mindset will not ensure that students will be prepared for the opportunities and work environments that will be presented in the digital age. The wave of new technology and digital tools allows educators to continually contemplate ways to better serve students and empower them with skills to better communicate, collaborate, and engage in authentic learning experiences.

When students approach learning tasks that they find to be personally meaningful, and they are provided the guidance to build leadership skills along the way, they benefit from the out-of-the-box thinking that a PBL and PL approach to education brings forth. Although many of the tools and trends they experience in today's classroom will be obsolete by the time they enter the workforce, students will be equipped with the skills to solve intricate problems and change the world in ways we can only imagine. Educators who incorporate PBL and PL into their curriculum will employ the following ISTE standards for students and for themselves as educators.

ISTE STUDENT STANDARDS ADDRESSED IN THIS CHAPTER

Standard 3: **Knowledge Constructor**	Knowledge Constructor: Students critically curate a variety of resources using digital tools to construct knowledge, produce creative artifacts and make meaningful learning experiences for themselves and others.
Standard 4: **Innovative Designer**	Innovative Designer: Students use a variety of technologies within a design process to identify and solve problems by creating new, useful or imaginative solutions.
Standard 7: **Global Collaborator**	Students use digital tools to broaden their perspectives and enrich their learning by collaborating with others and working effectively in teams locally and globally.

ISTE EDUCATOR STANDARDS ADDRESSED IN THIS CHAPTER

Standard 3: **Citizen**	Educators inspire students to positively contribute to and responsibly participate in the digital world.
Standard 4: **Collaborator**	Educators dedicate time to collaborate with both colleagues and students to improve practice, discover and share resources and ideas, and solve problems.
Standard 6: **Facilitator**	Facilitator: Educators facilitate learning with technology to support student achievement of the ISTE Standards for Students.

Questions and Reflections

- How does the PBL framework complement your current curriculum?

- Who are the stakeholders that should be consulted about including a PBL approach to classroom/schoolwide instruction?

- Which community partnerships might you need to enlist to have a successful project? (These partnerships will vary based on the community needs and the project topic.)

- What steps will you need to implement within your classroom management and routines to support independence and student-driven inquiries?

- What digital tools could you use to organize the management of a personalized learning approach to teaching?

- How prepared are staff to make the change to an individualized, student-centered approach to education? What trainings would be most helpful to make the shift?

- How will you prepare and empower students to develop a leadership role in all aspects of their education?

Further Resources to Get Started

Open Educational Resources (Free)

The Buck Institute for Education
(www.bie.org) Dedicated to creating, gathering, and sharing high-quality PBL instructional practices with teachers, schools, and districts.

Edutopia
(www.edutopia.org/project-based-learning-getting-started-resources) This article references a variety of resources within Edutopia.

High Tech High
(www.hightechhigh.org/student-work/student-projects/#) Descriptions of past projects at the high school level.

PBLU
(pblu.org) A variety of customizable, gold-standard projects that are aligned to content standards to use with your classroom.

Powerful Learning Practices
(plpnetwork.com/pbl-resources) Free PBL resources to inspire, launch, and troubleshoot projects.

The Teaching Channel
(www.teachingchannel.org/videos?q=ProjectBasedLearning) Videos on PBL in practice.

West Virginia University

(wvde.state.wv.us/teach21/pbl.html) Rich bank of project ideas, tools, and frameworks that align with standards, grades 2–12 and AP, all academic subject areas including dance, visual arts, music, and theater.

Intel® Teach Elements

(www.intel.com/content/www/us/en/education/k12/teach-elements.html) Free, on your own time professional development courses providing deeper exploration of digital age learning concepts, including PBL.

ISTE

(www.iste.org/explore/ArticleDetail?articleid=11) Personalized learning resources and blog.

KnowledgeWorks

(www.knowledgeworks.org/resource-room) Personalized learning resources.

Edutopia: 6 Steps to Help Personalize with PBL

(www.edutopia.org/blog/6-strategies-truly-personalize-pbl-andrew-miller) A useful blog post with strategies for trying PBL.

Education Elements: The Core Four of Personalized Learning

(www.edelements.com/hubfs/Core_Four/Education_Elements_Core_Four_White_Paper.pdf) A guide to incorporating PL for educators and districts.

Other Resources (For Purchase)

The Buck Institute for Education

(shop.bie.org/store-c2.aspx) The Buck Institute has done cutting edge research on Project Based Learning and offers professional development and consulting services.

KnowledgeWorks

(www.knowledgeworks.org) Knowledge works runs multiple schools (High Tech High Schools) and offers support for professional development and resources for PBL.

Books That May Be of Interest

Boss, S., & Krauss, J. (2014). *Reinventing project-based learning: Your field guide to real-world projects in the digital age* (2nd ed.). Eugene, OR: International Society for Technology in Education.

CHAPTER 6

Efforts toward Bridging the Digital Divide

To push for excellence today without continuing to push for access for less privileged students is to undermine the crucial but incomplete gains that have been made.

—Ernest Boyer

We believe connectivity is a human right. Connectivity cannot be restricted to just the rich and powerful.

—Mark Zuckerberg

In This Chapter:

- What is known about the past and current issues in digital equity?

- What examples exist on the ways digital equity is being addressed in schools?

- In what ways is digital equity being addressed in the larger community and nation?

Background and Current Status

Educators and researchers have recognized since the 1990s that new technologies present an opportunity to either lessen or eliminate existing educational inequalities (Warschauer, Knobel, & Stone, 2004). As the prevalence of digital materials and the necessity for digital fluency continue to increase, the need to address digital equity in education is magnified. "The Consortium for School Networking's 2016 IT Leadership Survey found that at least 50 percent of learning resources and content are expected to be digital within the next three years" (Krueger & James, 2017, p. 15). Inequity in digital fluency significantly affects students' educational opportunities throughout their school careers and particularly as they prepare for higher education and careers. This in turn can serve to exacerbate existing socioeconomic disparities (Martin, 2016). One definition raises the issues quite well:

> Digital Equity is a condition in which all individuals and communities have the information technology capacity needed for full participation in our society, democracy and economy. Digital Equity is necessary for civic and cultural participation, employment, lifelong learning, and access to essential services. (National Digital Inclusion Alliance, n.d., n.p.)

This same organization has crafted a definition that explores what Digital Inclusion would include and look like. Specifically,

> Digital Inclusion refers to the activities necessary to ensure that all individuals and communities, including the most disadvantaged, have access to and use of Information and Communication Technologies (ICTs). This includes 5 elements: 1) affordable, robust broadband internet service; 2) internet-enabled devices that meet the needs of the user; 3) access to digital literacy training; 4) quality technical support; and 5) applications and online content designed to enable and encourage self-sufficiency, participation and collaboration. Digital Inclusion must evolve as technology advances and requires intentional strategies and investments to reduce and eliminate historical, institutional and structural barriers to access and use technology. (National Digital Inclusion Alliance, n.d.)

Several recent documents underscore current data that paint the picture of broadband access and its implications:

- The Pew Research Center found that 5 million households with school-age children do not have broadband access. Low-income families make up a heavy share of those households.

- According to the Bill & Melinda Gates Foundation, 42% of teachers reported that their students lack sufficient access to technology outside of the classroom.

- Results from CoSN's 2016 Annual Infrastructure Survey show that 75% of district technology leaders ranked addressing the lack of broadband access outside of school as a "very important" or "important" issue for their district to address.

- In the same survey, 68% of respondents reported that affordability is the greatest barrier to out-of-school broadband access. (Alliance for Excellent Education, 2016)

The CNA Education organization conducted research in 2017 about the "leaks" in the STEM pipeline in Virginia, and it created an infographic (Figure 6.1) to describe their results. It shows a gender disparity and may be considered representative of other states.

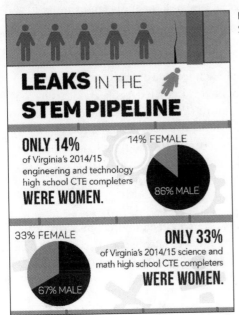

Figure 6.1. Leaks in the STEM pipeline.
Source: CAN Education (tinyurl.com/yc96b53l).

Digital equity research initially focused on equitable physical access to computers and the internet. Although inequalities in physical access still exist, they are declining. For example, in 1998 the ratio of students to instructional computers with internet access in U.S. schools with more than 50% minorities was 17:2, while in low minority schools it was 10:1. By 2001, those ratios had shifted to 6:1 and 4:7 (Kleiner & Farris, 2002, cited in Warschauer et al., 2004, p. 564). However, even though gaps in physical access are decreasing, researchers are finding increasing disparities in how technology is used and applied (Martin, 2016; Warschauer et al., 2004).

Reviewing the research in 2004, Warschauer et al. concluded that, "What emerges from this research is not a single construct of a digital divide but rather a number of factors that shape technology's amplification of existing inequalities in school and society" (p. 565). Accordingly, research has shifted to a wide range of issues focusing on what students actually do with technology and including access outside the school environment.

Based on their study of eight southern California high schools, Warschauer et al. concluded, "The introduction of information and communication technologies ... serves to amplify existing forms of inequality" (2004, p. 584). In low socioeconomic status (SES) schools, remedial activities and drills are more common, while in high-SES schools there is greater emphasis on research, analysis, and simulations (Greenhow, Walker & Kim, 2009; Warschauer et al., 2004). Factors influencing how students use technology in low-SES schools include higher numbers of English language learners and students below grade level and increasing pressure to prepare for state and national tests. In addition, low-SES schools have lower percentages of credentialed teachers, and these teachers may be less knowledgeable about technology and how to integrate it into the curriculum (Warschauer et al., 2004). After studying internet use among teens, Greenhow et al. also suggested that preservice and in-service teachers may be reluctant "to structure technology-enhanced learning projects with students they perceive as more technologically savvy than they are or with students they perceive as lacking out-of-school internet access or technology skills" (2009, p. 63).

As the demands and expectations for learning and using technology outside of school rise, researchers stress the criticality of students' out-of-school access. To take advantage of educational opportunities, access to high-speed network connectivity, mobile devices such as smart phones, and computers is required. However, research has demonstrated unequal access to both devices and high-speed network connectivity for low-SES families, a disproportionate percentage of whom are Hispanic or Black. Smart phones are increasingly needed for learning contexts as well as social interactions, but, in 2016, 27% of teens in the U.S. had access to only a basic cell phone or to none at all (Martin, 2016, p. 34). Martin notes that lack of smart phones is important to consider "because teens gain digital fluency through use of social media and digital technology." Mobile-only access, however, is considered underconnected and insufficient. One quarter of families earning below the median income level access the internet only through mobile devices and many quickly reach data limits or at times are unable to pay for phone service. Additionally, in low-SES families, mobile devices are often shared among numerous family members and each person's time is limited. Martin's research found that "Youth with computer access at home created more complex projects. This was partly because they had more time to develop, modify, and problem-solve their projects" (2016, p. 35).

Although federal programs such as FCC LifeLine, Connect Home (HUD), EveryoneOn, and US Ignite are addressing home connectivity, many students, primarily low-SES youth, continue to have limited home internet and computer access (Krueger & James, 2017). Greenhow et al. (2009) advise teachers to consider students' out-of-school digital contexts and recognize that low-SES students are less likely to have home access and are thus more reliant on public facilities, namely schools and public libraries. They observed, "Instructors can expect a large majority of their students—including those from low-income families—to have broad experience with internet-based technology. However, students' sophistication in their understanding of technology or internet-use strategies varies" (2009, p. 66). Teachers can support students' access in numerous ways, including designing learning activities to address inequities "in level of sophistication and duration of technology and internet use between low-income and high-income students" and offering time extensions for assignments requiring heavy internet use.

International researchers echo similar findings. In 2010, Gudmundsdottir (2010) analyzed access and information and communication technology (ICT) competence among seventh grade students in four Cape Town, South Africa, schools. This research demonstrated notable inequities correlated to socioeconomic status and home language. Students from low-SES families and whose home language is not English had significantly less access and ICT competence. Yuen, Lau, Park, Lau, & Chan (2016) found that, among eighth grade students in Hong Kong, students from high-SES families not only had more home access, but also received more parental guidance and mediation in their use of technology.

Lack of devices and high-speed network connectivity also significantly affects students in U.S. rural areas. In 2017, New America Weekly reported that:

> Despite the Telecommunications Act of 1996 mandating equal access for those in rural areas, only 62 percent of rural Americans have broadband installed in their homes, and those who do often pay exorbitant prices for sluggish speeds. In fact, 39 percent of rural Americans are unable to purchase internet service that meets the Federal Communications Commission's minimum standards for high-speed access—25Mbs/3Mbs—at all." Further, 40 percent of small libraries in rural areas cannot meet the FCC standards for libraries. (Lahanas, 2017)

Rural districts are seeking innovative ways to address this gap. For example, in 2014, rurally distressed Montgomery County Schools in North Carolina used a $3.5 million Department of Education Investing in Innovation (i3) grant "to update the school's wireless infrastructure, begin to provide 1:1 devices, and outfit school buses with wireless access" (Smith, 2016). Many of the district's students "spend three or four hours on the bus every day—time they're now able to devote to learning" (Smith, 2016, n.p.). School administrators stress that the success of this endeavor is based on including and maintaining communications with students, parents, staff, and the entire community.

The growing role of technology in education and the shift from static print to flexible digital materials also have the potential to expand educational opportunities for struggling readers and students with print disabilities, who can be found in every classroom. However, there is a danger these materials will create new barriers to student access and use of assistive devices and thus participation and achievement if this population is not considered in the development of digital materials (Bowser & Smiley Zabala, 2012). They suggest that to take advantage of new alternatives and ensure instructional materials are available to all students, teachers integrate digital tasks and accessible formats in all learning activities. "To increase equity for struggling readers and students with print-related disabilities, it's important that educators know the options for acquiring" accessible instructional materials (AIMs) (p. 16). They recommend educators become familiar with available AIM resources, which include purchased material; free materials, such as those available through the

National AIM Resource Center; and teacher-created materials, for example scanning or enlarging print materials or recording lectures. They also advocate professional development about the use of AIMs for all classroom teachers and greater attention to students who can benefit from them in all phases of resource acquisition.

Forming "smart partnerships" with local, state, national and international businesses, governmental agencies, universities, and nonprofit organizations (NGOs) is an emerging strategy to address the digital divide. Krueger and James discuss several examples of such partnerships, including one with local government in Massachusetts, another with a university and an NGO in North Carolina, and one in Kansas City with a community-based nonprofit (2017, p. 15). As mentioned earlier, Smith describes a successful endeavor in a distressed rural district that took advantage of an i3 grant to increase access and connectivity (2016). Partnerships are developing internationally as well. Charania and Davis (2016) discuss a multi-stakeholder partnership in India that was formed by schools, parents, and both domestic and international NGOs to decrease digital inequity by providing learning centers clustered in district-level villages for underserved adolescents. Research on smart partnerships, however, is limited, and Leahy et al. (2016) concluded that more research is needed on this topic.

Just as digital equity is a complex, multifaceted issue, there is no single approach to addressing digital inequity. The necessity for educators to keep in mind students' out-of-school context when seeking ways to bridge the digital gap is stressed in the literature. Successful endeavors need to include not just educators but also students, parents, and the entire community. To get started, Krueger and James recommend that educators survey and assess the current situation and what is available where; engage the entire community, including community and business leaders; consider out-of-the-box solutions for connectivity, and "ensure sustainability through community assets" (2017, p. 16).

Richard Culatta, CEO of the International Society for Technology in Education (ISTE), has a passion for digital equity and explains that in Spotlight 6.1.

SPOTLIGHT 6.1

Digital Equity

International Society for Technology in Education (@ISTE)

—— Richard Culatta (@rec54), CEO

In the book *Abundance: The Future is Better Than You Think,* authors Peter Diamandis and Steven Kotler make the case that opportunity gaps are often not a matter of scarcity of resources but a matter of access to them.

They predict that exponentially evolving technologies will enable us to make greater gains in closing access gaps over the next two decades than we've made in the previous 200 years.

As I read the book, I couldn't help thinking that nowhere is closing opportunity gaps more needed than in education. As internet connectivity becomes increasingly available in our schools and homes, we have a great responsibility to make sure we are using this tool to increase access to learning opportunities. In my role as CEO of the International Society for Technology in Education (ISTE), I see four specific opportunities where technology can help increase access to learning opportunities.

Access to learning resources

It's no surprise that schools with more money are able to buy updated equipment and newer books, while struggling schools cope with outdated textbooks and learning materials. A number of years ago, I worked at a school in Guatemala that couldn't afford to buy any textbooks—even outdated ones. It seemed a losing battle to try to provide the students in that school with the resources they needed to be globally competitive. Then we tried a crazy idea (remember, this was 15 years ago)—we created a satellite internet connection to the school. For the first time, students who for generations had been left behind had access to the same information as their wealthier peers around the world. By tapping into the wealth of knowledge available on the internet, technology can democratize access to high-quality learning materials.

Of course, access to learning resources goes beyond textbooks. Take for example the STEM School in Chattanooga, Tennessee. Students there have access to a scanning electron microscope, and not because the school can afford the whopping $1 million price tag. Schools in Chattanooga are connected to a gigabit internet network. Since the microscope can be controlled remotely, a team at the University of Southern California, connected to the same network, put a high-definition camera on its microscope, allowing students to experience science equipment that their school could never afford. Technology provided access to learning resources that would otherwise be beyond reach.

Access to expertise

The geographic location of learners also affects equitable access to learning opportunities. It can be difficult to find advanced math teachers or computer science teachers in rural or inner-city schools. That was the case in Omak, Washington, where an open position for a math teacher languished for five years.

But technology can bridge the expertise gap. Free videoconferencing tools give students access to a world of experts who can beam into their classroom, opening doors to learn from leaders in any field. Online learning programs allow students to be part of a global classroom participating in courses that their geographic location couldn't otherwise support.

Access to expertise is just as important for teachers as it is for students. I still remember that the thing that most surprised me when I first started teaching high school was how lonely it felt. I knew that there were more experienced teachers around the world, doing a much better job of teaching Spanish than I was, but I had no way to access them. I often think about how different my experience would have been if online teacher networks, like ISTE's Professional Learning Network (PLN), had existed back then. The PLN—think of it as professional learning on demand—allows teachers, regardless of geographic location, to tap into peers and mentors around the world.

Access to personalized learning

It's not uncommon for students to experience skills gaps—foundational learning concepts they haven't mastered. Absences, frequent school transfers, or a difficult topic that wasn't taught well can leave students forever behind because a critical building block is missing. I recently visited Pleasant View Elementary in Providence, Rhode Island, which until five years ago had been one of the lowest-performing schools in the state. On paper, the students of this school have everything stacked against them—low socioeconomic status, high special education population, limited family support—yet for five years now they have been outperforming students in other schools in the region. At the root of their transformation was a personalized learning approach, using technology to monitor student progress.

Technology enables personalized learning that can bridge this gap by helping teachers quickly visualize where students need extra support and recommend learning activities based on their individual progress. When learning can be tailored to the needs of each student, those who need help mastering a particular concept are no longer left behind just because other students aren't struggling with the same gap at the same time.

Access to planning for higher education

Navigating postsecondary education is incredibly complex. Deciphering the actual cost of college is difficult as scholarships, tuition rates, and financial aid options vary widely based on individual student circumstances. There is a slew of deadlines that students must be aware of. In addition to college applications themselves, there are required tests, FAFSA and other financial aid applications, and so on. Simple data-driven web-based tools and mobile apps can support students in making more informed decisions about their postsecondary experiences. When I worked for the U.S. Department of Education, we made annual tuition costs and average graduate salary available for each college in the US available online through a simple college scorecard—something that had never existed before.

Planning for a successful higher education experience doesn't end with college acceptance. Many barriers, including family responsibilities, work requirements, transportation, healthcare issues, and more lead to students leaving before they have completed their degree. Using technology, innovative universities are beginning to identify these potential barriers and provide support services before a student is forced to stop their work. Georgia State University has been on the forefront of using technology to identify and support student needs—one of the only institutions in the world with no gaps in graduation rates by demographic or socioeconomic status.

We have a lot of work to do to eliminate long-standing opportunity gaps in education. Every day, students around the world struggle to overcome geographic and socioeconomic barriers, racial and cultural injustices, and physical and cognitive disabilities. Technology provides us with a powerful new set of tools to increase access to learning opportunities to help close those gaps. When these tools are wielded by educators who understand their potential, are supported in mastering them, and are deeply committed to providing access to all learners, we can begin to overcome a false sense of scarcity and fling open the doors of opportunity.

■ ■ ■ ■ ■

School Districts Respond

In a report from the Center for Digital Education (2016), a true inequity exists in access to digital information. Given that seven in ten teachers report assigning homework that requires access to broadband (Aspen Institute, 2016, cited in Center for Digital Education, 2016), it is important to find ways to diminish the inequality. According to a U.S. Census Bureau report, 29 million homes do not have access to the internet at home, and five million of those are in low-income households (U.S. Census Bureau, 2013, cited in Center for Digital Education, 2016). This report does provide information about ways that schools are working to resolve this situation; a few of these are described below, However, it is worth noting that, according to a COSN study, "Most districts have not yet begun to address issues of home and off campus access. 82% of districts reported that they are not providing any type of off campus services for their students at this time" (COSN, 2014, p. 22). And the most recent COSN study (COSN, 2017) found that "budget constraints are ranked as the top challenge for the third straight year" (p. 4).

Florence County School District Three

Florence County School District Three (Lake City, South Carolina) has received a five-year, $9.1 million Magnet Schools Assistance Programs grant from the U.S. Department of Education's Office of Innovation and Improvement. The grant will be used for the district's Project C3 Explores: Colleges, Cultures, & Careers initiative. The district is one of the poorest in South Carolina, and the grant offers students new opportunities to develop career paths while also learning new skills and knowledge.

"The magnet school concept will give our parents and students choice, while enabling all students to be involved in rigorous, engaging programs," said Renee Kirby, Florence County School District Three Director of K–8 Literacy, Math and Academic Assistance, who will serve as the project director for the grant. "Also included in the grant is the opportunity for teachers to participate in professional development to gain the tools to provide personalized, innovative, theme-based instruction. We are over-the-moon excited for this opportunity that will push us closer to our goal of ensuring all of our students are ready for college and career." Principal Allana Prosser says, "Introducing STEM learning at an early age plays a key role in cognitive development. At the elementary level, students are still learning visually and with their hands. They learn through drawing and manipulating objects, therefore robotics makes it possible for them to work through problems visually and experiment with the various concepts they are learning. Not to mention, STEM learning is listed as the world-class knowledge needed in the *Profile of the South Carolina Graduate*. We not only want our students to be able to solve problems through inquiry and problem-based learning, but we also want them to be able to have an idea of the careers that are out there so that they can build their pathway for college and career at an early age." District Three Superintendent Laura Hickson adds, "This grant will ensure our students are exposed to many educational experiences and career pathways. Our vision is to become a premier district of choice. This grant is yet another piece toward accomplishing this goal" (Hickson, personal communication, 2017).

Cincinnati Public Schools

Cincinnati Public Schools is providing all students in 17 high schools access to Advanced Placement (AP) courses through the AP Blended Learning (APBL) program. This program uses technology to give students an opportunity to complete AP courses. All APBL students receive a laptop and Kajeet hot spot that goes home with them to complete class assignments. Teachers of this program incorporate a variety of technology applications to engage students in their learning and are often traveling between schools to see their students twice a week, which is why technology is pivotal to this program. Students engage in discussion boards, collaborative work, and one-on-one communication through online programs such as Schoology and G-Suite. Without technology, this program could not provide equity and access to all students to AP courses.

Wi-Fi Buses and Hotspots

Other school districts have chosen ways to make their Wi-Fi available to families and learners. Some wire their buses so that students may do their homework on their ride to and from home; other districts turn their Wi-Fi on broadly for the community when school is not in session (Godfrey-Lee, Wyoming, Michigan; Coachella Valley Unified School District, California). The buses are also parked overnight in neighborhoods where internet access is not otherwise available (McCrea, 2015). Some districts provide mobile devices for students to take home to level the access and provide for the connections, and others negotiate with local internet providers to lower the cost for families with students in the district. For example, Beekmantown Central School District in West Chazy, New York has a HotSpot program available to students enrolled in any of its four schools (tinyurl.com/ycrachsp). The district offers free wireless hotspot devices to students who do not have internet access at home; they provide devices for learners without them, and the district pays for both the device and the monthly access cost. The funding comes from an Extended Learning Time (ELT) grant, which is designed to help the students have access to digital resources to provide educational equity to all the learners.

In North and South Carolina, the Caldwell County Public School District and the Berkeley County School District partnered with Google and community groups to launch the Rolling Study Halls Pilot Program (RSH). RSH takes long school bus commutes and turns them into learning spaces for students by providing internet, devices, and an onboard teacher to allow students to work on classwork and homework.

School City of Mishawaka

In Indiana, the School City of Mishawaka worked with Sprint® to create a program to diminish the "homework gap" that persists in many communities. This program included handing out free smartphones to offer internet access to hundreds of high school students who have little or no access at home. Students without internet access, according to the School City of Mishawaka officials, "can face difficulty in communicating with teachers and keeping up with homework, which now often involves online elements" (Sheckler, 2017, n.p.). "We know there are students or families who don't have access at home, so that prevents kids from achieving their full potential," said Eric Johnson, the district's director of technology. "If I can't research efficiently or produce a digital document—that's not a situation I want our students to struggle with" (Sheckler, 2017, n.p.).

Public-private partnerships are still at work in communities across the country, with fifty low-income middle schools from diverse communities across the U.S. participating in the Dynamic Learning Project (edu.google.com/dynamic-learning-project). This pilot program, orchestrated by Digital Promise with support from Google, sponsors embedded technology coaches who help empower educators with the skills, tools, and training they need to use classroom technology in effective and meaningful ways. This program is part of Google's commitment to help underserved communities deliver on the promise of technology, both in the classroom and after school.

Libraries Respond, Too

Libraries Ready to Code is an initiative of the American Library Association (ALA), sponsored by Google, which aims to ensure that libraries have the resources, capacity, and inspiration to embrace activities that promote computational thinking and computer science among our nation's youth. In June 2017, the ALA announced a competitive grant program, also sponsored by Google, to fund a cohort of school and public libraries to develop resources to help get U.S. libraries "Ready to Code." This pilot program is an ongoing collaboration between ALA and Google, which donated $500,000 to the program. Ultimately, 25 to 50 participating libraries will receive funding from ALA, along with consulting expertise and operational support from Google. Individual libraries may use funding for devices, staffing, marketing, and other costs associated with piloting an educational toolkit developed in partnership, by libraries, for libraries. In addition, a toolkit released in conjunction with National Library Week in April 2018 includes computer science resources that libraries find most useful for designing and implementing youth computer science programming.

Dr. Albert Ritzhaupt, a professor at the University of Florida, has studied this challenge and presents the following assessment of the current status.

SPOTLIGHT 6.2

Digital Divide Within Schools: An Evolving Phenomenon

University of Florida, School of Teaching and Learning

Albert Ritzhaupt, Associate Professor, Educational Technology

The digital divide remains an important educational problem in the digital age, both within and outside the U.S. The digital divide originally expresses a host of socioeconomic variables (e.g., age, location, or income) between those with access and those without access to information and communication technology (ICT) resources. In an age of e-commerce, e-government, and e-learning, the digital divide has the potential to widen if not carefully addressed by interested stakeholders. Internationally, the digital divide is an issue of access in many developing nations; however, within the U.S. and other developed nations, this phenomenon has evolved from an issue of mere access to one of use, knowledge, skills, and dispositions. That is, the digital divide is a multilayered phenomenon with different concerns at each layer.

Since educational institutions are often perceived to be the bridges to correct this social inequity, emphasis has been placed on equipping educational institutions with ICT resources to support teachers, students, parents, and the communities in which they reside. Within schools, the digital divide can be characterized in three layers, as shown in Figure 6.2. At the first level, the model describes school infrastructure and access to appropriate ICT resources for students and teachers to integrate ICT into their personal and professional lives. The second level of the model characterizes how students and teachers are actually using the ICT resources in their classroom environment. The third and final layer of the model designates students to have the knowledge, skills, intent, and dispositions to create original artifacts with ICT resources.

Although much effort has been put forth to address the digital divide in formal educational settings, recent research demonstrates that the digital divide remains a concern for parents, legislators, administrators, teachers, librarians, and students (Hohlfeld, Ritzhaupt, Dawson, & Wilson, 2017; Ritzhaupt, Liu, Dawson, & Barron, 2013). For instance, Ritzhaupt et al. (2013) addressed the third level of the model and showed a digital divide in students' ICT literacy by gender, income, and ethnicity. Hohlfeld et al. (2017) showed that most disparities at level one have been addressed, but there remain differences in how students and teachers use ICT resources at level two of the model. Put simply, the digital divide has evolved from a problem of access to a problem of use, knowledge, skill, and attitude among important participants.

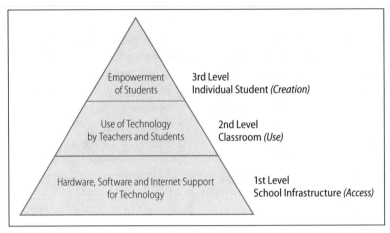

Figure 6.2. Levels of the Digital Divide in Schools. Adapted from: Levels of the Digital Divide in Schools (Hohlfeld, Ritzhaupt, Barron, & Kemker, 2008, p. 1649).

Fortunately, the educational community has put forth a number of potential solutions to the problem of the digital divide in formal educational settings. At a school level, programs like 1:1 device and bring-your-own-device (BYOD) initiatives have addressed student access issues. At a state and federal government level, programs such as the E-rate program have been widely adopted to ensure that students have access to reliable broadband internet connections to access appropriate ICT resources. Open Educational Resource (OER) initiatives have been emerging in the past decade to assist school districts with the immense costs associated with procuring quality educational materials for students and teachers to use.

▪ ▪ ▪ ▪ ▪

Community Approaches to Digital Equity

The city of Seattle created what may have been the first Digital Equity Manager to support its initiatives at bringing digital equity to all its residents. David Keyes was previously the first community technology planner; in that role, he directed the City of Seattle's Community Technology Program. In his work with the city, his leadership is responsible for the development of the Technology Access and Adoption Indicators research project, Technology Matching Fund community grants program, and cable broadband for nonprofit organizations' programs.

One such project was Seattle's Technology Matching Fund, which has been in existence for more than 20 years to support community organizations that improve access to the internet and digital skills training for Seattle residents (City of Seattle, n.d.) According to its website, "The goal of this fund and initiative is to ensure all residents and neighborhoods have the information technology capacity needed for civic and cultural participation, employment, lifelong learning, and access to essential services." The city strives to eliminate historical barriers to equal access through their intentional strategies, which they say will accomplish goals of better quality of life, offer educational and economic opportunities, make certain that all residents can use the electronic services now available, and ensure that all residents can connect through social media and mobile devices.

Portland, Oregon

Another example of a city taking steps to provide digital equity to all its residents is Portland, Oregon. The Portland City Council unanimously adopted its Digital Equity Action Plan on April 6, 2016, after hearings that brought to light the need for digital equity from residents. Its Digital Equity Action Plan (DEAP) outlines a series of operational and policy proposals for public and private agencies, along with nonprofits, in Portland and the greater Multnomah County to advance the cause of digital equity. The DEAP mission is to "bridge the digital divide for excluded members of our community with affordable access, training and tools" and its vision is "that all residents of Portland/Multnomah County will have barrier-free access to high-speed broadband internet at home and school, an affordable computing device and the training to use them effectively" (City of Portland, n.d.).

Portland has taken another step to provide equity and access. The Multnomah County Library offers one-on-one sessions, most of which involve computer skill support; it also offers a Free Geek earn-a-computer program (freegeek.org) in which digitally excluded populations gain skills and knowledge and then are given their own refurbished computer.

The U.S. Department of Housing and Urban Development (HUD) created a program to help mitigate the lack of access and equity. Its "HUD ConnectHome" seeks to provide individuals with the support they need to access the internet at home. This program began in 2015 by negotiating with internet service providers, nonprofit organizations, and private-sector entities to offer broadband access, technical training, digital literacy programs, and even devices for residents in assisted housing units.

Recently, Drs. Paul Resta and Robert T. McLaughlin launched a new organization focused on this topic. Their story is below.

SPOTLIGHT 6.3

National Collaborative for Digital Equity (NCDE)

Paul Resta (Co-Founder, NCDE; Ruth Knight Millikan Centennial Professor, Department of Curriculum and Instruction, College of Education, The University of Texas at Austin) and Robert T. McLaughlin (@DrBobDigital), (Co-Founder, NCDE; Associate Dean and Chair, Education, New England College)

In our increasingly global, digital age economy, it is becoming increasingly the case that, without digital access and skill, one cannot find out about, apply to, or qualify for living wage jobs. *Digital equity*—equitable access to essential technology resources for educational and economic opportunity and civic engagement—is rapidly becoming a prerequisite for economic and educational opportunity and justice.

The National Collaborative for Digital Equity (NCDE) was founded on the premise that investments in digital equity are vitally needed both for opportunity and social justice for low-income learners of all ages and their families, as well as community vitality (e.g., a reduction in the school-to-prison pipeline experienced by low-income students of color in many American communities). As digital access and skill become more and more of a prerequisite for learning about and gaining participation in living wage career paths, the nature and extent of the technology resources that are "essential" have evolved and will continue to do so. Therefore, NCDE has advocated intensively for policies that encourage public and private investments in digital equity to address this increasingly high-stakes and constantly evolving digital divide.

Our advocacy persuaded the Federal Reserve to issue guidance in August 2016 to encourage the nation's banks to use some portion of the funds they invest for economic opportunity, under the federal Community Reinvestment Act, to support digital equity (Federal Reserve Bank of Dallas, 2016). Banks annually spend more than $100 billion for economic opportunity in low- and moderate-income communities to meet their CRA obligation; our aim has been to encourage the banking industry to voluntarily commit eventually just 1% of these funds for digital equity, as this would unleash $1 billion each year to close the digital divide.

However, we know that simply to advocate for substantially increased investments in digital equity is not sufficient to ensure that such investments are successful and, therefore, likely to be sustained and scaled. Drawing on more than two decades of experience in P–12 technology infusion efforts—such as installing a computer lab in the school or providing every child with an iPad— we know definitively that providing all low-income learners in a high-poverty community with affordable home access to broadband and a computer will not ensure that they are given the other supports they will need to use these resources successfully. When we realized our advocacy on CRA policy was going to be successful, we realized we faced an urgent challenge—how to help banking leaders, foundations, and other potential digital equity investors to understand why and how to support local digital equity efforts that are systemic.

NCDE held a national convening of state and national thought leaders in education technology, to inform them of the policy shift and of the need to bring together thought leaders in banking, philanthropy, education technology research, school system and community leadership, and workforce development to develop a national strategic plan to (a) educate local leaders on how to develop funding proposals for systemic digital equity keyed to locally determined priorities for economic and educational opportunity; (b) educate banking, foundation, corporate philanthropy, and other digital equity investors on why and how to support only those digital equity efforts that are sufficiently multidimensional and evidence-based that their prospects for success are good; and (c) mobilize the educational technology research community to support dissemination of existing research on effective practices, as well as to undertake new studies needed to provide investors and community leaders with guidance.

■ ■ ■ ■ ■

Another national organization, the Consortium for School Networking (CoSN), has been involved in issues of digital innovation for many years; one of its main foci is to assist school districts in developing policy and plans around the issue of digital equity.

 SPOTLIGHT 6.4

"Digital equity is the civil rights issue of our time"

Keith Krueger (@keithkrueger), CEO, Consortium for School Networking (@cosn) (@leaddigitalleap)

There's Still a Gap

The growing ubiquity of internet access and pervasive use of online information has changed the learning landscape forever. Students continue to benefit from enhanced connectivity throughout the formal school day, thanks to a $1.5 billion increase in E-rate funding in late 2014. However, demand and expectations for learning outside the school day are on the rise, and there are still many students struggling to complete homework online, causing a challenging homework gap.

In 2017, the Pew Research Center reported that despite light-speed development in technology, in households where income is less than $30,000 annually, less than half the adults have home broadband services, own a smartphone, or own a traditional computer or tablet (Anderson, 2017).

If you were to simply ask lower-income families if they had Wi-Fi and a device, the majority would say yes. However, the Joan Ganz Cooney Center, a team of researchers funded by the Bill and Melinda Gates Foundation, who undertook such a mission, reported "Access to the internet and digital devices is no longer a simple yes/no question. Whether families have consistent quality connections and the capabilities to make the most of being connected is becoming just as important" (digitalequityforlearning.org, 2016).

Clearly, there is a great deal of work that needs to be done to narrow the inequitable homework gap. This issue constitutes a new civil right: the right to digital equity; the right to connect to needed resources—anywhere, anytime. This is a civil right that cannot be achieved by school leaders alone. A holistic approach will ensure that school-aged children aren't reduced to little, or no access. It calls for community leadership that is connected and collaborative.

Together, We're Better

The CoSN Digital Equity Toolkit was first launched in February 2016; it is a free resource designed to provide school districts and their communities with the information necessary to support students and families in achieving equity in out-of-school learning. Since that time, there have been many school pioneers breaking ground and making a difference in narrowing the gap. The Digital Equity Toolkit (2.0) offers an interactive window into their leadership and provides tools and resources to get underway. Most schools and districts working in this space have found their key to sustainable success has been to partner with community members. They have been working together to accomplish digital equity challenges, many of which are impossible to accomplish in isolation.

- Boulder Valley School District in Colorado is partnering with an internet company allowing the provider to place equipment on one of their elementary buildings in exchange for them providing free internet access to their low-income elementary families.

- Green Bay Unified School District in Wisconsin is collaborating with the state network on a proof-of-concept LTE (high-speed wireless) solution as well as a TV whitespace solution to get internet into students' homes.

- In the rural Lindsay Unified School District in California, the district used a variety of solutions, including a door-to-door campaign asking designated residents to host repeater devices to extend Wi-Fi connectivity into their students' homes.

- Beekmantown Central School District in New York has installed Wi-Fi on buses to help students maximize school activity and commuting times.

- In North Carolina, a nonprofit was started by a middle school student to bring digital equity to fellow students and their families by hosting citywide lemonade stands!

- In Kansas City, Missouri, a wide and diverse collaboration has developed and is implementing a metro area digital equity plan.

Explore CoSN's interactive Digital Equity Toolkit at cosn.org/digital-equity-toolkit for more compelling examples. Gather your team and get underway to grow the digital equity footprint within your community!

■ ■ ■ ■ ■

Summary

This chapter has focused on the enduring challenge of the digital divide and the efforts underway to ensure digital equity and access for all citizens of the world. It offered encouraging and creative solutions to providing opportunities for individuals who may not have the ability to complete their homework, take part in civic endeavors, or compete for access to resources. Luckily, schools, organizations, and cities are stepping up to help solve this ongoing difficulty. Educators who incorporate efforts to bridge the digital divide within their classrooms, schools, and beyond will be addressing the following ISTE standards for students and for themselves as educators.

ISTE STUDENT STANDARDS ADDRESSED IN THIS CHAPTER

Standard 1: Empowered Learner	Students leverage technology to take an active role in choosing, achieving and demonstrating competency in their learning goals, informed by the learning sciences.
Standard 2: Digital Citizen	Students recognize the rights, responsibilities and opportunities of living, learning and working in an interconnected digital world, and they act and model in ways that are safe, legal and ethical.
Standard 7: Global Collaborator	Students use digital tools to broaden their perspectives and enrich their learning by collaborating with others and working effectively in teams locally and globally.

ISTE EDUCATOR STANDARDS ADDRESSED IN THIS CHAPTER

Standard 2: **Leader**	Educators seek out opportunities for leadership to support student empowerment and success and to improve teaching and learning.
Standard 3: **Citizen**	Educators inspire students to positively contribute to and responsibly participate in the digital world.
Standard 6: **Facilitator**	Educators facilitate learning with technology to support student achievement of the 2016 ISTE Standards for Students.

Questions and Reflections

- Is it possible to identify the current situation in your classroom, school, district, or community regarding the issues related to equity and access to digital resources and devices?

- Are there things you are aware of that are designed to improve equity and access for all learners?

- Is your city or community engaged in supporting access for all its citizens? Is there a project your learners might take on to identify a challenge and discover a solution?

Further Resources to Get Started

Open Educational Resources (Free)

eSchool News
(www.eschoolnews.com/2014/11/12/digital-equity-access-938/2) This article offers an overview of the issues in digital equity.

Getting Smart
(www.gettingsmart.com/categories/topics/equity-access)
Offers resources, articles, and ideas.

Edutopia: Engage Parents as Partners to Close the Digital Divide
(www.edutopia.org/blog/engage-parents-partners-close-digital-divide-suzie-boss)
Edutopia consistently offers support on digital implementation; this article provides
actions to engage the entire community in addressing the issues.

COSN Digital Equity Toolkit
(www.cosn.org/focus-areas/leadership-vision/digital-equity-action-agenda) This set
of resources addresses the challenges, and offers multiple suggestions and ideas for
addressing the equity challenges.

**The Joan Ganz Cooney Foundation: Opportunity for All? Technology and Learning
in Lower-Income Families**
(joanganzcooneycenter.org/publication/opportunity-for-all-technology-and-learning-
in-lower-income-families) This is another guide with many suggestions and ideas
for local districts to address the disparity.

eSchool News: 7 Reasons Digital Equity Is a Social Justice Issue
(www.eschoolnews.com/2014/11/12/digital-equity-access-938) This article provides
a good overview of the issues on this topic.

New America Weekly: The Future of Broadband in Underserved Areas
(www.newamerica.org/weekly/edition-173/future-broadband-underserved-areas)
This is one more look at ways to overcome the challenges of digital access for all.

Books That May Be of Interest

Bauerlein, M. (2011). *The digital divide: Arguments for and against Facebook, Google,
texting, and the age of social networking.* New York, NY: TarcherPerigee.

Muschert, G. W., & Ragnedda, M. (2015). *The digital divide: The Internet and social
inequality in international perspective.* New York, NY: Routledge.

Spotlight on Digital Media and Learning. (2014). *Digital divide.* New York, NY:
MacArthur Foundation Digital Media and Learning Initiative.

CHAPTER 7

Blending of Formal, Nonformal, and Informal Education

I never teach my pupils, I only provide the conditions in which they can learn.

— Albert Einstein

Learning is not the product of teaching. Learning is the product of the activity of learners.

— John Holt

In This Chapter:

- What is known about formal, nonformal, and informal education?

- What examples exist on the importance and use of informal and nonformal education?

- What ways are formal educational systems and informal entities collaborating?

What Is Known About Formal, Nonformal, and Informal Learning?

How did you learn to bake a cake or to change a tire? In all likelihood, someone in your family helped you learn. We know that much of what any individual knows is not learned in a formal classroom setting; after all, we spend far more time out of school than in it. Reflection on the idea of the relationship between formal schooling and out-of-school learning, for example in science education, has the potential to "work through conceptions of partnerships that will help erase boundaries among cultures, practices, teaching and learning, constitutive of life-long, life-wide, and life-deep science learning, science teaching and science education, and that in the end, will be transformative" (Rahm, 2014, p. 395).

Hung, Lee, and Lim (2012) define formal education as "school curriculum in which learning might be characterized as focusing on structured content, extrinsic motivation, and strict assessments" (p. 1072). Two terms are often applied to out-of-school learning. "Dividing of out-of-school learning into informal and nonformal categories helps to achieve a better understanding of the characteristics of out-of-school learning" (Esach, 2007, p. 173). First is the term *nonformal*, which occurs in a planned but highly adaptable manner in institutions, organizations, and situations beyond the spheres of formal educational entities. Second is the term *informal learning*, which can be defined "generally as learning that occurs at home, work and during leisure hours in order to increase some form of new knowledge, skills, abilities and understandings" (Strimel et al., 2014, p. 45). According to Rogoff, Callahan, Gutiérrez, & Erickson (2016), "Informal learning is nondidactic, is embedded in meaningful activity, builds on the learner's initiative or interest or choice (rather than resulting from external demands or requirements), and does not involve assessment external to the activity" (p. 356). Informal learning occurs more spontaneously in situations in life such as within the family circle, the neighborhood, and so on. Hung et al. (2012) defined informal education as:

> less structured activities, in which learning outcomes might not be explicitly foregrounded. Time and space is given for exploration, experimentation, developing interests, and intrinsic motivations. Assessments are less formal and might take the form of peer-recognition and critique to co-inform likeminded peers in their pursuits. (p. 1072)

As you might expect, many people have their own ways of expressing these differences. Gerber, Marek, and Cavallo (2001) stated, "In essence, the informal learning can be defined as the sum of activities that comprise the time individuals are not in the formal classroom in the presence of a teacher" (p. 570).

However the concepts are defined, the idea of blending nonformal and informal learning with learning into formal educational settings has expanded during the last decades, and technology has played a role in the potential and reality. Further, schools are beginning to consider a new way of thinking about learning within the concept of a learning ecology, one that proposes "while students learn differently in school and out-of-school settings, learning can take place across boundaries, and what has been learned out of school can help shape what is learned in school" (Lai, Khaddage, & Knezek, 2013, p. 415).

Focus on Science and STEM

Informal science learning is everywhere around us. The University of Pittsburgh has created the Center for Advancement of Informal Science Education (CAISE) with a focus on informal science education, which they define as "lifelong learning in science, technology, engineering, and math (STEM) that takes place across a multitude of designed settings and experiences outside of the formal classroom" (Center for Advancement of Informal Science Education, 2017, n.p.).

The U.S. Department of Education created the 21st Century Community Learning Centers program (21st CCLC) in order to support learners in multiple ways:

> This program supports the creation of community learning centers that provide academic enrichment opportunities during non-school hours for children, particularly students who attend high-poverty and low-performing schools. The program helps students meet state and local student standards in core academic subjects, such as reading and math; offers students a broad array of enrichment activities that can complement their regular academic programs; and offers literacy and other educational services to the families of participating children. (U.S. Department of Education, 2017)

Funding for these programs is given to the states, which in turn accept grant applications from entities in that state. Many applications are from school districts, but others come from Boys and Girls Clubs, local community centers, and other organizations. They vary widely in the ways in which the grants are implemented, but all are required to include innovative programming, homework help, and snacks.

The Illinois State Board of Education (ISBE) organized their funding to sponsor an innovative program that has supported the creation of 456 centers to provide academic and social enrichment opportunities during nonschool hours. To date, the initiative has reached more than 70,000 students across the state, with a special focus on serving students from high-poverty communities. Education Development Center (EDC) is conducting an evaluation of the statewide 21st CCLC programs and is working with ISBE to determine how well the centers are meeting their programmatic goals. Dr. Leslie Goodyear, who spearheads the evaluation of this and other 21st CCLC programs, said, "Many exciting things are happening in these centers. They work to connect the schools and the families. One center has the attendees prepare and serve dinner once a week; another held a project, Science of Medieval Villages, in which they studied levers and catapults, and another studying the Science of Fashion" (personal communication, 2017). In particular, centers that are run by school districts seem to have a well-developed blending of formal and informal learning experiences, but Dr. Goodyear also explained that many are now creating their plans to align with ESEA.

Alaska has also established its share of 21st CCLCs. In Sitka, Alaska, the school district runs a center in its four Title I schools, out of five total, and as expected, it is deeply involved in both academic efforts and informal educational opportunities. Program coordinator Ryan Haug said, "Academics are important, but we also focus on social emotional learning, and the notion of grit and resilience" (personal communication, 2017). The programs vary by grade level, but all learners do have the obligation to complete their homework. Academic assistants provide support for the learners' schoolwork, and, because the centers are in the schools, it is not unusual to have an academic assistant and a student seek out the student's teacher after school to ensure what work is expected or to seek clarification.

The Blatchley Middle School has an especially strong formal/informal relationship with the Sitka Sound Science Center. The 21st CCLC has its typical routine Monday through Thursday, but each Friday is "Fab Friday" at the science center. Janet Clarke, the education manager for the Science Center, discussed the many opportunities for the students at the center. The science center includes the oldest fish hatchery, an aquarium, tidal basins, and eco-discovery opportunities. The goal is to have a semester-long project for the Fab Fridays to engage the students in authentic activities, building on their interests and the affordances of a location such as Sitka, Alaska.

Sometimes it is university researchers who take innovative programs into the community. Spotlight 7.1 shares the story of two science educators who have a unique approach to blending formal and informal learning.

SPOTLIGHT 7.1

Informal STEM Programs

Angela Calabrese Barton (@calabresebarton), Michigan State University.
Edna Tan, University of North Carolina, Greensboro.

Professors Calabrese Barton and Tan have been changing the nature of STEM education through a series of NSF-funded projects, and the results are exceptional. They have created a model that encourages participants, typically underrepresented populations in the STEM careers, to become "community ethnographers." Rather than just asking, "What do you want to make?" they assist learners in collecting data to investigate what their community needs, and then to collectively identify problems and design solutions with community stakeholders, in response to those community challenges.

These researchers work with Boys and Girls Clubs near both universities, and they strive for longitudinal explorations of "equity-oriented STEM-rich making experiences." They have been conducting these programs since 2007 and have seen results that provide encouragement for what they are doing.

One example concerns safety in a difficult neighborhood, particularly given the requirement that youth not wear hoodies at public schools. One young man worked diligently to find a way to push back on this mandate, but to also provide support for his neighborhood friends. He spent a number of months prototyping a "phantom hoodie" powered by wind turbines attached to the shoulders of the hoodie, that would allow the wearer to power the cells to emit a siren should he or she be accosted. One of the highlights of this program is a focus on sustainability and renewable energy; thus, the wearer is able to generate the electricity for the cells by turning a crank. This could allow others to come and protect someone being harassed and demonstrates the goals of inventing, social justice, persistence, and STEM.

Another example from this project is equally impressive. In the winter, Michigan experiences many long hours of darkness, and one participant felt that he and his friends were unable to play football in the dark. He determined that a solution would be to develop a prototype of a football that lights up in the dark. This proved to be quite a challenge: he had to ensure that the lights would not generate so much heat that they burned the skin, the battery power had to avoid changing the balance of the ball, and so on. For months he persisted and eventually was able to produce a successful model, with assistance from his peers, community club mentors, his mother, and undergraduate university engineering students, among others. Interestingly, when he asked to show the football in his science class, he was denied that opportunity; however, his physical education teacher was thrilled and allowed him to demonstrate his results, and this formal recognition for his informal learning proved to be a powerful success!

To encourage the blending of this informal/formal space, these researchers have provided deep professional development for teachers. They have invited classroom teachers into the community club making spaces during summer workshops, where teachers are encouraged to participate in ways that the participants do and to begin to understand the nature of this new model of community engagement as ethnography. Educators have recognized that they might have overorganized such a space but, in watching some of the students, they began to see the power of the inquiry- and community-based open-ended activities.

Two of the youth who have been involved in the program for several years have taken it upon themselves to create a little free library for STEM, and have even made small "maker kits" for other students who are not involved in the program, so that they can begin to experience the same exciting activities. Calabrese Barton and Tan argue that STEM, engineering, and making should not be divorced from youths' everyday lives and the social relationships important to them, and that by leveraging community wisdom and insight in the process of robust, technical, STEM-rich making, such activities can lead to transformative outcomes for the youth and their community, even as youth learn to deal with frustration during the iterative design process. As Kairree, a 13-year-old girl reflected of her work designing and prototyping a heated bus seat for public riders in her city,

> The process of designing and prototyping this [artifact] was like going to Hell and back. It takes a lot of work and time to put into this, and some parts I messed up and had to redo. Sometimes I just got it completely done in just one step, not two. That felt magnificent.

■ ■ ■ ■ ■

Learning and Science Museums

Many of the collaborations between formal education and nonformal learning take place in science museums. Rogoff, Callahan, Gutiérrez, & Erickson (2016) suggested, "In designing exhibits and spaces, the goal is often to provide opportunities for informal learning that is self-driven and active" (p. 385). The content found in these entities offer a wide range of possible subjects to challenge and engage learners. As Rahm (2014) suggested, "Informal science education is a broad field of research marked by fuzzy boundaries, tensions, and muddles among many disciplines, making for an unclear future trajectory (or trajectories) for the field of study" (p. 395).

Phillips, Finkelstein, and Wever-Frerichs (2007) found that more than 70% of science-rich cultural institutions in the U.S. have programs specifically designed for school audiences. These settings offer experiences that promote different kinds of engagement and support various types of learning styles. Filippoupoliti and Koliopoulos (2014) provide a comprehensive definition:

> A science centre has a distinct experimental philosophy that moves from the display of the authentic object to create an original/meaningful museum experience through active visitor participation. Beyond object worship, it is the exhibition space that matters more as it assimilates the laboratory, a gallery of research and a place of demonstration. (p. 783)

SPOTLIGHT 7.2

Spreading Science Literacy

Singapore Science Centre (@ScienceCentreSG)

Dr. TM Lim, Chief Executive

Dr. TM Lim is the Chief Executive of the Science Centre Singapore. He is trained as a zoologist and is a biology professor, and eight years ago the Singapore government seconded him from his university to transform the Science Centre into what he describes as Science Centre 2.0.

During these past eight years, he has moved in multiple directions to accomplish his four primary goals, which overall seek to popularize science. First, he wants to make sure that the centre is considered as an alternate classroom where learning of all types occurs. He has developed myriad ways to encourage individuals of all ages to come to the science centre; he explained that the birth rate is falling and if he focused only on young children, he would soon run out of attendees and participants! One exhibit focuses, for example, on the science of aging.

Second, he wants this centre to be known as the preferred or desired partner for public and private organizations. To that effort, he has sought out opportunities so that the Science Centre is visible to all.

Third, Dr. Lim has a plan to make sure that the museum is a science centre without walls. To accomplish this, the center strives to take the learning and experiences into many locations. Finally, he is determined to spread science literacy. He eloquently speaks about the center as a community-owned and cocreated entity.

He has done many things during his almost nine years as the Chief Executive to demonstrate and move toward these goals. For example, in 2012 they launched a mini Maker Faire, which brought in about 50 makers and 1,000 visitors; it was a bold and innovative step into a relatively new field. The most recent Maker Faire attracted more than 1,000 makers and almost 13,000 visitors and generated so many applications from those involved in making who wanted to show off their efforts, that they had to limit the number of participants. The centre helped develop a Science Carnival in Beijing that proved highly successful and did not cost the Singapore centre any funding; Italy asked for assistance in a similar pursuit, and again, Dr. Lim was happy to help.

When asked about the relationship with formal educational organizations, Dr. Lim was very eager to discuss his accomplishments. He developed an overarching effort called the Youth Science Movement, which includes three significant activities. First, he created the Singapore Academy of Young Engineering and Science: SAYES (say yes!). This organization is for secondary students who are interested in science; as he explained, it is for youth and by youth. Although it began as a more social club for those with this content as their strong interest, it is now conducting real science and tackling authentic challenges.

The second initiative, CRADLE, encourages youth to actually participate in research and applied sciences with hands-on learning. They have assigned secondary teachers to be research mentors who promote a bottom-up approach that involves authentic science fairs, industrial partners who provide insight into real-world challenges for sciences, and even includes a summer work experience program.

Finally, Dr. Lim wanted to make a difference in schools that the community and government did not consider to be particularly strong. A former Minister of Education challenged the education community, specifically in neighborhood schools, to reach a goal of becoming "good schools" in one focus area of effort, and many wanted to become STEM schools. Most impressive was the manner in which this was approached. The original goal was to scale up half of these neighborhood schools (62 of the 124), but they have managed to transform 73. The STEM Inc., created by Dr. Lim, included engaging curricula specialists, using real-world science and engineering, and doing away with examinations. Moreover, the changes had to take place during the school day rather than after school or on weekends. In order to be accepted, schools had to agree to changing their thinking to include a systems approach to learning science, the school leader had to be completely on board, and the schools had to embrace this as a way to change their learners' outcomes and potential. There are three tiers to the STEM Inc. plan: Tier 1 is compulsory for all 13-year-old learners, Tier 2 and 3 are optional and offer enhanced learning opportunities. Schools typically partner with an industrial partner; these partners recognize the power of helping create a pipeline of future scientists and engineers.

The programs in the Science Centre, in the schools, and in the wider community will continue to grow and expand, remain relevant and support all individuals in lifelong learning, and promote a greater understanding of, and appreciation for, science. As Dr. Lim put it, the Science Centre 2.0 is for everyone from cradle to grave!

■ ■ ■ ■ ■

With well-documented support that informal science programs improve children's attitudes about science, raise their interest in STEM careers, and meet the needs of "specific subgroups of students, (e.g., females; non-Caucasians)" (Crawford & Huscroft-D'Angelo, 2015, p. 2), many projects have sought to expand the reach of informal programs. For example, the Challenger Learning Center in Southern Colorado offers a simulated space mission on site to students from 50 different schools, representing 25 school districts in grades 6–8.

> Students completed one of three missions: (1) Return to the Moon, (2) Rendezvous with a Comet, or (3) Voyage to Mars. The three missions share a common role-playing element with students acting as astronauts, engineers, scientists, and/or mission controllers. The element of teamwork is embedded throughout all of the missions and if students do not learn to work together during their mission, it inevitably fails. For example, in Return to the Moon, students establish a permanent lunar base in order to conduct scientific observations and studies. (Crawford & Huscroft-D'Angelo, 2015, p. 7)

In the evaluation of the program, these authors found that perception of and interest in space and STEM in general did improve; however, there were still differences between males and females, and among racial groups. This example brought up more questions and ideas on how to reduce these discrepancies.

Spring Street International School (SSIS) in Friday Harbor, Washington, promotes collaborative projects (for more information about SSIS, see Chapter 5). For example, its Salish Sea Sciences Program provides a 26-day immersive research adventure for motivated science students ages 14–18. This program, between SSIS and the

University of Washington Friday Harbor Laboratories, offers students the opportunity to learn what it takes to be effective collaborators with working scientists. The experience takes place each summer in June and July, culminating in a five-day longboat expedition in the great inland ocean called the Salish Sea (see salishseasciences.org).

Virtual Field Trips

According to Trevesa, Viterbob, & Haklay (2015), "Research into virtual field trips (VFTs) started in the 1990s but, only recently, the maturing technology of devices and networks has made them viable options for educational settings" (p. 97). Importantly, educators see that field trips do connect with the curriculum; they see field trips (virtual or actual) as opportunities to reinforce or expand upon the classroom curriculum by providing an additional perspective or a more meaningful connection, provide firsthand, rich, novel, and new learning experiences, and foster students' interest and motivation (Eshach, 2007). Additionally, "Scientific field trips to science centers can generate a sense of wonder, interest, enthusiasm, motivation, and eagerness to learn" (Eshach, 2007, p. 178). All virtual field trips should include the following attributes: clear objectives, authenticity, interactivity, multimedia, constructivist approach, problem-based and inquiry pedagogy, teacher support materials, and an evaluation component, including collecting data of student attention (Stoddard, 2009; Trevesa et al., 2015).

Niemitz et al. (2008) stated that virtual connections with professional experts and scientists provide students with excellent opportunities to experience and understand scientific processes and enhance student aspirations for science careers. Ball State University (apso.bsu.edu/eft) has been offering VFT for more than a decade and, in some ways, their lessons are useful to anyone considering offering or taking a VFT. They have a four-step approach that includes video broadcast with authentic scientists, park rangers, or other appropriate experts; a website with exploration tools to deepen understanding; teacher resources; and on-demand video content to expand the learning concepts.

For many years, Dr. Barbara Levin has been preparing future educators to teach social studies and to embed technology appropriately into their curriculum. She offers these suggestions for virtual field trips.

SPOTLIGHT 7.3

Virtual Field Trips

University of North Carolina, Greensboro

Barbara B. Levin, Professor, Teacher Education and Higher Education

Imagine taking your students to George Washington's home at Mt. Vernon (mountvernon.org/site/virtual-tour) in the morning and then visiting the National Gallery of Art in Washington, DC, (nga.gov) in the afternoon where more than 40,000 images are available—all from the safety of your school. Then you can use Google Earth to locate and show examples of different kinds of ecosystems or landforms around the globe, and later go on a Google Lit Trip (googlelittrips.org) to Japan to see the setting for *Sadako and the Thousand Cranes* by Eleanor Coerr. You can also take your students to the Statue of Liberty, Mt. Rushmore, and other famous landmarks around the world in 3-D using Google Cardboard, and also go inside the human body or under the ocean on a virtual reality (VR) field trip (edu.google.com/expeditions). Such learning opportunities are virtually unlimited! Literally thousands of virtual field trips (VFTs) and potential sites for VFTs are available on the internet as lesson plans that you can modify for your needs. Or, you can design your own VFT to help your students learn more about science, the arts, social studies, English language arts, and even mathematics without getting permission slips or paying for a bus. The main requirement for going on VFTs is access to the internet and, in the case of Google Cardboard, garnering increasingly inexpensive VR headsets.

One important thing about VFTs is selecting age-appropriate places to visit, including finding websites with lots of images (plus some text for older students), and hopefully the added ability to see 360° panoramic images of a site. Some sites also have sound, but even kindergarten students can go on VFTs with some guidance. The most important thing about VFTs is to provide a trip guide for students so they know what to look for and what your objectives are for taking them on a VFT. After all, students should learn something during a VFT! Trip guides, however, should not be simple scavenger hunts to look for right answers. Instead, trip guides should ask students open-ended questions that encourage them to use higher-order thinking about what they are seeing and reading. For example, at Mt. Vernon you might ask students to list five new things they learned about George Washington and if they would have liked to live there in Washington's lifetime and why. You could also send them to Thomas Jefferson's home at Monticello and ask them to compare and contrast the estates of these two presidents. Or, while viewing the four presidents on Mt. Rushmore, you could ask students to nominate a fifth person to add and explain why they think their nominee deserves this honor. Or, after virtually visiting several monuments, you could ask students to design a new monument that honors our history or our democracy. The possibilities for VFTs of all kinds are endless! In fact, one research report included VFTs among the top nine keys to student achievement and cost effectiveness, explaining that students taking monthly VFTs have higher degrees of success: "With more frequent use, virtual [field] trips are more powerful. The best schools do these at least monthly" (Greaves, Hayes, Wilson, Gielniak, & Peterson, 2010, p. 12).

■ ■ ■ ■ ■

Not every teacher will have connections to offer students the opportunity for virtual field trips and other types of live connections to interesting people and places. Microsoft offers a program for teachers and learners in the U.S. and around the world to connect with others:

> Skype in the Classroom is an online community that enables thousands of teachers to inspire the next generation of global citizens through transformative learning over Skype. You can connect your students with other classrooms around the world and collaborate on projects or one-off calls, or invite an expert to talk to your students over Skype. (Microsoft, 2018, n.p.)

There are four distinct types of interactions: Skype collaborations, virtual field trips, guest speakers, and classroom-to-classroom connections. The program also offers professional development and badging for educators. One educator tells her story in Spotlight 7.4 below.

SPOTLIGHT 7.4

Skype Enriches My Students' Experiences!

Amy Rosenstein (@SkypeAmy), Third Grade Teacher

Using Skype in my classroom over the last nine years has been magical. There is so much inherent in the experiences! From researching before the calls, to using speaking and listening skills during the conversations, to reflecting afterward in writing, podcasts, or digital stories, students learn more than they realize. I teach in a third grade classroom in Westchester County, New York. I started using Skype in my classroom when a parent in our community moved with her two boys (former students of my elementary school) to Hong Kong. That year, our curriculum changed to focus on China, and we decided to give Skype a try. I had never heard of this being done before, but decided to take the leap, and the results were astounding. Connecting with young children, live, across the world was powerful. Just seeing that it was nighttime there, while we had just begun our school day, really hit home for the eight-year-olds in front of me.

Before the calls take place, my students conduct research. For the calls that are focused on culture, we use a website called Culturegrams, where students can get a strong in-depth background about the country we are about to call. The research pushes students to ask thoughtful questions. The idea is for students to avoid inquiries that can be answered through search engines. Students also "visit" the location with apps like Barefoot World Atlas. This process has taken place for countries from India to Uganda to Brazil to Russia. During the calls, students take notes in a variety of ways. Over the years, we've used graphic organizers, Thinking Maps, and other note-taking methods.

After the calls, students use their notes to create detailed reflections. These include what they learned, queries they still have, comments on the technology, and more. At times, students have created podcasts and digital stories based on the Skype experiences. Since this began, my third-graders have Skyped with people on every continent and more than 40 countries. We've met experts and authors. We've taken virtual field trips, and we've had many cultural exchanges and Mystery Geography Skype calls. We've integrated the United Nations Sustainable Development Goals into an increasing number of our calls, and we've learned a lot about empathy, understanding, and respect along the way.

I can't imagine teaching without it and I'm so proud of my students as they've developed into true global citizens. At the end of the year, I often receive photo books from the class in which students state their favorite memories of third grade; almost all are about Skype! Just a few are:

"I can't forget how excited I was before our first Skype session with China." —Liz

"My favorite time this year was when we Skyped with Israel. I found it very interesting." —Josh

"Social Studies is not my favorite subject, with Skype, you made it a blast." — Kaitlyn

After Virtual Field Trip (with Fabien Cousteau):

"It felt amazing to Skype underwater!" —Jason

"When I looked out the window of Aquarius, I was amazed! I saw big fish, small fish, bright fish, and dark fish! No fish looked alike. Fabien says that he feels very lucky to be experiencing what he's experiencing. I felt the same way today to have such an amazing, once in a lifetime opportunity to Skype with someone underwater!" —Dylan

Figure 7.1. Students share their artifacts via Skype.

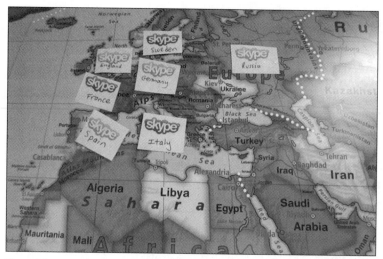

Figure 7.2. Locations of our Skype connections.

Figure 7.3. We have seen penguins as part of our studies.

Figure 7.4. We demonstrate our love for international interactions!

Microsoft has helped in innumerable ways. I remember starting to use Skype in my classroom before "Skype in the classroom" existed. Soon after, teachers came together through SITC and the rest is history. There were 1,000, then 10,000, then 20,000 teachers and now there are more than 500,000 members of the Microsoft Educator Community. It's a powerful way to make connections all over the world in countless subjects. It's simple to filter, so I can find exactly what I'm looking for, and I also post my own lessons and collaborations so that others can easily find me.

■ ■ ■ ■ ■

While virtual field trips are exciting and engaging, we now have the possibility of virtual reality field trips, using Google's Cardboard viewer, its app, and the more than 200 possible places to experience. According to Catapano (n.d.),

Virtual reality offers a more interactive, immersive experience. Instead of sitting passively, students stand up. Instead of looking at one aspect of an image, they literally turn their heads and move their eyes to view angles of an image. Instead of remaining aware of their classroom environment, they are immersed inside of a virtual reality setting. (n.p.)

For a small fee per pupil, to purchase the reusable cardboard viewer, the class or a subset of the learners can engage in an experience that is almost like being in the location. For example, if you are studying Shakespeare, you can take your class backstage to the Royal Shakespeare Theater in Stratford on Avon. If you are studying Antarctica, your class can experience its marine wildlife or its glaciers. Or perhaps one learner is eager to explore what it might be like to be a surgeon; she can spend one day in a surgeon's life.

The National Park Foundation offers a variety of engaging, more traditional, virtual field trips. These include history, nature, interactive and visitor center tours; unfortunately, these experiences include steps that provide information and educator notes, but do not represent the collaboration that could produce the type of ongoing investigative challenges that engage students. Purdue zipTrips offer opportunities that include live 45-minute interactive programs with four core components: in-studio and remote/off-site audiences, live interaction with scientists, prerecorded segments, and integrated activities for in-studio, web, and broadcast audiences. With a specific focus on teaching comparative biology, zipTrips aim to enhance student understanding, interest, and perceptions of life-science research, researchers, and career opportunities. According to Adedokun et al., 2012), the trips are deeply engaging. For example, "The 8th grade, *It's a Gene Thing!* zipTrips provides opportunities for interactions between students and real-world geneticists. A scientist studying mutations in mice helps students understand how her work in animals informs our knowledge of human disease" (p. 609).

Non-STEM Foci

It is important to remember that not all collaborations between formal and non/informal education are related to STEM. For example, Chris Anagnos, Executive Director of The Association of Art Museum Directors (AAMD), discussed the partnerships in learning that were supported by the U.S. Department of Education (aamd.org/partnersinlearning). In 2015, she stated,

> Art is a powerful tool for education, and museums provide invaluable access to arts education for students in this country. More than just field trips, these museum-school partnerships result in more innovative programs than ever before, with a focus on long-term community engagement with students and teachers alike. (n.p.)

The U.S. Department of Education sponsored a celebration of this effort, *Museums: pARTners in Learning 2015* and reported that the collaborations encourage "21st-century skills," including creativity, innovation, critical thinking, problem solving, communication, cultural awareness, and collaboration. A few of the many school and museum collaborations are discussed below.

Museum of Modern Art

The Museum of Modern Art (moma.org), perhaps the most well-known museum in New York, has a number of resources and offerings for educators. It provides a wide variety of professional development courses (on site and online) and resources for teachers and learners (moma.org/learn/moma_learning). It offers a number of onsite sessions, including interactive engagements with 3–4 artworks in the galleries, or an interactive engagement followed by a hands-on exploration of materials and processes, along with previsit and postvisit lessons. Additionally, MoMA offers community programs. Since not everyone lives in or near New York City, the online resources serve to support educators throughout the world (moma.org/research-and-learning/teachers/online).

Whitney Museum of American Art

Another of the popular museums in New York is the Whitney Museum of American Art. The Whitney has developed a program of school partnerships, which includes guided visits, hands-on art making, classroom visits, family programs, and professional development for teachers. The education staff at the Whitney works closely with teachers to design customized programs that are tailored to the specific needs of their students and map to their school curriculum (whitney.org/Education/K12/SchoolPrograms/SchoolPartnerships).

Phillips Collection

In Washington, DC, the Phillips Collection has developed a series of arts-integrated programs for the District of Columbia Public Schools (DCPS) named Art Links to Learning (phillipscollection.org/learn/k-12-education/museum-school-initiatives). Art Links is a project that weaves the visual arts into subject areas to improve student learning outcomes. The goal is to develop higher order skills such as critical thinking and problem-solving. This program provides professional development for educators, brings activities into classrooms, and also offers classroom visits to the Phillips. Students create multidisciplinary projects from these experiences.

Madison Museum of Contemporary Art's Art on Tour

Partnerships are not unique to the east coast. The Madison Museum of Contemporary Art's Art on Tour (aamd.org/node/2442) selects original works of art from the permanent collection and takes them to nine public elementary and middle schools in Dane County, Wisconsin. Art on Tour offers authentic masterpieces to schools so that students can learn about the art, but also to inspire students to explore their own creativity. It has reached more than 4,500 learners with its program to teach about observing, analyzing, and interpreting the artwork.

Joslyn Art Museum

The Joslyn Art Museum in Omaha, Nebraska, offers a variety of resources for educators and students in its geographic area, as well as virtually. It provides lesson plans, professional development, and "outreach trunks" that include many materials for lessons that teachers can borrow. It routinely provides downloadable tours for mobile devices of special collections or as a preview for a visit. It is particularly proud of its Kent Bellows Mentoring Program (aamd.org/node/2441) which is an amazing experience for many teens. Professional artists are engaged to serve as students' mentors as the project strives to create an inclusive community that supports creativity and brings together students from more than 25 regional high schools. Teens identify their interests from a variety of self-directed options and they establish themselves as artists. In addition, the museum has an outreach of this studio program at the Boys Town National Research Hospital for those unable to come to the museum.

High Museum and Seattle Art Museum

Local museums are working hard to connect to educators and students, as well as to the larger community. The High Museum in Atlanta has established academic affiliations with a number of schools in the Atlanta area (high.org/students-and-educators). These collaborations allow for the sharing of resources to further integrate visual arts into educational curriculum. The Seattle Art Museum (SAM) also provides opportunities for both educators and learners that are designed to stimulate creativity and curiosity, as well as foster critical thinking. (seattleartmuseum.org/programs-and-learning/schools-and-educators).

Technology Assistance: Blending Formal and Informal

In a number of locations, informal education has rapidly developed in an effort to provide opportunities to students outside of school. Lai, Khaddage, and Knezek (2013) suggested educators consider the "importance of recognizing students' technology-enhanced informal learning experiences and develop pedagogies to connect students' formal and informal learning experiences to meet the demands of the knowledge society" (p. 414). In a number of locations, informal education has rapidly developed in an effort to provide opportunities to students outside of school.

Cox (2013) reminded us, "Research into students' use of IT outside formal settings has shown that many school students use IT outside school even more than in school, and learning outside school is equally important in young peoples' development" (p. 15). Barron (2006) submitted that the literature on the importance of authenticity to learning is focused on either the formal or informal curriculum; therefore, it is important to look more closely at the interaction between the two. Literature on informal learning suggests that participants are "inclined to tinker, experiment, and 'mess around' with things as settings are relaxed and the stakes are low" (Hung et al., 2012, pp. 1077–78); more importantly, it is essential to find ways to blend both (Shimic & Jevremovic, 2012). Erstad (2012) encouraged a view of "learning lives" as a way to examine all aspects of the ways in which learning occurs throughout one's life experiences. She reported that the two most time-consuming aspects of youths' living are formal school and media use and suggested that "young people as learners move between different contexts of learning, both offline and online, in a constant flow of activities" (p. 26).

One example is the Pittsburgh Kids+Creativity effort to bring together libraries, museums, and other entities to support both STEM and makerspaces under the umbrella term of Remake Learning. (Read more about this program in Spotlight 8.4.) Gregg Behr of the Grable Foundation stated, "Today, new pioneers—gamers, roboticists, technologists, and designers—are working alongside educators in and out of schools to inspire and provoke creativity and curiosity among children and youth in the Pittsburgh region" (Behr, personal communication, 2017). While this effort has produced amazing results, they are also interested in bringing together the formal educational experiences of learners. Recently, the groups involved in all aspects of these efforts in western Pennsylvania and West Virginia joined together to form a new organization, the Remake Learning Council.

According to Jones, Scanlon, and Clough (2013),

> Mobile technologies can support learning across different contexts as their portability enables them to be used by the learner in whichever context she or he is in. They can be particularly beneficial in informal and semiformal contexts where learners have more control over their learning goals and where motivation is often high. (p. 22)

Museums, for example, bring students in for focused experiences—not just once but for ongoing learning opportunities. Many libraries offer multiple opportunities for students to explore their creativity. Additionally, grants are given to universities to develop actual technology systems for schools using design-based development and rapid prototyping.

An example is the Providence After School Alliance (PASA), developed by a collaborative group in Providence, Rhode Island, and supported by the Providence City Council. They offer middle and high school students an opportunity outside their regular school program; designed around a "personalized student experience," students can earn elective high school credit as well as digital badges. Digital badges are "an assessment and credentialing mechanism" that are managed online and are a way to make visible the learning that occurs in formal and informal settings (macfound.org/programs/digital-badges). The PASA organization supports learners by promoting validation that these badges act as public signifiers of the skills each student has acquired outside the classroom. These badges are placed in online portfolios, and potential employers, community members, and college admission offices can see the badges and the work that led to them.

It is worth considering this thoughtful reminder from Vygotsky (1997),

> Ultimately, only life educates, and the deeper that life, the real world, burrows into the school, the more dynamic and the more robust will be the educational process. That the school has been locked away and walled in as if by a tall fence from life itself has been its greatest failing. Education is just as meaningless outside the real world as is a fire without oxygen, or as is breathing in a vacuum. The teacher's educational work, therefore, must be inevitably connected with his (or her) creative, social, and life work. (p. 345)

Other Examples

Vossoughi, Hooper, and Escudé (2016) call for attention to pedagogy in ways that provide an explicit focus on the role of elders and mentors in young people's development, so that the creation of social relationships is truly the primary outcome rather than a secondary one. There is a debate surrounding the value of informal learning as it relates to measurable outcomes and the impact of such learning on performance in the workplace or classroom (Strimel et al., 2014, p. 49). This leads to the nature of the trend now to integrate formal and informal learning opportunities to expand what either can do alone. It is also important to consider the teacher's role; teachers have expressed their challenges and the difficulty of giving up "control" of the classroom, letting go of the techniques and philosophy that were emphasized in their teacher training (Steele, 2001).

NASA has developed projects designed for learners of all ages and has connected these projects to schools. As an example, during the August 2017 total solar eclipse, they promoted the idea of everyone collecting data and sending it back to the scientists. Through its Global Learning and Observations to Benefit the Environment (GLOBE) project, NASA sent an invitation for all to become citizen scientists (nasa.gov/feature/goddard/2017/nasa-invites-you-to-become-a-citizen-scientist-during-us-total-solar-eclipse). The GLOBE project is a NASA-supported research and education program that encourages students and citizen scientists to collect and analyze environmental observations. GLOBE Observer is a free, easy-to-use app that guides citizen scientists through data collection (available at observer.globe.gov/about/get-the-app). This program routinely has a few challenges going at any one time.

Blending Formal and Informal for Preservice and Practitioners

A number of studies have looked at the use of informal learning for preservice and in-service educators, with a general conclusion that the involvement of all teachers in nonformal educational settings such as science museums should be part of teacher training and professional development (DeWitt & Osborne, 2007). For example, Kelly (2000) incorporated visits to the Museum of Science and History into a science methods course and found that it increased their content and pedagogical knowledge; further, the future science teachers exhibited increased confidence in becoming excellent educators. Anderson, Lawson, and Mayer-Smith (2006) investigated the impact of a three-week aquarium practicum experience on secondary preservice biology teachers; their study demonstrated improved awareness of connections between practice and theory and increased their ability to plan curriculum. An unexpected outcome was their increased awareness of the role of collaboration.

Further, Popovic and Lederman (2015) sought to increase teachers' understanding of the relationship between mathematical concepts and scientific phenomenon by investigating mathematics in science museum exhibits. They found that "by investigating mathematics in the science museum exhibits, the teachers became aware of the ways in which mathematical concepts could be used to explain scientific phenomena" (p. 138). They concluded, "In particular, mathematics content courses should include modeling real-world phenomena activities, which will provide prospective teachers with opportunities to apply their knowledge of concepts covered in class to solving real-world problems" (p. 139).

Summary

This chapter has focused on the effort and collaboration between formal, nonformal, and informal educational entities to improve education and opportunities for all students. It explored the rich context of 21st Century Community Learning Centers and the incredible opportunities available to learners in a wide variety of locations. It also provided information about museums, both science- and nonscience-related, and the ways in which they are engaging with schools, the general community, and often, distant audiences. It offered a glimpse into virtual field trips, including new virtual reality trips. Educators who reach out to blend the formal/nonformal/informal educational experiences will be incorporating the following ISTE standards for students and for themselves as educators.

ISTE STUDENT STANDARDS ADDRESSED IN THIS CHAPTER

Standard 1: Empowered Learner	Students leverage technology to take an active role in choosing, achieving and demonstrating competency in their learning goals, informed by the learning sciences.
Standard 3: Knowledge Constructor	Students critically curate a variety of resources using digital tools to construct knowledge, produce creative artifacts and make meaningful learning experiences for themselves and others.
Standard 4: Innovative Designer	Students use a variety of technologies within a design process to identify and solve problems by creating new, useful or imaginative solutions.

ISTE EDUCATOR STANDARDS ADDRESSED IN THIS CHAPTER

Standard 4: Collaborator	Educators dedicate time to collaborate with both colleagues and students to improve practice, discover and share resources and ideas, and solve problems.
Standard 5: Designer	Educators design authentic, learner-driven activities and environments that recognize and accommodate learner variability.
Standard 6: Facilitator	Educators facilitate learning with technology to support student achievement of the 2016 ISTE Standards for Students.

Questions and Reflections

- What organizations (museums, libraries, zoos, aquariums, etc.) are in your town, region, or state that may be potential collaborators?

- In what ways could these resources enhance or expand your learners' interests and experiences?

- What organizations around the country or the world have electronic resources or offer electronic field trips to expand or deepen your curriculum?

- Who are the stakeholders who will need to support or approve these relationships?

- What resources (fiscal, material, etc.) will you need to secure to support this relationship?

Further Resources to Get Started

Open Educational Resources (Free)

Education Development Center

(www.edc.org/resources) A nonprofit organization that works to improve education, health, and economic opportunity worldwide, offering many free resources.

Smithsonian Kids

(www.si.edu/Kids) Resources for children from across the Smithsonian Institution, including access to each museum's webpage. A separate educator page hosts activities and a forum.

NGAKids

(www.nga.gov/content/ngaweb/education/kids.html) The National Gallery of Art's webpage offers resources, games, and interactive art projects. Children can download images from the collection search page.

Exploratorium

(www.exploratorium.edu) Resources for children include virtual science labs. Educator resources include Tools for Teaching and Learning.

MoMA

(www.moma.org/learn/kids_families/index) The Museum of Modern Art offers classroom resources and an online search of the collection. Children ages five to eight can explore works of art, artists, and their techniques at the interactive Destination Modern Art (www.moma.org/interactives/destination/#).

British Museum

(www.britishmuseum.org) Among its many online offerings is Teaching History With 100 Objects (www.teachinghistory100.org), which includes information and teaching ideas.

North Carolina Museum of History

(ncmuseumofhistory.org) This museum offers opportunities to explore their exhibits from a distance to educators and families.

Carnegie Museum of Art

(www.cmoa.org/kids-and-families) This is a great site to suggest to families to allow exploration of works of art.

National Building Museum

(www.nbm.org; www.nbm.org/familieskids/teens-young-adults/cityvision.html) This site offers opportunities to study architecture and buildings as an informal activity.

Making Teachers Nerdy: Best Online Interactive Museum Exhibits for Students

(mrssmoke.onsugar.com/Best-Online-Interactive-Museum-Exhibits-Students-2871369) This is a rich resource to help teachers infuse museum opportunities for all ages.

Smithsonian National Air and Space Museum

(airandspace.si.edu/explore-and-learn/topics/discovery) A microsite devoted to the space shuttle Discovery.

Smithsonian National Museum of American History

(amhistory.si.edu/starspangledbanner/default.aspx) A microsite devoted to The Star-Spangled Banner.

United States Botanic Gardens

(www.usbg.gov) Take a tour of the U.S. botanical gardens as part of a learning center or embedded in a curricular activity.

Digital Public Library of America

(dp.la/primary-source-sets) Offers digital primary sources, plus other electronic resources.

Books That May Be of Interest

Philips, L., & Aaron, R. (2012). *The artistic edge: 7 skills children need to succeed in an increasingly right brain world.* New York, NY: Author.

Rosenstein, A. (2014). *10 fresh ways to incorporate technology into your classroom.* New York, NY: Scholastic.

CHAPTER **8**

Lessons Learned, Emerging Themes, and Looking Forward

If you attempt to implement reforms but fail to engage the culture of a school, nothing will change.

—Seymour Sarason

Give the pupils something to do, not something to learn; and the doing is of such a nature as to demand thinking, learning naturally results

—John Dewey

In This Chapter:

- What lessons and themes can be extracted from the previous chapters to inform your practice?

- How do these themes and educational imperatives interact and inform each other?

- What exemplars can we look to for guidance in making changes within a school? A district? A community? Within a larger context?

- What newer technologies are heading toward educational environments?

Lessons Learned and Emerging Themes

The most exhilarating and interesting thing about writing a book like this one is our ability to learn lessons from fabulous educators (in formal, nonformal, and informal locations) who we meet in person, online, or serendipitously through colleagues! If one only reads about education in the popular press, one might imagine that nothing very innovative or challenging is happening in the educational environment. We know that is absolutely not the case. As we explained in the Introduction, we have only scratched the surface in finding amazing stories, but from those we have investigated, several themes and lessons have emerged.

Overall, we consistently and continuously encountered four themes in our observations and interviews with our respondents around the globe, and we found the same recommendations from the literature. These themes represent sound educational practice and were evident in public and private schools, whether they were small or large, rural or urban. Of course, none of them were surprising, but it was reassuring that those findings of success were exhibiting similar plans and strategies.

In general, those who were having success were tackling challenges in addition to all the typical things they had to accomplish; that is, they recognized the need to prepare students to take high-stakes tests, yet they were able to modify typical school time allocations, reconfigure spaces, and rethink curriculum to accomplish things they felt were important. Let's unpack the following four areas of innovative implementation.

Theme One: Personalized Learning is Not Just for Learners

As Chapter 5 described, personalized learning (PL) for students has been around for some time, and has gained great popularity, particularly as employed with project-based learning (PBL). This concept includes the idea of providing choices of content, ways to demonstrate knowledge learned, and options for inquiry. However, we witnessed a new approach to employing this concept in assisting educators in their own professional development by applying the same principles and model of personalized learning to them. Rather than a one-size-fits-all model of professional development (especially when this includes bringing in an outside "expert" for a one-day lecture), the schools we saw were allowing individuals to have input into their own professional growth plans.

Educators were allowed to customize the topics they learned about in new and exciting ways. They were free to select or pursue an area of interest, but they were also given the resources to begin to implement their dreams. They might be recognized as a local expert, or even become globally known as an expert in their chosen area of focus. They were encouraged to gain their professional development (for credits, noncredit, or badges), and were given choices as to how they accomplished their goals. They often were given the option of whether to learn online or face-to-face, in small groups or one to one. Their school leader or district often gave them recognition by inviting them to conduct professional development for others, or by giving them leadership responsibilities in their area of expertise. In whatever manner these efforts were personalized, educators were able to celebrate their own skills and knowledge rather than learn something deemed as important for everyone.

Theme Two: Distributed Leadership Supports Innovation

We recognized this model of leadership, as described by Spillane, Halverson, and Diamond (2001) in almost every situation we learned about. The notion behind this concept is that leadership looks beyond what one person can do and looks instead at what each person might bring to a situation, identifies the strengths of the group, and then takes on a challenge collaboratively. Thus, leadership is best understood as moving "beyond an analysis of individual knowledge and consider[s]" what groups can do together (p. 25).

In many of the stories we have described, we witnessed leaders encouraging, celebrating, and sharing individuals' expertise. Someone with knowledge of gamification, for example, was asked to lead an initiative to explore options regarding its implementation for a school. We heard about schools in which local expertise was shared and teachers were given time to support others who had an interest in a particular topic. Teams of teachers were encouraged to find their passion and identify ways to learn about it.

As Spillane et al. reported, "New curricular materials can potentially influence teachers and students, but their potential to effect change in instruction is also dependent on the teachers and students who use the materials" (2001, p. 27). It was clear that the school leaders we interviewed had a deep understanding of the need to involve all stakeholders in implementing any new program, idea, curriculum, or technology for it to succeed and truly change practice. In Chapter 2, we reported about a school in North Carolina that took advantage of an early-release day to give students and teachers options to learn new skills or explore interests that may seldom get time during a typical school week. The enthusiasm was evident from the learners, but also from the teachers who had the chance to share their passions with all age groups.

Theme Three: The Lens of Equity and Access Is Everywhere

It was eye-opening and reassuring to find that many schools and districts filter each and every activity, idea, and plan through the question of equity and access. If some schools do not offer enough Advanced Placement (AP) classes in a large urban district, then how do we level the playing field? Cincinnati Public Schools came up with a creative solution so that the learners can take AP classes online; they were given a laptop and wireless access for their home use. Some districts put Wi-Fi on buses or repositioned their servers so that the community can use them when school is not in session. Some negotiated lower-cost options and packages for Wi-Fi, devices, and internet access for families that need it, and some built community spaces and solutions that involved an entire city.

It is also encouraging to see the number of national and international efforts that are specifically designed to address the inequity of access to digital resources. In particular, nongovernmental agencies, international organizations, and others are working together to solve problems that belong to the entire world. Nemer (2013) conducted research in the favelas of Rio de Janeiro, where one might expect to find no digital resources; however, he investigated the ways in which the community came together to become part of the digital world. Through houses that serve as local area networks (LANs), where high-speed connectivity is available for residents to use for small fees, students and others are accomplishing their own work and studies. According to Omari:

> The internet has become an indispensable part of life in Rio's favelas as much as it has anywhere else in the world. For residents of these communities, internet access and its ability to further a more democratic society are vital for day-to-day living. Accordingly, the availability of the material technologies (namely desktop computers, laptops, tablets, mobile phones, or LAN houses) that facilitate access is essential for a broad range of social, cultural, financial, and political activities that govern life in the favela. (2015, n.p.)

Most importantly, it is clear that the need for equal access (at school, at home, in communities, and beyond) is enormous. In a conversation about digital equity and the many small victories that school districts, organizations, and even cities had accomplished, Dr. Sheryl Abshire, Chief Technology Officer of Calcasieu Parish Public Schools in Lake Charles, Louisiana, became thoughtful and stated, "These are wonderful examples, but it is a much broader problem. To really solve the problem, nationally, the federal and state governments are going to have to step up, put necessary resources behind it, and truly commit to solving the problem" (personal communication, 2017). Thus, this is not an issue that can be ignored; however, it will require a large effort to resolve.

Theme Four: It Takes a Community

The most successful stories we found included attention to cultural norms and history, took advantage of local resources, celebrated students' input and interests, and incorporated the entire world into its plans. From the Sitka 21st Century Community Learning Center program that embraced Native American cultural experiences, to Friday Harbor's Spring Street International School's integration of flora and fauna, to Hong Kong's Harbour School's embrace of its location, and even bringing sharks into a classroom in Ohio, schools everywhere are building curriculum on authentic resources and options.

The reality is that we now have technology widely available to allow the type of interactions described by Amy Rosenstein and her third grade students in Chapter 7, as they Skype with classrooms around the globe. No longer do geography or finances dictate limitations to learners' opportunities. In fact, very few limitations exist if educators and institutions are willing to embrace the opportunities around. We have seen amazing examples of individual classrooms and schools taking advantage of the possibilities. Some of the examples are in a single school, while others are in a district, a community, or the larger educational enterprise.

We invited Dr. Kecia Ray (@keciaray), CEO of the Center for Digital Education (@centerdigitaled), to tell us what she sees as the largest issues facing full implementation of digital education:

> Even though we have a tremendous amount of technology in the world at large, most people use it as an interface for productivity. In general, teacher education programs don't adequately prepare teachers to use technology as an instructional or learning tool. We must help teachers develop a higher level of comfort in adopting technology as a part of their instructional toolkit and we must help them understand how to maximize their teaching

through the use of technology. Additionally, there is a misconception in our society that everything we use in a classroom must improve student achievement. I say misconception because not everything can possibly have a direct correlation to achievement, especially technology. Laptops should never be associated with student achievement any more than a car would be correlated to a safe driver. Instructional software could have such correlation if the teacher and student are using the software properly. We want a silver bullet in our education and we think sometimes that it will be a piece of technology. It is my belief that we have the silver bullet in a caring, effective teacher. The lack of people going into the teaching profession will create a bigger challenge for the quality of public education than any piece of technology ever could. (personal communication, 2017)

She has spoken eloquently about the ways in which we need to think about digital education, and she addresses these themes as well. They are woven through the pages of this book and, more importantly, in schools throughout the world that are moving forward to address disparity and challenges.

Examples Within a School

Some of the examples discussed were in one school, while others were in a district, a community, or the larger educational enterprise. Here are a few very exciting stories that document this interweaving of the themes seen in gathering data for this book.

 SPOTLIGHT 8.1

Supporting Students to Succeed

P.K. Yonge Developmental Research School (@pkyongedrs)
at the University of Florida

Lynda Fender Hayes (@LyndaHayesPKY), Director

P.K. Yonge Developmental Research School is a publicly funded K–12 laboratory school affiliated with the University of Florida since 1934. The school's planning and decision-making framework is shaped by an overriding commitment to equity—equity in opportunity, and success for each and every student no matter who they are or where they come from. The 1,155 students on campus are selected by lottery to intentionally represent the diversity of Florida (and the nation).

P.K. Yonge is in the midst of designing and implementing a K–12 personalized, mastery-based education system that ensures every student has a learning experience that fully prepares them for education and career opportunities beyond high school—that is, P.K. Yonge is moving beyond every student graduating from high school to every student graduating prepared and skilled, and with a plan and a vision for their future.

Striving for equitable learning environments drives P.K. Yonge's goal setting and planning. Professional learning, facility and infrastructure improvements, curriculum choices, instructional strategies, and the implementation of technologies are considered through a Universal Design for Learning framework to design for and respond to learner variability.

P.K. Yonge's ambitious goals drive school planning and choices: every student demonstrating reading proficiency by the end of third grade; every eighth grade student enrolling and succeeding in Algebra I; every ninth grade student taking Biology Honors and Geometry Honors and passing the state end-of-course exams; every student succeeding in an advanced high school math class; and every student successfully completing at least one college course prior to graduation. Most recently, P.K. Yonge collapsed course tracks and now offers an inclusive (both gifted and special education), honors-only learning experience for every student. All teachers are trained in Universal Design for Learning principles to help them embrace and think about designing for learning differences to support student success.

Technology is leveraged as a tool to help teachers reach every student and realize P.K. Yonge's ambitious goals. Technology does not replace P.K. Yonge teachers. Teachers recognize that personal relationships and skilled coaching are instrumental to student learning, engagement, and success. P.K. Yonge now works in a 1:1 learning environment supported by campus-wide wireless access points, extended library hours that provide internet access to all students beyond the end of the school day, and remote internet access for those students lacking such at home. P.K. Yonge issues a personal digital device to every student in grades 6–8, and teachers provide anytime/anywhere learning support through a common learning management system.

P.K. Yonge has been intentional in helping teachers learn how to design curriculums, assessments, and grading practices that afford multiple pathways for students to achieve and demonstrate mastery of essential knowledge and critical skills. In spring of each year for the past six years, P.K. Yonge has offered mini-grant opportunities, called Waves of Innovation, to support teachers' engagement in school-designed online professional learning that leads to teacher-driven curriculum redesign completed during the summer. At the close of each school year, teachers are invited to share their learning and uses of technology to support student learning during a one-day, teacher-led, panel-to-round table, drive-in conference.

P.K. Yonge teachers are engaged in continuous cycles of inquiry as they examine their practices and various sources of data to understand the impact of their work on their students. All faculty members identify an area of practice that they believe can be altered to improve the learning experience of individual students. Each school year now begins with a day devoted to publicly sharing and discussing what each teacher learns through their inquiry during P.K. Yonge's *Annual Inquiries and Investigations Symposium*. Together, P.K. Yonge teachers are designing and testing approaches that inform P.K. Yonge's vision for a personalized, mastery-based education system: a rigorous, meaningful, and engaging learning experience that supports the success of every student, no matter who they are or where they come from.

■ ■ ■ ■ ■

We wonder how many of us would welcome the opportunity to create a new school: to create the structure, identify the vision, and invent the way learners interact and teachers collaborate might be a dream come true. In Queenstown, New Zealand, a community is doing just that. Shotover Primary School started three years ago to meet the needs of a boom in all areas and population growth, and it is an excellent example of developing an educational system that works for all. Their story is in Spotlight 8.2.

SPOTLIGHT 8.2

Embracing Creativity

Shotover Primary School (@shotoverprimary), Queenstown, NZ

Emma Watts (@emmerw), Design, Arts, Technology, and Science (DATS) Specialist

Ms. Watts explained that the vision for the school and for all children is to Create a Climate of Possibility (influenced by Sir Ken Robinson's work). Why bold? Their goal is to "cause learning to happen and to create an environment that does not limit the imagination of the children entrusted into our care" (Shotover Primary School, n.d.). Now in its fourth year, the student population has grown from 80 to more than 450, with learners from first entry until the end of Year 8 (approximately 13 years old). The curriculum of the school is focused on deep learning, and each year a concept is identified for students to learn to learn, through their learning model, activation of their school values (curiosity, growth mindset, collaboration, thinking, and joy), and their capacities (dispositions).

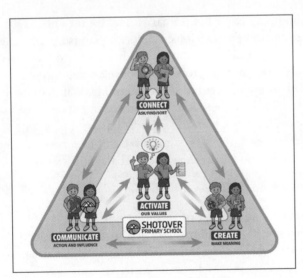

Figure 8.1. Shotover inquiry learning model.

The school is organized into *habitats* that encompass up to four teachers and four classes of learners and that are driven by collaboration, customizable teaching spaces, and a commitment to support each learner's needs. Some are age-specific, but most of them encompass two or three grade levels. The teachers in each habitat plan and work together, personalize learning for students, and live up to the goals of the school.

Ms. Watts' role is to bring all the areas of DATS into the habitats, and she does it with many options for the school. Each habitat has a makerspace, stocked recycled materials, paints and painting tools, hot-glue guns, paper, cardboard, craft knives, glue, and more. There is also one larger central makerspace for the school that includes a 3-D printer, vinyl cutter, and laser cutter, as well as the typical things one might find. Ms. Watts is also very enthusiastic about the coding and robotics program, which includes a wide variety of robots, including Spheros, Edisons, LEGO Mindstorms EV3, Cubettos, mBots, and Blue-Bots. She especially appreciates that the coding with robotics lets learners take their learning into the real world. She ensures, through the many choices, that all learners have the opportunity to explore and participate, rather than only having older learners use the programs.

This school is impressive in many ways, but primarily because the entire staff and community take its vision and goals seriously. Before a plan is implemented or an idea started, it is measured against the vision. It is not assumed that each teacher is an expert in collaboration, thus professional development occurs within each habitat and also among the entire school staff. Ms. Watts compared it to the notion of "hard fun." Part of the school's vision statement on its website includes, "As a 21st century school, teachers and support staff will be highly skilled and work collaboratively to foster safe, supportive and inclusive learning environments that will prepare students to engage in a 21st century world."

It appears that this school lives up to that promise.

Concepts are timeless, abstract, and broad, can be shown through a variety of examples, support an integrated curriculum approach, and help learners to develop generalisations (insight/enduring understanding). This year their concept is "relationships," which gives teachers and learners many possible ways to conceptualize, investigate, and gain deeper understanding of what that means.

▪ ▪ ▪ ▪ ▪

Some examples occur throughout an entire district. Spotlights 8.3 and 8.4 provide two exciting stories about districts making systemwide changes.

SPOTLIGHT 8.3

CPS Tech Truck (@IamCPS)

Megan Safko-Preslin (@msafko27), Technology Training Administrator

Cincinnati Public Schools' *My Tomorrow* initiative is designed to expressively expand equity, access, and opportunity for all students by rethinking the approach of how to build great neighborhood schools. As part of this multiyear and multiphase plan, all schools in the district are working to ensure that all students are prepared with the real-world skills, knowledge, and technical aptitude they need to be successful in the workplace. At the pinnacle of this program is proficiency navigating and using technology. As our world is propelled by technology, CPS understands that it is imperative to shift how we prepare students to not only use technology, but also to be adaptable with its use, as these skills are what jobs of tomorrow will require. In addition to learning how to use state-of-the-art digital devices and software, students are engaged in deeper understandings about the importance of being a responsible digital citizen as they navigate social networks and online platforms.

With all of the emphasis on developing technological aptitude for students, the district recognizes the importance of meeting the professional development needs to retain staff, as well as to attract talented staff who are charged with the implementation of *My Tomorrow*. It was important for the district to create innovative ways for teachers to develop the skills needed to use and teach the latest in technology tools and software. In order to most effectively meet the needs of professional development for a large district with more than 2,300 teaching staff, CPS designed a Digital Learning Truck (Tech Truck for short) as a state-of-the-art mobile classroom outfitted with the technology tools available in the district. The truck and its expert staff travel to all 57 school campuses, on a rotating basis throughout the school year, to train staff on the use of new technology, software, and applications. It is here, in an unintimidating environment, where staff can get hands-on experiences, obtain answers to questions, see new technologies, receive one-on-one training, or even collaborate with their colleagues. Teachers recognize the Tech Truck as a unique and valuable resource to help support their use of technology in the classroom. This on-site, small-group approach has been instrumental in providing the necessary support for teachers to use and incorporate the latest technology into their instruction.

Figure 8.2. Cincinnati Public School teachers engaged in ongoing professional development in the Digital Learning Truck.

Figure 8.3. Inside Cincinnati Public Schools' Digital Learning Truck.

Figure 8.4. Cincinnati Public Schools' Digital Learning Truck ready to roll.

One thing that cannot be overestimated in making an impact is the value of the school leader. Spotlight 8.4 shares the story of one small district and its superintendent's focus on transformative change.

SPOTLIGHT 8.4

Superintendent as Talent Scout!

Sitka School District, Sitka, Alaska

Mary Wegner (@MaryWegnerSitka), Superintendent

Sitka School District is the public school for residents of Sitka, Alaska, which is located on the western edge of Baranof Island in the southeast part of the state. Our community faces the open ocean and is accessible only by boat or plane. In other words, we live on a rock at the edge of the ocean, and as a result we have a strong sense of community and respect for the individual contributions each person offers.

Today Sitka Schools is a proud member of the League of Innovative Schools; however, only a few short years ago, high school students went to our school board to express concern that they were not being adequately prepared for their future, as at the time we did not have a wireless network and the technology we did have was unreliable. Consequently, teachers throughout the district were reluctant to use technology with students. Luckily, the school board listened to the students and made a subsequent commitment to invest in technology, infrastructure, and professional learning so students would be prepared to enjoy success in life.

It is within this context that my leadership skills evolved, first as an assistant superintendent and now as superintendent in Sitka Schools. I entered the scene the first year of implementation of the new technology-rich vision, and within a year and a half our teachers went from little to no use of technology in the classroom to 90% of teachers being at least proficient on the ISTE Standards for Educators. I have long considered myself to be a transformational leader, and I had experienced a great deal of success implementing districtwide educational technology initiatives in my previous positions; however, this was a transition and timeline that not even I expected. We achieved this total transformation through professional learning communities where small groups of teachers explored one aspect of educational technology on a topic of their choosing (e.g., the use of cell phones as a learning tool, technology in a literacy center in a primary classroom, Web 2.0 resources, student-centered learning in a media-rich classroom), coupled with reliable and accessible technology, and yes, wireless broadband.

From those early beginnings, I became a talent scout looking for teachers and groups of teachers who had an idea that pushed the envelope of educational technology use. We then made sure that these teachers had the resources and learning opportunities they needed to implement their idea. The teachers became the lighthouse examples of what can be, which helped their colleagues see in practice what they were learning about in their professional learning communities. Because students were so excited about the learning happening in these teachers' classrooms, parents also became supportive of the district's new direction. I wanted the lighthouse teachers to have a metaphorical microphone to share their ideas and impact, and I helped to amplify their voices and message at every opportunity. The excitement for learning with and through technology spread like wildfire throughout the district and community. In essence, my philosophy and approach gave teachers permission to think expansively about how technology can be used as a learning tool that fosters student voice and agency. A few examples of this includes second grade students using coding skills to solve problems, gamifying a middle school social studies class, students designing the parameters of our district's digital safety technology guidelines, and first grade students learning about wants and needs by programming Ozobots to travel around a community that they socially designed.

The same talent scout process continues today. As I visit classrooms around the district, I am always looking to better understand each teacher's ideas and passion for using technology in their classroom, and I support teachers with resources and encouragement. I consider my efforts to be similar to listening to instrumental music where it is the multitude of specific sounds that helps me to best appreciate the experience the music offers. In essence, I am building an orchestra of teachers, each with their unique voice and passion, who collectively contribute to a culture where students are encouraged to find their own voice and passion.

■ ■ ■ ■ ■

Examples Within a Community

Often multiple stakeholders in a community gather together to improve the entire educational landscape for students across school districts and institutions. Gregg Behr, Executive Director of the Grable Foundation, has promoted and encouraged an educational network known as Remake Learning in the greater Pittsburgh, Pennsylvania, area. He describes the ways in which it has supported innovative educational experiences for all learners in one large community and beyond.

SPOTLIGHT 8.5

Remake Learning (@Remakelearning)

Gregg Behr (@greggbehr), Executive Director, Grable Foundation

Remake Learning's Purpose

Tomorrow's graduates will be asked to face enormous challenges, from climate change to hunger. We believe that to truly prepare learners for this future, we need to move beyond teaching discrete chunks of subject matter. We need to equip them not only with interdisciplinary content knowledge and high-tech tools but also the skills and creativity needed to navigate a rapidly changing society.

What is Remake Learning?

We're a network of more than 500 schools, universities, libraries, start-ups, nonprofits, museums, and others in the Pittsburgh region who work together to ignite engaging, relevant, and equitable learning opportunities for every student. Our members—community leaders, makers, educators, technologists, and more—form partnerships that draw upon and amplify the network's strengths. The Children's Museum of Pittsburgh, for example, works with Carnegie Mellon University to design a makerspace grounded in the latest learning science. Or an edtech firm partners with local teachers to develop a classroom app for kindergartners. A school district shares professional development by opening its cutting-edge STEAM institute to educators from across the region. The learning opportunities our members create leverage technology, art, and science to help learners thrive amid dramatic social and technological shifts.

Where We've Been, Where We're Going

We started as an experiment in collaboration among educators, researchers, mentors, and caring adults. Over the past decade, we've become a movement—one that affects thousands of learners and educators. Together, we're working to turn the region itself into a campus—a place where both formal and informal learning spaces collaborate to help kids think critically, solve complex problems, and collaborate and communicate across cultures. We're working to engage learners by giving them the support and encouragement they need to become active problem solvers, creators, innovators, and advocates. We're working to make learning relevant by connecting it to learners' interests, goals, and lives. And we're working to make it equitable by directing more resources and support to the learners of greatest need.

Moving forward, we're striving to grow our movement by lifting up the voice of every learner, especially those who've been forgotten or pushed aside. Here in Pittsburgh, that means paying particular attention to working alongside learners in poverty, learners of color, learners in rural areas, girls in STEM, and learners with exceptionalities. In 2017, we revamped our mission, vision, and values to reflect this renewed focus. We envision a future in which all the places where learners live, work, and play empower learners to identify and solve problems that affect themselves and their communities; to question, examine, and dissect social systems; to explore, play, and follow their curiosity; and to form deep and caring relationships with families, peers, educators, and mentors.

Lessons Learned Thus Far

We've deliberately designed Remake Learning with a supportive infrastructure that helps our members connect and exchange knowledge across sectors, grow their own professional capacity, and help shape the vision and direction of the network. A small staff provides day-to-day support to network members, coordinates working groups and special initiatives, and champions Remake Learning in communities and in the media. We've also established the Remake Learning Council—a panel of more than 40 regional leaders from the education, government, business, and civic sectors that helps guide our work. We've built partnerships with local and national funders to provide our members with the means to put their ideas into action, whether through small grants that serve to encourage innovation and experimentation or through strategic, sustained initiatives. And we've engaged parents, families, and communities by launching Remake Learning Days, an annual showcase of transformative teaching and learning that draws tens of thousands of people from across the region and around the world, sparking excitement and dialogue about remaking learning.

■ ■ ■ ■ ■

Another way to think about community engagement is one group of educators, or one group of learners, at a time. Chris Clay from Auckland, New Zealand, has developed an interesting approach to opening teachers' thinking up to science and creativity.

SPOTLIGHT 8.6

Open Exploration and Inquiry

Chris Clay (@chrisclaynz), Educational Consultant, Auckland, NZ

If I have seen further, it is by standing on the shoulders of giants.

—Isaac Newton

Whilst we often consider great achievements to be the result of individual endeavour, they are more likely the result of the collective endeavours of an entire knowledge ecosystem. In such an ecosystem, the documented failure of one person increases the likelihood of success of others within the community to which they belong.

James Surowiecki supports this notion in his book, *The Wisdom of Crowds*, and the scientific community is a good example of this in action. Each scientist has a degree to which they are able to operate independently, which leads to the community as a whole developing a wider range of unique ideas. However, rather than simply going off in their own direction, they remain closely connected through conferences, journals, and other media. No single scientist is as intelligent as their crowd, and all scientists benefit from the wide range of ideas and experiences of the crowd to which they belong.

Despite all this, the experiences of students learning science and technology at school are mostly built around highly structured activities. These involve students following predetermined instructions in order to reach an outcome that has also been predetermined by the teacher. Such a structured experience may be of use when guiding an exploration of specific concepts, but it does not reflect the messy and divergent nature of the disciplines of science and technology. If we are to help students learn to deal with our increasingly diverse and multicultural communities and the wicked problems of the Anthropocene, something else is required!

Whilst there has been widespread recognition of the need for students to work collaboratively, in my experience this rarely moves beyond having students cooperate with one another. This is a significant contrast to individuals or small groups working independently and then engaging actively with other people trying to overcome similar challenges using different approaches. If a group is really collaborating, it is more valuable than the sum of its parts. A group of effective collaborators will actively engage in debate and identify areas of consensus and conflict. This will establish the validity of different ideas as well as set the direction for future exploration. Developing these kinds of communities within classrooms became the goal for my own programme of STEM workshops and professional development resources.

The workshops have two main objectives:

- Promote divergent thinking and experimentation between groups
- Develop collective intelligence across groups

Like most practical STEM activities, our workshops are built around open-ended engineering challenges (e.g., how to design and build the loudest possible paper cup speaker). The challenge is presented to students through what we call a "shoddy demonstration" that allows us to provide just the right amount of direction to prevent students from being overwhelmed but not so much they all take the same approach. This should take no more than 5 minutes and is immediately followed by a 20-minute period of open exploration where students prototype in their own small independent groups.

At the end of the 20-minute period of open exploration, the classroom community is convened for a conference. At this point the teacher facilitates a whole-class discussion modeled around the peer-review process, with the aim of building collective intelligence across the group as a whole.

Just like a real scientific conference, our classroom conference involves students making claims about the factors that positively or negatively affect their designs—for example, factors that affect the volume of a paper speaker. At this point the teacher facilitates a class discussion where claims are evaluated based on the critique of any supporting evidence. Finally, each claim is placed along a "consensus vs. conflict continuum" depending upon degree to which the class as a whole agrees or disagrees with the claim. The students are then released to go back into their groups for a second period of open exploration, armed with new insights gathered from the wider community.

During this second period of open exploration, the ideas improve rapidly as a result of the conference. This serves as a great example of the importance of diversity and collective intelligence within a community of innovators. Further conferences are sometimes convened depending upon the collaborative abilities of a group as they seek to develop new practices to help them make the most of their community.

As of this writing, we have started to consider how this might work in other creative areas such as filmmaking, creative writing, and even learning about the future. To find out more, visit www.education-unleashed.com

■ ■ ■ ■ ■

A Bigger Picture

Sometimes the lessons and themes can be seen within a larger context. Below are three examples of implementation and innovation that stretch beyond the walls of a community.

Cincinnati Public Schools (CPS) has created an innovative project as a pilot with the Smithsonian Institution and General Electric Aviation Division (GE). Washington, DC is famous for its museums, of course. The Smithsonian offers the Center for Learning and Digital Access, the History Explorer, Science Game Center, Smithsonian Learning Lab, and a 3-D viewer, including datasets to print some of the museum's artifacts on 3-D printers! It has created these resources for those who can come in person, but also for those who want to visit electronically. They pride themselves on offering more than a million resources, within all content areas, that allow one to create a personal collection of materials. But recently they determined that they needed to do more to engage schools throughout the country in a more formal manner.

SPOTLIGHT 8.7

Virtual Field Trips and Interactive Video Conferences

The Smithsonian Air and Space Museum (@airandspace) and
Cincinnati Public Schools (@IamCPS)

Sandi Sumerfield (@ssumerfield), Consultant

Cincinnati Public Schools (CPS) has partnered with the Smithsonian National Air and Space Museum (NASM) and General Electric Aviation Division (GE) to provide virtual field trips paired with hands-on learning where students experience the Washington, DC, museum without ever leaving their classroom. This exciting project has created a robust partnership that brings real-world STEM experiences to Cincinnati Public Schools students in grades 4–6 via an interactive video conference (IVC). The IVC experience connects to the Ohio Learning Standards in Science and the Next Generation Science Standards (NGSS) for each grade level. The IVCs provide a complement of experts who have contributed to the STEM fields of aerospace engineering, geology, astronomy, chemistry, biology, additive technology, and much more.

During an IVC, students are given global learning experiences on STEM topics, through hands-on application and opportunities to demonstrate their knowledge with one-on-one engagement via videoconference in real time. With the guidance of National Air and Space Smithsonian Explainers (high school and college students specially trained to help visitors interact with museum artifacts), students engage in complex and rich topics such as identifying the importance of learning about gravity, behaviors of light, and why scientist use various types of technology to explore remote celestial bodies, to name just a few. As an example, sixth grade students studying the makeup of rocks and soil have researched characteristics about planets and begun to wonder what equipment scientists would need to explore in conditions very different from those found on Earth. Students are then charged with creating their own version of a Mars Rover that is equipped to operate effectively and efficiently in the challenging conditions it would encounter on the planet. After their research, students build a prototype to present during an IVC. Each experience includes opportunities for students to practice presentation skills to help develop self-confidence and to communicate their research findings and project details. During the presentation, the student-scientists will explain each feature they chose and provide a justification for the need of that specific feature. Explainers provide feedback and then engage students in conversations replete with probing questions to challenge deeper thinking. After their presentations, students will hear from NASA scientists who explain the actual features they considered in creating the Mars Rover, and Explainers will show the real rovers that are located on the floor of the museum.

In addition, students are exposed to information gained in past research, as well as research that is currently underway. This includes up-close historical artifacts that are housed in the museum that have been, and some still currently are, used to conduct the research that they have previously seen from the flat page of a school textbook. Following the IVC, students are engaged in post-IVC activities in their classroom that synthesize information from their independent research with the new concepts learned from their engagement with the explainers. Students and teachers at one CPS location, Rothenberg Academy, were so inspired by the effect the IVC experiences had on students' desire to explore STEM careers that they raised funds to take a trip to Washington, DC, and visit the Air and Space Museum.

These deeply invested partners have created a close relationship and together have painstakingly developed IVC experiences to ensure that the experiences are meaningful and complementary to districts' interactive and engaging science curriculum and provide student exposure to the scientific community as well as STEM careers that are available to them. Engaging lesson plans have been developed that accompany the current district curriculum, while also building student background knowledge prior to the IVC. During the IVC experience, students have an opportunity to present their work, receive feedback from the Explainers, and engage in dialogue that scaffolds their understanding of complex scientific topics they encountered with their projects. After the IVCs, teachers and students engage in post-IVC activities to reinforce big concepts and merge the new learnings to ensure meaningful connections to everyday experiences. "This project is multifaceted in that you have high school and college Explainers unlocking and delivering the national treasures to students in grades 4–6 in an interactive way and aligned to standards," said Mark Kornmann, Associate Director, Education and Public Engagement, Smithsonian National Air and Space Museum (personal communication, 2017).

Michelle Hughes-Linnere (@mission64u), Cincinnati Public Schools Science Curriculum Manager, reflects on the experiences:

> I enjoy seeing the "wow" factor and curiosity illuminated in our students. They find common ground in the fact that scientists, whose research has helped our understanding of natural phenomena and space exploration, were once curious elementary students just like them. This empowers our students to dream big and see themselves as STEM professionals. We have great students who are curious, energetic, and bold dreamers. This is an exciting time for CPS students. I am looking forward to the contribution of these future scientists and engineers. Our role is to provide the inspiration that gives them confidence for their aspirations. I see our students in one of my favorite quotes by Karen Ravn, "Only as high as I reach can I grow, only as far as I seek can I go, only as deep as I look can I see, only as much as I dream can I be." (Hughes-Linnere, personal communication, 2017)

Ultimately, the goal of this incredible experience is to see more CPS students pursuing careers in STEM fields. With this incredible partnership, the goal of equitable access for students has taken a positive step forward; most importantly, it has ignited a passion for the possibilities a STEM career may hold for many.

Figure 8.5. CPS students participating in an IVC. Photo Credit: Sandi Sumerfield, 2016.

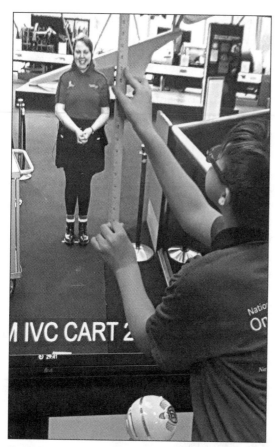

Figure 8.6. CPS student engaging with NASM Explainers during an IVC. Photo Credit: Sandi Sumerfield, 2017.

■ ■ ■ ■ ■

New Zealand is a relatively small country but has taken aim at providing digital age access to every school in the country in a unique way that demonstrates equity of access as well as commitment to a digital age education.

SPOTLIGHT 8.8

New Zealand Network for Learning (@N4LNZ)

Carolyn Stuart (@carolynstuart), Deputy Chief Executive, Education

Network for Learning (N4L) is a government-owned company established in 2012 to provide schools with technology that "just works." Our biggest project to date has been a fully funded "managed network" for New Zealand schools, providing teachers and students with an internet connection that is fast, reliable, and safe. Ninety-eight percent of schools in New Zealand have taken advantage of this initiative.

Teachers can now confidently plan to use technology with their classes without having to worry about what to do if the internet doesn't work. Students have access to a great internet experience that is safe. Leaders can rest easy knowing that we manage any cyber-attacks on their network. All schools on the N4L managed network have access to our web filtering and firewall service, which can be used effectively to protect their school's network against online threats, such as viruses, and to block access to inappropriate content.

We indirectly support teaching about digital citizenship through our close liaison with schools around content filtering. We believe that it is important that everyone is educated around potential threats and viruses. In New Zealand, we work with several other government-funded agencies to ensure that there is a safety net under all users. Our Ministry of Education also provides advice and support to schools on how to keep their students safe online. Each school manages its own policies and procedures around responsible use.

We have built a platform called Pond through which teachers can share and access recommended content with which to deliver the New Zealand curriculum. The New Zealand Qualifications Authority have been using Pond to surface content for teachers, especially in subjects where teachers have found New Zealand-specific content difficult to locate.

N4L was set up originally to ensure that all schools were provided the same equitable digital access regardless of whether they are large, small, or remote, or whatever their socioeconomic status. In addition to our main mission, we are in the early stages of exploring how to provide students from low socioeconomic backgrounds with access to our managed network outside the school day. We understand the disadvantage these students experience when they cannot go home and get online in the same way as their more advantaged peers can. As the person responsible for the education side of the company, I expend quite a lot of time and energy in promoting a national conversation about the rising exponential technologies, and how they might affect education.

■ ■ ■ ■ ■

Finally, let's look at one organization, Google, that has entered the world of education in a very dramatic and robust manner. Its products, Google Apps for Education (GAFE), and many programs are described in the spotlight below.

SPOTLIGHT 8.9

Google and Education: Just the Beginning!

Jaime Casap (@jcasap), Google Education Evangelist

Today, more than half the nation's primary- and secondary-school students—more than 30 million children—use Google education apps such as Gmail and Docs (Singer, 2017). The company's Chromebooks now account for more than half the mobile devices shipped to schools. Equally impressive are the tools available for K–12 schools, which include virtual reality expeditions to "practically anywhere," academic articles through Google Scholar, researching the globe with Google Earth, and lessons to teach students searching skills. Mr. Casap, Google Education Evangelist, explained, "Businesses were using these tools and some educators were, too; we simply added some layers to ensure safety, security, and ease of use, to make these tools better for the educational enterprise" (personal communication, 2017).

Mr. Casap began with Google in 2006 when he was hired to develop new business at Arizona State University in Tempe. He recognized an opportunity; the students were already using Gmail, thus he suggested replacing it with a free version of Google tools. Impressively, a vast majority of the university's approximately 65,000 students signed up in one semester.

From this very successful venture into the postsecondary education market, it was not a difficult transition to the K–12 educational system. In 2010, the Oregon Department of Education made Google applications available to all schools. From there, the spread was rapid and extensive.

Most importantly, Google understands that transformation of education is not a simple or quick process and is not solely connected to the technology. Mr. Casap stated, "I think transformation happens as a constant shift, constantly moving forward. Tools are not the solution; so it happens on Monday, Tuesday, Wednesday, and so on" (personal communication, 2017).

To support this steady and challenging transformation, Google developed support for educators, leaders, and others; it also developed its transformation framework to assist in the process. The framework includes: Vision, Learning, Culture, Professional Development, Technology, Funding & Sustainability, and Community Engagement. They also "set up dozens of online communities, called Google Educator Groups (google.com/landing/geg/groups), where teachers could swap ideas for using its tech. It started training programs with names such as Certified Innovator (edutrainingcenter.withgoogle.com/certification_innovator) to credential teachers who wanted to establish their expertise in Google's tools or teach their peers (edutrainingcenter.withgoogle.com/certification_trainer) to use them" (Singer, 2017, n.p.).

Google continues to develop support and applications for learners. The Chromebook has specific apps and an educational browser with no advertisements. They recognized the disparity that still exists in access to digital resources and the internet; thus, they have worked on a way for learners to use their Chromebooks offline at home and upload their homework when they return to school. It is conducting research on myriad topics, including machine learning. And perhaps most interestingly to schools and universities, they intend to be involved and dedicated to transformation for the foreseeable future.

■ ■ ■ ■ ■

A Look into the Future—Where Do We Go from Here?

Each year the Horizon Report conducts research to gauge the current status of educational technology and to ask leaders in the field to peer into the future to estimate what the next technologies will be and when they may be adopted by mainstream educational institutions. The guiding philosophy behind this study is, "If a school adopts a culture of innovation, then deeper learning is a possibility, plain and simple" (Freeman et al., 2017, p. 3). We have seen rapid implementation of the makerspace movement and a spread in the belief that coding and robotics support STEM initiatives and are useful to assist learners in computational thinking. These two examples are now assumed to be in the category of "time to adoption" of one year or less.

Looking at the areas ready for adoption widely within two to three years, we find the following two specific trends. First, analytics technologies will become much more prevalent in schools. If you think about the ways in which some consumer organizations track your spending, searching, and interests, you will understand how these tools work. While an online video company can recommend the next video you may be interested in, based on what you have seen and enjoyed previously, we can take the same concept to "track student activities, behaviors, performance, and interests to tell a story about individual learners' experiences" and to take these technologies into educational settings to "move from data-rich and information-poor scenarios to data-driven, AI and machine learning" (Freeman, et al., 2017, p. 44).

The second area expected within two to three years is the growth of virtual reality (VR). Virtual reality refers to "computer-generated environments that simulate the physical presence of people and/or objects and realistic sensory experiences" (Freeman, et al., 2017, p. 46). These may be high-end headsets (for example, HTC VIVE or Sony Playstation VR) or more modest sets, such as Google Cardboard. In general, "These content creation tools along with the viewers can make learning more authentic, allow for empathetic experiences, and increase student engagement" (p. 46).

In four to five years, according to estimates (Freeman, et al., 2017), two more technologies will have an impact on education. These are artificial intelligence (AI) and the internet of things. Basically, AI could take tedious tasks away from educators, and instead use massive data sets to assist in students' metacognition or assume virtual assistant tasks (for example, as Amazon's Alexa does). Cortez (2017a, n.p.) suggests, "Of all the areas where AI might work in K–12, the article indicates the potential to create adaptive learning features that personalize tools for each student's learning experience is the biggest." Is it possible that a machine will do all the grading of assignments? Brown (2017) suggests that AI will increase the ability of educators to personalize learning; for example, it could be used to level reading groups, evaluate grammar, and grade mathematical calculations. This would free teachers to work on the more creative or intuitive aspects that we hope students acquire.

The internet of things (IoT) is the second innovative technology that is expected to affect K–12 schools within four to five years (Gupta, 2017). IoT is the connection of smart physical devices to track and monitor life; these devices transmit data via the internet to the cloud, which makes the user's experience "smarter." For example, your exercise tracker lets you know continuously how many steps you've taken, and your refrigerator may keep track of your shopping list. Smart schools are already using connected technologies to keep track of buses or to keep attendance through the use of student smart cards or radio frequency identification (RFID). Using the technology, real-time information could be sent to students, rather than having instantly out-of-date textbooks. Interactive whiteboards, of course, are already in schools and offer potential for the IoT to enhance the experience of using them. Consider whiteboard paint that allows any wall to become a whiteboard; now there is embedded software that allows a wall to work similarly to an interactive whiteboard.

With both of the technologies, however, it is important to consider ways to safeguard privacy and the safety of information and intellectual property. Is it any wonder that schools are a bit overwhelmed by the waves and waves of new technologies; this is especially true when one considers that there is no reduction in the number of things that schools are responsible for. Testing does not disappear; schools are still required to be compared to each other through test scores, even when not all schools have the same resources.

Summary

This chapter has focused on the themes, efforts, and strategies of successful educational entities that have simultaneously integrated technology into learners' lives while being guided by the imperatives of equity, new pedagogy, and the changing landscape of informal and nonformal education. The chapter has offered examples specific to one school, throughout school districts, and to the larger communities and beyond. It challenges others to identify ways to learn from these exemplars, to weave these ideas through one's own culture, context, and demographics.

We again asked Dr. Kecia Ray to think about the future, and to tell us what makes her most hopeful about education and the future. She replied,

> When I began my teaching career in 1983, I couldn't imagine having access to the tools we have access to today as teachers and as learners. Today, teachers are able to use technologies to engage students, to facilitate student collaboration within their school and beyond, and students are able to create products they could never have created in the early '80s. Several studies show that the use of technology for blended learning increases academic achievement by at least 10%. Learners today are comfortable with technology and the classroom shouldn't be absent of tools they would have ready access to in their world. (personal communication, 2017)

Education offers the opportunity to support learners in authentic and meaningful learning, help them recognize the interconnectedness of our world, and level the playing field so that each of them may reach his or her own goals and full potential.

It is an exciting time to be an educator, a parent, or a learner!

Epilogue

This book has brought together information from currently popular areas of technology implementation within a framework of the forces that have always been important and valuable to educators and to education in general. What is most impressive is the manner in which the educators presented in this book, and the thousands of others not in this book, are able to manage to balance on the tightrope that spans all the imperatives required of today's education professionals.

The demands on the educational system will continue to increase, and this is happening at a time when fewer individuals choose to become teachers. It is therefore incumbent on all of us to make their career path a desirable one, to celebrate those master teachers who remain steadfast in their commitment to education, and to elevate the importance and value of their work and of the learners in each classroom.

References

Abel, N. (2016, February 17). *What is personalized learning?* [Blog post]. Retrieved from www.inacol.org/news/what-is-personalized-learning

Abram, S., & Dysart, J. (2014). The maker movement and the library movement: Understanding the makerspaces opportunity. *Feliciter, 60*(1), 11–13.

Acedo, M. (2017). 10 specific ideas to gamify your classroom. Retrieved from www.teachthought.com/pedagogy/how-to-gamify-your-classroom

Adedokun, O. A., Hetzel, K., Parker, L. C., Loizzo, J., Burgess, W. D., & Robinson, J. P. (2012). Using virtual field trips to connect students with university scientists: Core elements and evaluation of zipTrips. *Journal of Science and Educational Technology, 21*, 607–618. doi.org/10.1007/s10956-011-9350-z

Alimisis, D. (2013). Educational robotics: Open questions and new challenges. *Themes in Science & Technology Education, 6*(1), 63–71.

Alliance for Excellent Education. (2017). *About personalized learning.* Retrieved from all4ed.org/issues/personalized-learning/key-resources/about-personalized-learning

Alliance for Excellent Education. (2017). Advancing digital equity—education groups urge leaders to address national challenge [Press release]. Retrieved from all4ed.org/press/advancing-digital-equity-education-groups-urge-leaders-to-address-national-challenge

Anderson, D., Lawson, B., & Mayer-Smith, J. (2006). Investigating the impact of a practicum experience in an aquarium on preservice teachers. *Teaching Education, 17*(4), 341–353.

Anderson, M. (2017). Digital divide persists even as lower-income Americans make gains in tech adoption. Retrieved from www.pewresearch.org/fact-tank/2017/03/22/digital-divide-persists-even-as-lower-income-americans-make-gains-in-tech-adoption

Association for Experiential Education. (n.d.). *What is experiential education?* Retrieved from www.aee.org/what-is-ee

Azriel, J. A., Erthal, M. J., & Starr, E. (2005). Answers, questions, and deceptions: What is the role of games in business education? *Journal of Education for Business, 81*(1), 9–13.

Barron, B. (2006). Interest and self-sustained learning as catalysts of development: A learning ecology perspective. *Human Development, 49,* 193–224.

Basye, D. (2016, October 23). *Personalized vs. differentiated vs. individualized learning* [Blog post]. Retrieved from www.iste.org/explore/articledetail?articleid=124

Beckett, G. H., Hemmings, A., Maltbie, C., Wright, K., Sherman, M., & Sersion, B. (2016). Urban high school student engagement through CincySTEM iTEST projects. *Journal of Science Education and Technology, 25*(6), 995–1007. doi.org/10.1007/s10956-016-9640-6

Bendici, R. (2017). Flexibility for the future. *District Administration, 53*(8), 32–36.

Benesch, S., Ruths, D., Dillon, K. P., Mohammad Saleem, H., & Wright, L. (2017). Considerations for successful counterspeech. From the research project, *Evaluating Methods to Diminish Expressions of Hatred and Extremism Online.* Retrieved from publicsafety.gc.ca/cnt/ntnl-scrt/cntr-trrrsm/r-nd-flght-182/knshk/ctlg/dtls-en.aspx?i=119

Benitti, F. B. V. (2012). Exploring the educational potential of robotics in schools: A systematic review. *Computers & Education, 58*(3), 978–988.

Bers, M. U., Flannery, L., Kazakoff, E. R., & Sullivan, A. (2014). Computational thinking and tinkering: Exploration of an early childhood robotics curriculum. *Computers & Education, 72,* 145–157. doi.org/10.1016/j.compedu.2013.10.020

Bevan, B., Petrich, M., & Wilkinson, K. (2015). Tinkering is serious play. *Educational Leadership, 72*(4), 28–33.

Bolkan, J. W. (2014). 13 resources to help you teach digital citizenship. *THE Journal, 42,* 21–23.

Boss, S., & Krauss, J. (2014). *Reinventing project-based learning: Your field guide to real-world projects in the digital age* (2nd ed.). Eugene, OR: International Society for Technology in Education.

Bozkurt Altan, E., & Ercan, S. (2016). STEM education program for science teachers: Perceptions and competencies. *Journal of Turkish Science Education, 13*(Special Issue), 103–117.

Brahms, L., & Wardrip, P. S. (2014). *Learning practices of making: An evolving framework for design.* Pittsburgh, PA: Children's Museum of Pittsburgh.

Brahms, L., & Wardrip, P. S. (2016a). Learning practices of making. *Teaching Young Children, 9*(6).

Brahms, L., & Wardrip, P. S. (2016b). Making with young learners. *Teaching Young Children, 9*(5).

Brahms, L., & Werner, J. (2013). Designing makerspaces for family learning in museums and science centers. In M. Honey & D. E. Kanter (Eds.), *Design, make, play: Growing the next generation of STEM Innovators* (pp. 71–94). New York, NY: Routledge.

Bray, B., & McClaskey, K. (2014, June 11). Personalize your learning environment [Blog post]. Retrieved from www.iste.org/explore/ArticleDetail?articleid=11

Brown, A. (2017, October 12). AI is on the upswing in optimizing K–12 education. *Ed Tech Magazine.* Retrieved from edtechmagazine.com/k12/article/2017/10/ai-upswing-optimizing-k-12-education

The Buck Institute for Education. (2013). *Research summary: PBL and 21st-century competencies.* Retrieved from www.bie.org/object/document/research_summary_on_the_benefits_of_pbl

Bullock, S. M., & Sator, A. J. (2015). Maker pedagogy and science teacher education *Journal of the Canadian Association for Curriculum Studies, 13*(1), 60–87.

Burguillo, J. (2010). Using game theory and competition-based learning to stimulate student motivation and performance. *Computers & Education, 55,* 566–575.

Burke, J. J. (2014). *Makerspaces: The practical guide for librarians.* Lanham, MD: Rowan & Littlefield.

Burrows, A. C. (2015). Partnerships: A systemic study of two professional developments with university faculty and K-12 teachers of science, technology, engineering, and mathematics. *Problems of Education in the 21st Century, 65,* 27–38.

California Tinkering Afterschool Program. (2017). California tinkering afterschool network. Retrieved from www.exploratorium.edu/education/california-tinkering-afterschool-network

Campbell, P. J. (2016). Coding for all? [Editorial]. *The UMAP Journal, 37*(4), 333–337.

Catapano, J. (n.d). Technology in the classroom: Google's virtual field trips. *TeachHub.com*. Retrieved from www.teachhub.com/technology-classroom-googles-virtual-field-trips

Center for Advancement of Informal Science Education. (2017). What is informal Science? Retrieved from informalscience.org/what-informal-science

Center for Digital Education. (2017). *Closing the homework gap with digital equity.* Folsom, CA: Author.

Centers for Disease Control and Prevention. (2016). The 2015 youth risk behavior surveillance system. Retrieved from www.cdc.gov/healthyyouth/data/yrbs/index.htm

Change the Equation. (2015). Solving the diversity dilemma: Changing the face of the STEM workforce. Retrieved from changetheequation.org/solving-diversity-dilemma

Charania, A., & Davis, N. (2016). A smart partnership: Integrating educational technology for underserved children in India. *Educational Technology & Society,* 19(3), 99–109.

Children's Museum of Pittsburgh. (2014). Making Spaces. Retrieved from makeshoppgh.com/2017/04/06/making-spaces

Chin, J.-C., & Tsuei, M. (2014). A multi-modal digital game-based learning environment for hospitalized children with chronic illnesses. *Educational Technology & Society,* 17(4), 366–378.

Chung, C. J. C., Cartwright, C., & Cole, M. (2014). Assessing the impact of an autonomous robotics competition for STEM education. *Journal of STEM Education,* 15(2), 24–34.

City of Portland, Oregon. (n.d.) *Digital Equity Action Plan (DEAP)*. Retrieved from www.portlandoregon.gov/revenue/73863

City of Seattle. (n.d.) Seattle information technology | Technology matching fund. Retrieved from seattle.gov/tech/initiatives/digital-equity/technology-matching-fund

Clapp, E. P., Ross, J. , Oxman Ryan, J., & Tishman, S. (2016). *Maker-Centered Learning: Empowering Young People to Shape their Worlds*. San Francisco, CA: Jossey-Bass.

ClassCraft. (2014). The classroom is changing. Retrieved from classcraft.com/overview

Code.org. (2018). Promote computer science. Retrieved from code.org/promote

Code.org. (2018). About us. Retrieved from code.org/about

CodeClub. (n.d.). About code club. Retrieved from www.codeclub.org.uk/about

Collier, A. (2017, July 18). 6 takeaways from 20 years of Net safety: Part 1. Retrieved from www.netfamilynews.org/6-takeaways-20-years-writing-net-safety-part-1

Consortium for School Networking (CoSN). (2014). *CoSN's 2nd annual E-rate and infrastructure survey.* Washington, DC: Author.

Consortium for School Networking (COSN). (2017). *2017 K–12 IT leadership survey report.* Washington, DC: Author.

Cortez, M. B. (2017a, July 12). AI in education will grow exponentially by 2021. *Ed Tech Magazine.* Retrieved from edtechmagazine.com/k12/article/2017/07/ai-education-will-grow-exponentially-2021

Cortez, M. B. (2017b, August 30). Student privacy: A back-to-school refresh. *EdTech Magazine.* Retrieved from edtechmagazine.com/k12/article/2017/08/student-privacy-back-school-refresh

Costa, C. (2017). Robotics K-12 and your district: The essence of STEM education and the e-ticket to unlimited possibilities. *Leadership, 46*(4), 32–35.

Cox, M. (2013). Formal to informal learning with IT: Research challenges and issues for e-learning. *Journal of Computer Assisted Learning, 28*(1), 85-105.

Crawford, L., & Huscroft-D'Angelo, J. (2015). Mission to space: Evaluating one type of informal science education. *Electronic Journal of Science Education, 19*(1), 1–25.

Darling-Hamilton, L., Zielezinski, M., & Goldman, S. (2014). *Using technology to support at-risk students' learning.* Palo Alto, CA: Alliance for Excellent Education, Stanford Center for Opportunity Policy for Education.

Davee, S., Regalla, L., & Chang, S. (2015, May). Makerspaces: Highlights of select literature. Retrieved from makered.org/wp-content/uploads/2015/08/Makerspace-Lit-Review-5B.pdf

Deci, E. L., & Ryan, R. M. (2000). Intrinsic and extrinsic motivations: Classic definitions and new directions. *Contemporary Educational Psychology, 25*(1), 54–67. doi.org/10.1006/ceps.1999.1020

Delaney, M. (2014, October 9). Meet the new school of digital citizenship. EdTech Magazine. Retrieved from edtechmagazine.com/k12/article/2014/10/upright-citizens-brigade

Deterding, S., Dixon, D., Khaled, R., & Nacke, L. (2011). From game design elements to gamefulness: Defining gamification. In H. Franssila, C. Safran, & I. Hammouda (Eds.), *Proceedings of the 15th International Academic MindTrek Conference: Envisioning Future Media Environments* (pp. 9–15). New York, NY: AMC.

DeWitt, J., & Osborne, J. (2007). Supporting teachers on science-focused school trips: Towards an integrated framework of theory and practice. *International Journal of Science Education, 29*(6), 685–710.

Dickey, M. (2007). Game design and learning: A conjectural analysis of how massively multiple online role-playing games (MMORPGs) foster intrinsic motivation. *Educational Technology, Research and Development, 55*(3), 253–273.

Digital Equity. (2016). Digital equity + opportunity for all. Retrieved from digitalequityforlearning.org

Divjak, B., & Tomic, D. (2011). The impact of game-based learning on the achievement of learning goals and motivation for learning mathematics – literature review. *JIOS, 35*(1), 15–30.

Dixit, A., & Nalebuff, B. (2008). Game theory. *The Concise Encyclopedia of Economics.* Retrieved from www.econlib.org/library/Enc/GameTheory.html

Dotterer, G., Hedges, A., & Parker, H. (2016). Fostering digital citizenship in the classroom. *Education Digest, 81,* 58–63.

Dourda, K., Bratitsis, T., Griva, E., & Papadopoulou, P. (2014). Content and language integrated learning through an online game in primary school: A case study. *Electronic Journal of E-Learning, 12*(3), 243–258.

Echegaray, C. (2015, February 5). Mobile makerspace provides patients tools to create, inspire. *ResearchNews @Vanderbilt.* Retrieved from news.vanderbilt.edu/2015/02/mobilemakerspace-provides-patients-tools-to-create-inspire

Eguchi, A. (2010). What is educational robotics? Theories behind it and practical implementation. In D. Gibson & B. Dodge (Eds.), *Proceedings of Society for Information Technology & Teacher Education International Conference 2010* (pp. 4006–4014). Chesapeake, VA: AACE.

Ehrhardt, G. (2008). Beyond the "prisoner's dilemma": Making game theory a useful part of undergraduate international relations classes. *International Studies Perspectives, 9,* 57–74.

Erstad, O. (2012). The learning lives of digital youth: Beyond the formal and informal. *Oxford Review of Education, 38*(1), 25–43.

Eshach, H. (2007). Bridging in-school and out-of-school learning: Formal, non-formal, and informal education. *Journal of Science Education and Technology, 16*(2), 171–190. doi.org/10.1007/s10956-006-9027-1

Eseryel, D., Law, V., Ifenthaler, D., Ge, X., & Miller, R. (2014). An investigation of the interrelationships between motivation, engagement, and complex problem solving in game-based learning. *Educational Technology & Society, 17*(1), 42–53.

Farber, M. (2018). *Game-based learning in action: How an expert affinity group teaches with games*. New York, NY: Peter Lang.

Federal Reserve Bank of Dallas. (2016). Closing the digital divide: A framework for meeting CRA obligations. Retrieved from www.dallasfed.org/assets/documents/cd/pubs/digitaldivide.pdf

Feldstein, M., & Hill, P. (2016). Personalized learning: What is really is and why it really matters. *EDUCAUSE Review, 51*(2). Retrieved from er.educause.edu/articles/2016/3/personalized-learning-what-it-really-is-and-why-it-really-matters

Fesler, J., & Palmieri, C. (2017). Tribeworthy team creates a social network where everyone can practice media literacy. Available: medialiteracynow.org/tribeworthy-team-creates-a-social-network-where-everyone-can-practice-media-literacy

Filippoupoliti, A., & Koliopoulos, D. (2014). Informal and non-formal education: An outline of history of science in museums. *Science & Education, 23*, 781–791.

Fishman, B., Riconscente, M., Snider, R., Tsai, T., & Plass, J. (2014). *Empowering educators: Supporting student progress in the classroom with digital games*. Ann Arbor, MI: University of Michigan. Retrieved from: gamesandlearning.umich.edu/a-games/downloads

Fleming, L. (2015). *Worlds of making: Best practice for establishing a makerspace in your school*. Thousand Oaks, CA: Corwin.

Fleming, L. (2016). A maker culture. *Principal, 95*(4), 16–19.

Fleming, L. (2018). *The kickstart guide to making great makerspaces*. Thousand Oaks, CA: Corwin.

Fluck, A., Webb, M., Cox, M., Angeli, C., Malyn-Smith, J., Voogt, J., & Zagami, J. (2016). Arguing for computer science in the school curriculum. *Journal of Educational Technology & Society, 19*(3), 38–46.

Freeman, A., Adams Becker, S., Cummins, M., Davis, A., & Hall Giesinger, C. (2017). *NMC/CoSN Horizon Report: 2017 K–12 Edition.* Austin, TX: The New Media Consortium.

Gabrielson, C. (2013). *Tinkering: Kids learn by making stuff.* Sebastopol, CA: Maker Media.

Gee, J. P. (2005). *Why video games are good for your soul: Pleasure and learning.* Melbourne, Australia: Common Ground.

Gee, J. P. (2008). Learning and games. In K. Salen (Ed.), *The ecology of games: Connecting youth, games, and learning* (pp. 21–40). Cambridge, MA: The MIT Press. doi.org/10.1162/dmal.9780262693646.021

Gerber, B. L., Marek, E. A., & Cavallo, A. M. L. (2001). Development of an informal learning opportunities assay. *International Journal of Science Education, 23*(6), 569–583.

Gerstein, J. (2016). Becoming a maker educator. *Techniques: Connecting Education & Careers, 91*(7), 14–19.

Gibson, D., Coleman, K., & Irving, L. (2016). Learning journeys in higher education: Designing digital pathways badges for learning, motivation, and assessment. In D. Ifenthaler, N. Bellin-Mularski, & D.-K. Mah (Eds.), *Foundation of digital badges and micro-credentials* (pp. 115–138). New York, NY: Springer.

Gierdowski, D., & Reis, D. (2015). The MobileMaker: An experiment with a mobile makerspace. *Library Hi Tech, 33*(4), 480–496.

Gómez-Pablos, V., Del Pozo, M., & Muñoz-Repiso, A. (2016). Project-based learning through the incorporation of digital technologies: An evaluation based on the experience of serving teachers. *Computers in Human Behavior, 68,* 501–512.

Google Inc. & Gallup Inc. (2016). *Trends in the state of computer science in U.S. K–12 schools.* Retrieved from services.google.com/fh/files/misc/trends-in-the-state-of-computer-science-report.pdf

Google for Education. (n.d.).

Grant, S. L. (2017, January). Digital badging: The practice of recognizing discrete skills so students can communicate more meaningful aspects of who they are and what they know. *School Administrator,* 17–20.

Greaves, T., Hayes, J., Wilson, L., Gielniak, M., & Peterson, R. (2010). *The technology factor: Nine keys to student achievement and cost-effectiveness.* Shelton, CT: Marketing Data Retrieval.

Greenhow, C., Walker, J. D., & Kim, S. (2009). Millennial learners and net-savvy teens? Examining Internet use among low-income students. *Journal of Computing in Teacher Education, 26*(2), 63–68.

Gros, B. (2007). Digital games in education: The design of games-based learning environments. *Journal of Research on Technology in Education, 40*(1), 23–38.

Gudmundsdottir, G. B. (2010). From digital divide to digital equity: Learners' ICT competence in four primary schools in Cape Town, South Africa. *International Journal of Education and Development using Information and Communication Technology* (IJEDICT), *6*(2), 84-105.

Gupta, P. (2017, July 14). The Internet of things (IoT) and its significance in education. *EdTech Review.* Retrieved from edtechreview.in/trends-insights/trends/2855-internet-of-things-iot-in-education

Halverson, E., & Sheridan, K. (2014). The maker movement in education. *Harvard Educational Review, 84*(4), 495–505. doi.org/10.17763/haer.84.4.34j1g68140382063

Harris, W. (2013, December 12). Albemarle schools' maker spaces program gets national attention. *NBC29.* Retrieved from www.nbc29.com/story/24201428/albemarle-schools-maker-spaces-program-gets-national-attention

Haskell, C. (2015). *Play this, learn that* [iBooks]. Retrieved from itunes.apple.com/us/book/play-this-learn-that/id1000085917?mt=11

Hatch, M. (2014). *The maker movement.* New York, NY: McGraw-Hill.

Hernandez, P. R., Bodin, R., Elliott, J. W., Ibrahim, B., Rambo-Hernandez, K. E., Chen, T. W., & de Miranda, M. A. (2014). Connecting the STEM dots: measuring the effect of an integrated engineering design intervention. *International Journal of Technology and Design Education, 24*(1), 107–120.

Hohlfeld, T. N., Ritzhaupt, A. D., Barron, A. E., & Kemker, K. (2008). Examining the digital divide in K-12 public schools: Four-year trends for supporting ICT literacy in Florida. *Computers & Education, 51*(4), 1648–1663.

Hohlfeld, T. N., Ritzhaupt, A. D., Dawson, K., & Wilson, M. L. (2017). An examination of seven years of technology integration in Florida schools: Through the lens of the levels of digital divide in schools. *Computers & Education, 113,* 135–161.

Hung, D., Lee, S.-S., & Lim, K. Y. T. (2012). Authenticity in learning for the twenty-first century: Bridging the formal and the informal. *Educational Technology Research and Development, 60,* 1071-1091.

Intel. (2014). MakeHers: Engaging girls and women in technology through making, creating, and inventing. Retrieved from www.intel.com/content/www/us/en/technology-in-education/making-her-future-report.html

Jones, A. C., Scanlon, E., & Clough, G. (2013). Mobile learning: Two case studies of supporting inquiry learning in informal and semiformal settings. *Computers & Education, 61,* 21–32.

Jong, M. S.-Y., & Shang, J. (2015). Impending phenomena emerging from students' constructivist online game-based learning process: Implications for the importance of teacher facilitation. *Educational Technology & Society, 18*(2), 262–283.

Keeley, P. (2015). *Science formative assessment, Volume 1: 75 more strategies for linking assessment, instruction, and learning* (2nd ed). Thousand Oaks, CA: Corwin.

Kelly, J. (2000). Rethinking the elementary science methods course: A case for content, pedagogy, and informal science education. *International Journal of Science Education, 22*(7), 755–777.

Kilpatrick, W. H. (1918). The project method: Child-centeredness in progressive education. *The Teachers College Record, 19,* 319–334.

Knoll, M. (2010). "A marriage on the rocks": An unknown letter by William H. Kilpatrick about his project method. Retrieved from files.eric.ed.gov/fulltext/ED511129.pdf

KnowledgeWorks. (2017). *Building a vision for all students.* Retrieved from www.knowledgeworks.org/sites/default/files/u1/case-study-marysville-district.pdf

Krueger, K., & James, J. (2017). Digital equity: The civil rights issue of our time. *Principal, 96*(4), 12–16.

Lahanas, M. (2017). The future of broadband in underserved areas. Retrieved from www.newamerica.org/weekly/edition-173/future-broadband-underserved-areas

Lai, K.-W., Khaddage, F., & Knezek, G. (2013). Blending student technology experiences in formal and informal learning. *Journal of Computer Assisted Learning, 29,* 414-425.

Leahy, M., Davis, N., Lewin, C., Charania, A., Nordin, H., Orlič, D., Butler, D., & Lopez-Fernadez, O. (2016). Smart Partnerships to Increase Equity in Education. *Educational Technology & Society, 19*(3), 84–98.

Levin, B. B., & Schrum, L. (2017). *Every teacher a leader: Developing the needed dispositions, knowledge, and skills for teacher leadership.* Thousand Oaks, CA: Corwin.

Livingstone, S., & Third, A. (2017). Children and young people's rights in the digital age: An emerging agenda. *New Media & Society, 19*(5), 1461–4448.

Martin, C. (2016). A library's role in digital equity. *Young Adult Library Services, 14*(4), 34–36.

Martinez, S. L., & Stager, G. S. (2013). *Invent to learn: Making, tinkering, and engineering in the classroom.* Torrance, CA: Constructing Modern Knowledge Press.

McCrea, B. (2015, April 30). WiFi on wheels puts two districts on the fast track to 24/7 access. *THE Journal.* Retrieved from thejournal.com/articles/2015/04/30/wifi-on-wheels.aspx

McDonald, C. V. (2016). STEM education: A review of the contribution of the disciplines of science, technology, engineering and mathematics. *Science Education International, 27*(4), 530–569.

McKibben, S. (2017). A flight plan for coding in pre-K and beyond: As the demand for coding climbs, the logistics of implementation can feel up in the air. *Education Update, 59*(7), 2–6.

Microsoft. (2018). Skype in the classroom. Retrieved from education.microsoft.com/skype-in-the-classroom/overview

Milanesi, C. (2017, March 15). Why today's education system is failing our children. *Tech.pinions.* Retrieved from techpinions.com/why-todays-education-system-is-failing-our-children/49129

Minnigerode, L., & Reynolds, R. (2013). Don't give up: A case study on girls and video game design. *LEARNing Landscapes, 6*(2), 283–302. Retrieved from www.learninglandscapes.ca/index.php/learnland/article/view/617

Morgan, H. (2014). Using digital story projects to help students improve in reading and writing. *Reading Improvement*, 51(1), 20–26.

National Academies of Sciences, Engineering, & Medicine. (2005). *Rising above the gathering storm: Energizing and employing America for a brighter economic future.* Washington, DC: Author.

National Center for Education Statistics. (2016). Student reports of bullying: Results from the 2015 school crime supplement to the national crime victimization survey (Web tables). Retrieved from nces.ed.gov/pubs2017/2017015.pdf

National Digital Inclusion Alliance. (n.d.) Definitions | Digital inclusion. Retrieved from www.digitalinclusion.org/definitions

Nemer, D. (2013). *Favela digital: The other side of technology.* Vitória, Brazil: GSA Editora e Grafica.

Niemitz, M., Slough, S., Peart, L., Klaus, A. D., Leckie, R. M., & St. John, K. (2008). Interactive virtual expeditions as a learning tool: The school of rock expedition case study. *Journal of Educational Multimedia and Hypermedia*, 17(4), 561–580.

Nugent, G., Barker, B., Grandgenett, N., & Adamchuk, V. I. (2010). Impact of robotics and geospatial technology interventions on youth STEM learning and attitudes. *Journal of Research on Technology in Education*, 42(4), 391–408.

Oliver, K. M. (2016a). Professional development considerations for makerspace leaders, part one: Addressing "what?" *TechTrends, 60*, 160–166. doi.org/10.1007/s11528-016-0028-5

Oliver, K. M. (2016b). Professional development considerations for makerspace leaders, part two: Addressing "how?" and "why?" *TechTrends, 60*, 211–217. doi.org/10.1007/s11528-016-0050-7

Omari, J. (2015, March 10). Democracy through technology: Internet access in Rio's favelas. *RioOnWatch*. Retrieved from www.rioonwatch.org/?p=20426

Opal Charter School. (n.d.). Opal School guiding principles. Retrieved from www.portlandcm.org/teaching-and-learning/opal-school

Ormondale School. (n.d.). STEM. Retreived from ormondale.pvsd.net/academics/s_t_e_m.

Pane, J., Steiner, E., Baird, M., Hamilton, L., & Pane, J. (2017). *Informing progress: Insights on personalized learning implementation and effects* (Report No. RR-2042-BMGF). Santa Monica, CA: The Rand Corporation. doi.org/10.7249/RR2042

Papert, S. (1980). *Mindstorms: Computers, children and powerful ideas.* New York, NY: Basic Books.

Papert, S. (1986). *Constructionism: A new opportunity for elementary science education.* Cambridge, MA: Massachusetts Institute of Technology, Media Laboratory, Epistemology and Learning Group.

Papert, S. (1987). Computer criticism vs. technocentric thinking. *Educational Researcher, 16*(1), 22–30.

Papert, S. (1991). Situating constructionism. In S. Papert & I. Harel (Eds.), *Constructionism* (pp. 1–11). Norwood, NJ: Ablex.

Peppler, K., & Bender, S. (2013). Maker movement spreads innovation one project at a time. *Phi Delta Kappan, 95*(3), 22–27.

Perlis, D. (2015, June 22). Building miniature makerspaces [Blog post]. Retrieved from lighthousecreativitylab.org/2015/06/2548

Phillips, M., Finkelstein, D., & Wever-Frerichs, S. (2007). School site to museum floor: How informal science institutions work with schools. *International Journal of Science Education, 29*(12), 1489–1507.

Pocock, J. (2016). Maker movement 2.0. *ASEE Prism, 26*(3), 34–37.

Popovic, G., & Lederman, J. S. (2015). Implications of informal education experiences for mathematics teachers' ability to make connections beyond formal classroom school. *Science and Mathematics, 115*(3), 129–140.

Preddy, L. B. (2013). *School library makerspaces: Grades 6-12.* Santa Barbara, CA: Libraries Unlimited.

Prensky, M. (2001a). Digital natives, digital immigrants, part 1. *On the Horizon, 9*(5), 1–6. doi.org/10.1108/10748120110424816

Prensky, M. (2001b). Digital natives, digital immigrants, part 2: Do they really think differently? *On the Horizon, 9*(6), 1–6. doi.org/10.1108/10748120110424843

Rahm, J. (2014). Reframing research on informal teaching and learning in science: Comments and commentary at the heart of a new vision for the field. *Journal of Research in Science Teaching, 51*(3), 395–406.

Ravitz, J., & Blazevski, J. (2014). Assessing the role of online technologies in project-based learning. *The Interdisciplinary Journal of Problem Based Learning, 8*(1), 66–79.

Ribble, M. (2012). Digital citizenship for educational change. *Delta Pi Record, 48*, 148–151.

Ribble, M., & Bailey, G. (2007). *Digital citizenship in schools.* Eugene, OR: International Society for Technology in Education.

Ritzhaupt, A. D., Liu, F., Dawson, K., & Barron, A. E. (2013). Differences in student information and communication technology literacy based on socio-economic status, ethnicity, and gender: Evidence of a digital divide in Florida schools. *Journal of Research on Technology in Education, 45*(4), 291–307.

Rogoff, B., Callahan, M., Gutiérrez, K. D., & Erickson, F. (2016). The organization of informal learning. *Review of Research in Education, 40*, 356–401. doi.org/10.3102/0091732X16680994

Rondinelli, B. P., & Owens, A. M. (2017). Computational thinking. *School Administrator, 74*(5), 23–27.

Rosenheck, L., Gordon-Messer, S., Clarke-Midura, J., & Klopfer, E. (2016). Design and implementation of an MMO: Approaches to support inquiry learning with games. In D. Russell & J. M. Laffey (Eds.), *Handbook of Research on Gaming Trends in P-12 Education* (pp. 33–54). Hershey, PA: IGI Global.

Sancho, P., Moreno-Ger, P., Fuentes-Fernández, R., & Fernández-Manjón, B. (2009). Adaptive role playing games: An immersive approach for problem based learning. *Educational Technology & Society, 12*(4), 110–124.

Sanford, K., & Madill, L. (2007). Understanding the power of new literacies through video game play and design. *Canadian Journal of Education, 30*(2), 432–455.

Schön, D. A. (1983). *The reflective practitioner.* London, England: Temple Smith.

Sebugwaawo , I. (2017). High power bills inspire boys to build 'solar robot.' *Khaleej Times.* Available: www.khaleejtimes.com/nation/high-power-bills-inspire-boys-to-build-solar-robot

Sentance, S., Waite, J., Hodges, S., MacLeod, E., & Yeomans, L. E. (2017). "Creating cool stuff": Pupils' experience of the BBC micro:bit. *Proceedings of the 2017 ACM SIGCSE Technical Symposium on Computer Science Education,* 531–536. doi.org/10.1145/3017680.3017749

Shaffer, D. W., Nash, P., & Ruis, A. R. (2015). Technology and the new professionalization of teaching. *Teachers College Record, 117*(12), 1–30.

Sheckler, C. (2017, September 21). Free mobile devices to help Indiana students with Internet 'homework gap.' *South Bend Tribune.* Retrieved from www.centerdigitaled.com/k-12/Free-Mobile-Devices-To-Help-Mishawaka-Students-With-Internet-Homework-Gap.html

Sheridan, K., Halverson, E. R., Litts, B. K., Brahms, L., Jacobs-Priebe, L., & Owens, T. (2014). Learning in the making: A comparative case study of three makerspaces. *Harvard Educational Review, 84*(4), 505–535.

Shotover Primary School. (n.d.) Shotover Primary School home. Retrieved from shotover.school.nz/home

Shimic, G., & Jevremovic, A. (2012). Problem-based learning in formal and informal learning environments. *Interactive Learning Environments, 20,* 351-367.

Singer, N. (2017, May 13). How Google took over the classroom. *The New York Times.* Retrieved from www.nytimes.com/2017/05/13/technology/google-education-chromebooks-schools.html

Slaton, J. (2016). How one middle school gets creative to teach digital citizenship [Blog post]. Retrieved from www.commonsense.org/education/blog/how-one-middle-school-gets-creative-to-teach-digital-citizenship

Smith, T. (2016). Digital Equity: "A Moral Imperative": Part 3 www.techlearning.com/resources/digital-equity-a-moral-imperative-part-3

Spillane, J. P., Halverson, R., & Diamond, J. B. (2001). Investigating school leadership practice: A distributed perspective. *Educational Researcher, 30*(3), 23–28.

Stager, G. (2012). A good prompt is worth 1000 words. *Creative Educator.* Retrieved from creativeeducator.tech4learning.com/2012/articles/A_Good_Prompt_is_Worth_1000_Words

Stager, G. (2014). What's the maker movement and why should I care? Retrieved from www.scholastic.com/browse/article.jsp?id=3758336

Steele, K. (2001). A new teacher learning to share responsibility with parents. In B. Rogoff, C. Goodman Turkanis, & L. Bartlett (Eds.), *Learning together: Children and adults in a school community* (pp. 138–144). New York, NY: Oxford University Press.

Stoddard, J. (2009). Toward a virtual field trip model for the social studies. *Contemporary Issues of Technology in Teacher Education, 9*(4), 421–438.

Stone, D., & Mercado-Crespo M. C. (2017, September 14). New CDC resource can help states and communities prevent suicide among youth. Retrieved from www.stopbullying.gov/blog/2017/09/14/new-cdc-resource-can-help-states-and-communities-prevent-suicide-among-youth.html

Stopbullying.gov. (n.d.) What is cyberbullying. Retrieved from www.stopbullying.gov/cyberbullying/what-is-it/index.html

Stout, R. (2017, July 15). Simple steps to digital citizenship. *School Library Journal, (63)*7, 15.

Strimel, G., Reed, P., Dooley, G., Bolling, J., Phillips, M., & Cantu, D. V. (2014). Integrating and monitoring informal learning in education and training. *Techniques, 89*(3), 48–54.

Thompson, C. (2014, October 9). How videogames like *Minecraft* actually help kids learn to read. *Wired Magazine.* Retrieved from www.wired.com/2014/10/video-game-literacy

Trevesa, R., Viterbob, P., & Haklay, M. (2015). Footprints in the sky: Using student track logs from a "bird's eye view" virtual field trip to enhance learning. *Journal of Geography in Higher Education, 39*(1), 97–110.

Trolley, B. C., & Hanel, C. (2010). *Cyber kids, cyber bullying, cyber balance.* Thousand Oaks, CA: Corwin.

Tucker, A. W., & Luce, R. D. (1959). *Contributions to the theory of games* (Vol. 4). Princeton, NJ: Princeton University Press.

Tulloch, R. (2014). Reconceptualising gamification: Play and pedagogy. *Journal of Digital Culture and Education, 6*(4), 317–333.

Ullman, E. (2017). Digital citizenship lessons for everyone. *TechLearning, 38*(1), 18–22.

U.S. Department of Education. (2017). 21st Century Community Learning Centers. Retrieved from www2.ed.gov/programs/21stcclc/index.html

VanLehn, K. (2011). The relative effectiveness of human tutoring, intelligent tutoring systems, and other tutoring systems. *Educational Psychologist, 46*(4), 197–22.

Vossoughi, S., Hooper, P., & Escudé, M. (2016). Making through the lens of culture and power: Toward transformative visions for educational equity. *Harvard Educational Review, 86*, 206–232.

Vygotsky, L. S. (1978). *Mind in society: The development of higher psychological processes.* Cambridge, MA: Harvard University Press.

Vygotsky, L. (1997). *Educational psychology.* Boca Raton, FL: St. Lucie Press.

Wardrip, P. S., & Brahms, L. (2014, October). *Mobile MAKESHOP: Preliminary findings from two school sites.* Poster presented at Fablearn Conference, Stanford, CA.

Wardrip, P. S., & Brahms, L. (2015). Learning practices of making: Developing a framework for design. *Proceedings of the 14th International Conference on Interaction Design and Children.* New York, NY: Association for Computing Machinery (ACM).

Wardrip, P. S., & Brahms, L. (2016). Making goes to school. In K. Peppler, E. Halverson, & Y. Kafai (Eds.), *Makeology: Makers as learners* (Vol. 1). New York, NY: Routledge.

Wardrip, P. S., Brahms, L. Carrigan, T., & Reich, C. (2017). *Making + learning in museums and libraries: A practitioner's guide and framework.* Pittsburgh, PA: Institute of Museum and Library Services and Children's Museum of Pittsburgh.

Warschauer, M., Knobel, M., & Stone, L. (2004). Technology and equity in schooling: Deconstructing the digital divide. *Educational Policy, 18*(4), 562–588. doi.org/10.1177/0895904804266469

Wendell, K., & Rogers, C. (2013). Engineering design-based science, science content performance, and science attitudes in elementary school. *Journal of Engineering Education, 102*(4), 513–540.

Weppel, S., Bishop, M. J., & Munoz-Avila, H. (2012). The design of scaffolding in game-based learning: A formative evaluation. *Journal of Interactive Learning Research, 23*(4), 361–392.

The White House. (2015). Educate to innovate. Retrieved from obamawhitehouse. archives.gov/issues/education/k-12/educate-innovate

Willett, R. (2016). Making, makers, and makerspaces: A discourse analysis of professional journal articles and blog posts about makerspaces in public libraries. *Library Quarterly: Information, Community, Policy, 86*(3), 313–329.

Wolking, M. (2016, August 10). Reflections on personalized and project-based learning [Blog post]. Retrieved from www.edelements.com/blog/reflections-on-personalized-and-project-based-learning

Yuen, A. H. K., Lau, W. W. F., Park, J. H., Lau, G. K. K., & Chan, A. K. M. (2016). Digital equity and students' home computing: A Hong Kong study. *Asia-Pacific Education Research,* 25(4), 509–518. doi.org/10.1007/s40299-016-0276-3

Zieger, L., & Farber, M. (2012). Civic participation among seventh-grade social studies students in multi-user virtual environments. *Journal of Interactive Learning Research,* 23(4), 393–410.

Index